SCHOLAR *in the* WILDERNESS

Francis Adrian Van der Kemp

SCHOLAR *in the* WILDERNESS

Francis Adrian Van der Kemp

HARRY F. JACKSON

Syracuse University Press 1963

*This book
has been published
with the assistance of a
Ford Foundation grant.*

THIS BOOK HAS BEEN SET IN 10 POINT LINOTYPE
BASKERVILLE, LEADED 2 POINTS, WITH DISPLAY IN
JANSON; PRINTED ON 60 POUND P. H. GLATFELTER
ANTIQUE STANDARD WHITE TEXT PAPER, R GRADE;
BOUND IN COLUMBIA CHAMBRAY CLOTH; DESIGNED BY
FRANK MAHOOD; AND MANUFACTURED BY VAIL-BALLOU
PRESS, INC., IN THE UNITED STATES OF AMERICA.

To Mary Ruth

Contents

viii

Preface

FRANCIS Adrian Van der Kemp was a writer, minister and political leader of some prominence in his native Holland when he fled from religious and political persecution in 1788 to settle in central New York. He became one of the area's important citizens during its formative period.

When he arrived on the shores of Oneida Lake, Van der Kemp was the only scholar in the region. As a friend to both noted and common men in central New York, he provided a bridge between scholarship and responsible citizenship for many years. His active, inquiring mind ranged far beyond his rural village. Politics, religion, history, government, scientific agriculture, geology, the Erie Canal, the conduct of the War of 1812, and any threat to political or religious freedom stimulated him to research and writing.

On the national scene, Van der Kemp's opinions influenced many of the great leaders of America. John Adams credited him with a "vast view of civilization" and respected his advice. His warm friendship with John and Abigail Adams endured till their deaths, and John Quincy Adams continued the relationship. He shared Washington's interest in scientific agriculture after a visit to Mount Vernon, and persuaded Thomas Jefferson to publish one of the latter's religious works.

De Witt Clinton, an early acquaintance through his uncle, Governor George Clinton, sought Van der Kemp's views on the building of the Erie Canal. John Lincklaen of Cazenovia counted him as a valued friend. Jonas Platt, who rose from the position of a struggling young lawyer at

Whitesboro on the frontier to state Supreme Court judge, relied heavily on Van der Kemp, while Chancellor Robert Livingston made use of his knowledge of agriculture, conservation, and geology.

He was a member of learned societies, published numerous writings in leading religious journals, and moved easily in academic circles. He set a climate of scholarly pursuit stretching from the nation's capital to the frontier, from the banks of the Potomac to the banks of obscure Cincinnati Creek. Van der Kemp provided a dignity for scholarship from his wilderness that inspired leaders to apply learning to the problems of development.

As a justice of the peace, he helped to give decorum and integrity to the courts of the New York frontier. Deeply religious, he helped to establish one of the first churches in the area. As a translator, he rescued the early records of the Dutch colony of New Netherland from oblivion.

Van der Kemp already had a university education and theological training when he came to America. In his new country he applied himself diligently to intellectual search and research. His numerous letters probed for ideas and knowledge. His correspondence with John Adams over a period of forty years, largely intact, gives the best view of the scholar's intellectual strivings. A lengthy correspondence with De Witt Clinton, shorter exchanges with Thomas Jefferson and Robert Livingston and fragments of writings exchanged with many others help to round out the picture. Van der Kemp's own publications and manuscripts show gratifying results of his scholarship. A short autobiography and many records help to reconstruct his extremely busy life into an understandable, admirable picture of a man who, in spite of the handicaps of the frontier, an adopted language, and financial hardships, contributed much to the development of America.

Van der Kemp was always the scholar, whether in political or religious conflict, applying scientific knowledge to agriculture, or acting as intelligent observer of military tactics. He was firm in the belief that knowledge was a force for good and that ignorance was evil. By studying the past, Van der Kemp believed that he and other scholars could lead the way to a better future. By studying natural science, he believed that he and other scholars could design better and greater uses of natural resources. By studying religion, he sought to make a simple tie between good works on earth and a heavenly reward.

The Van der Kemp manuscripts owned by the Oneida Historical Society first provided the possibilities for study of his life. A careful reading of his autobiography, edited and enlarged by Helen Lincklaen Fairchild, encouraged the research for a full biography. The aid of Francis Cunningham, curator of the Oneida Historical Society, has been invaluable over the several years of study.

Utica College encouraged the project with favorable schedule arrangements, secretarial assistance and two summer grants. Miss Mary Dudley, the college librarian, was helpful in the search for materials. Dr. Robert V. Anderson assisted directly in the search, continually offered suggestions and responded to questions on the project. Mr. Craig R. Hanyan helped with the De Witt Clinton materials. Mrs. Dorothy Judd Sickels criticized parts of the manuscript and made valuable suggestions. Mrs. Marian Inglis typed rough drafts at both convenient and inconvenient times. Members of the Unitarian Church in Barneveld, Van der Kemp's church, have encouraged the biography by their interest. Their minister, the Reverend Frank Edson Robertson, has allowed the author to spend much time in the parsonage, imagining how it was when the Van der Kemps were its residents. To all of these people and to friends and family who have aided in less tangible ways, I am deeply grateful.

HARRY F. JACKSON

Utica, New York
1963

❧ I ❧

The Evolution of
the Scholar

THE province of Overyssel in the little country of the
Netherlands was a good place to begin life in 1752. The
country was not free of troubles, as later events would prove,
but the inhabitants had great opportunity to shape their
own lives. In most of Europe, in most of the world, men
were tied to a bit of the earth (like Gulliver) by the ropes
of ignorance, superstition, tyranny, class control, and mal-
nutrition. The Dutch had loosened or cut these bonds in
the century and a half before the birth of Francis Adrian
Van der Kemp. He, like most of his countrymen, needed
little more than opportunity; with it they earned necessities and added a good measure of comforts.

Overyssel was a farming land on the Issel River and the
Zuider Zee. The major town of Kampen had been a prominent and prosperous seaport in the days of the old Hanseatic
League. Now dependent on the regional economy, it retained and treasured historic memories. Several old gates
spoke of a time before national states were formed, when
powerful walls protected the town and its citizens. The
Groote Kerk, a handsomely decorated Gothic church, was
begun back in the fourteenth century. It now stood as one
of the finest religious monuments in the Netherlands, a
reminder of religious persecution in the past and tolerance
in the present—the tolerance of a people who welcomed

1

Huguenots, Portuguese Jews and Separatist Pilgrims, who allowed Lutherans, Dutch Reformed, Mennonites, and Catholics to live in religious peace. In the center of the town stood the *raadhuis* or city hall, built in the fourteenth century and reconstructed in the sixteenth. In passing, young Van der Kemp could look up at the stone figures of Brotherly Love, Moderation, Fidelity and Justice. He could see the iron cage once used for holding criminals in public view. The *raadhuis* bell tower, housing the great bell which rang out warnings to the public in olden days, rose in grandeur above the surrounding buildings. The impressive structure inspired confidence in local government and local justice, in government for the people if not always by the people.

Kampen lacked only a good university. In the latter half of the eighteenth century this deficiency could be minimized by sending promising youths to Groningen, Leyden, or Utrecht, where three of the best universities of Europe were located. Groningen was the nearest of the three, and there young Van der Kemp would go.

The Kampen townsmen had a reputation for droll stupidity. They delighted in the tale of the Kampen city fathers and the town bell. When a Spanish army approached the city the officials hurriedly took the bell from the old tower and loaded it into a boat. Out in the Zuider Zee they heaved the bell overboard with great relief. However, a townsman in the boat who admitted his inability to understand all the actions of city officials, asked how they would find the bell again. The indignant burgomaster thus challenged said firmly, "We'll mark the place where we heaved it overboard," as he quickly cut a notch in the boat's gunwale. Again, they reported the council had decided to double tax collections by doubling the number of gates where tariffs were collected.

In Kampen, with its historical traditions balanced by everyday humor, Francis Adrian Van der Kemp was born on May 4, 1752.[1] His mother was Anna Catharina Leydekker. His father was John, a captain in the military service.

They were proud of their ancestry—the Bax, the Van Drongelens and Van der Kemps on the one side, the Leydekkers, De Huyberts and De Witts on the other. From his parents Francis learned to respect his grandparents and great-grandparents and to treasure the inspiration gained from study of the past. The material inheritance of the Van der Kemps was apparently modest. On one occasion John abandoned a tract of land as not being worth the amount of the taxes.[2]

John was educated to be a merchant, but in the eighteenth century Dutch commerce had declined and the profession failed to hold his interest. He became a soldier, an honored and promising vocation in this time of naval decay. He and Anna Catharina Leydekker were married in 1747. John was stationed at Kampen when Francis was born, later moving to Zutphen, to Zwolle and to Bois-le-Duc.

John and Catharina hoped that Francis would be a scholar. As do many mothers, Catharina watched for a sign and found it. When the baby fretted and cried in the old Dutch cradle, placing a little book in his hands appeased him most often. How could any mother doubt this prophecy of scholarship?

The baby grew into a healthy boy with the knack of attracting the good will and affection of all around him, young and old, at school or at play. His early schooling included French to prepare him for Latin School. Francis began his classical training at the age of nine or ten when the family moved to Zutphen. Fifty or sixty years later in his autobiography for his son, Van der Kemp wrote: "My progress was rather slow, without any brilliant proficiency; yet when, the 14th of January, 1763, I left the first for the second class, I was rewarded with *Nieupoort de Ritibus Romanorum.*"

Zutphen, not far from Kampen, was farther inland on the Issel River in the province of Gelderland. Here the lowlands gave way to rolling hills, with many wheat fields and fine stands of fir trees. Here the cruel tyrant, Duke Alva,

had severely punished many Dutch citizens during the revolt against the Spanish rule. Hundreds had been put to
death. Two centuries later stories of these Dutch patriots
instilled a spirit of freedom and hatred of foreign domination in Van der Kemp and his young classmates.

The family's next residence was in Zwolle, the capital
city of Overyssel, also only a few miles from Kampen. Like
its neighboring town, Zwolle had its Groote Kerk, a fine
Gothic structure with excellent interior carving. Built
several centuries earlier, it had been taken over by Protestants during the Reformation and was now used by the
Dutch Reformed organization. The Sassenpoort, an old
gate with four splendid towers, was another inspiring land-
mark of the city. At Zwolle Thomas a Kempis lived, wrote,
and later was buried. Here the growing boy, Francis, continued his education. His progress was slower than his
parents expected. He passed step by step to the fourth
class, later reporting in his autobiography that he was
"never higher than third place." His parents began to doubt
the capacity of their son for a scholarly profession. When
Francis had reached the fourth class, his parents turned
for advice to their next door neighbor, a wise and respected
clergyman who knew the boy and understood scholarship.
He must have broken the parents' hearts and shaken a little
of their faith by expressing his doubt that Francis could
ever succeed as a man of letters and suggesting the choice
of a different profession.

John and Catharina were reluctant to believe their son's
scholastic ability was only mediocre, but hesitated to dis-
count the opinion of their counselor. Though Francis probably had a voice in the decision, independence for children
was a rare practice in 1764. By compromise, they decided
Francis should become a military cadet, but that he would
continue his study of Latin and Greek.

At this time the Duke of Brunswick was the chief ad-
viser to young William V, the stadholder. The duke, Lud-
wig Ernest von Brunswick-Wolfenbuttel, had entered the
Dutch military service in 1750, having served as a field

marshal in the Austrian army during the War of the Austrian Succession. He knew the armies of Europe well, having fought for or against some of the best. Now he wanted to strengthen and modernize Dutch military and naval forces, but was unable to overcome resistance to change. In this army young Van der Kemp became a cadet, first in the infantry regiment of Holtein Gottorp and later in John Van der Kemp's regiment.

What a Dutch boy learned in the army can only be guessed. In the company of other boys and men he surely learned cooperation and nationalism. He learned enough to assume the leadership of a small force in defense of a Dutch town some twenty years later. He learned enough to be intelligently critical, more than forty years later, of the competence of leaders in the War of 1812 at Sackett's Harbor, New York State. And he was proud to see his second son become a soldier for the United States.

While a cadet at Bois-le-Duc, Francis won prizes for accomplishment in the study of Greek and Latin literature in 1768 and 1769. He had private lessons in the study of Greek and Hebrew, the latter because of his father's serious hope to guide the boy into the ministry. Though he had some regret that his son was not to follow in his military footsteps, John had soon realized Francis had little liking for a military career and conceded that a scholarly contemplative life would be "more congenial" to his son's character.

However, the boy's decision to leave the army was unexpected. Years later in his autobiography Van der Kemp described the turn of his life in these words:

An encampment, which was ordered in 1769, would have been a serious and expensive obstruction to my studies, and useless if I quitted the military career; but my father peremptorily declined to intercede in my favor, to obtain an exemption; he could not brook a refusal, and would not ask it of the Prince of Hesse, but left it willingly to me to act as I deemed proper. I paid then a visit to his Highness, solicited the boon, and on his abrupt repulse instantly requested my dismission from the service, which I obtained. Scarcely had I returned under the paternal roof, than, in answer to the questions of my Father on the result, I threw my military accoutrements on the floor, and told him I had obtained my dismission.

No comment is made as to the father's reaction. Francis renewed his studies with vigor, and was admitted to the Univerity of Groningen in August, 1770.

The universities of the Netherlands offered the best in higher education. There were other good institutions of learning, chiefly in the provincial capitals, but not so prominent or attractive. The big Dutch universities were an unusual mixture of medieval and modern, with less state and religious control than in most European universities. They had no dormitories, but provided only the halls of learning and expected the students to look after their own material necessities. Students from near and far chose lodgings by recommendations of friends and relatives or burghers' signs indicating rooms to let. Meals could be eaten in one's room, at the table with the landlord, or at an inn. Students were not required to wear uniforms as at many European universities, and professors wore their colorful robes only on special occasions. Responsibility for success rested primarily on the students although professors often took personal interest in boys who attracted their attention.

The many foreign students in Holland gave an international atmosphere to the schools, perhaps more to Utrecht and Leyden than to Groningen. The journal of a young Englishman, James Boswell, recorded his academic life at Utrecht:

I have got a neat house of my own and an excellent servant. I get up every morning at seven. I read Ovid till nine, then I breakfast. From ten to eleven I read

Tacitus. From eleven to twelve I am shaved and dressed every day. From twelve to one I hear a lecture upon Civil Law. From one to three I walk and dine. From three to four my French master is with me. The rest of the day is spent in reading different books and in writing. This day I began to set about recovering my Greek. I have taken Cebes's *Table* and shall next read Xenophon, and so advance to greater difficulties.[3]

Coffee, then as now, was a welcome interlude between Greek and notes "of law and history." Wine and beer were reserved for complete relaxation in social gatherings at the close of the academic day or on weekends. Boswell spent, on one occasion, a gay evening with Dutch students. They were "all keen on meat and drink; then marching like schoolboys with *Kapitein* and frightening the street." [4] Van der Kemp must have enjoyed some of the same activities, as he later looked upon wine as a necessity for health and good living. One of his lighter writings, "Dutch Conviviality," described a discussion group in one of the homes at Oldenbarneveld, New York. It was similar to a discussion in a student room or inn at Groningen. At the close of the evening they drank toasts to the Fatherland and to the five V's—*Vrijheid, Vreede, Vriendschap, Vrouwen* and *Vrolijkkeid* (liberty, peace, friendship, women, gaiety) and sang a song before departing. One guest stayed for a *mantel pypje* and a *glasje of de val reep* (a pipe of tobacco with one's coat on and a drink for the road).[5] At the university, perhaps before, Van der Kemp learned to play cards, backgammon and chess.

Students often spent the night and early morning hours on discussion and study rather than sleep. Francis Van der Kemp, determined to rise "above mediocrity," entered into academic work with enthusiasm. He seldom slept more than five hours, frequently only two or three, and sometimes not at all. He attended lectures in Latin, Greek and oriental languages. He studied philosophy, "viz. Metaphysicks, Natural History, Cosmology." He studied English and German through private instruction and delved into chemical experimentation. Knowledge increased, but his health failed. On the advice of friendly Professor Petrus Camper, Francis gave up chemistry, increased his sleep, and studied "at a standing position," a frequently prescribed measure for good health. He also gratefully accepted Professor Camper's gift of glasses for nearsightedness. The boy recovered.

In the course of his academic strivings, Van der Kemp acquired the true scholar's love of books. He wanted his own copies to refer to and annotate as he pleased. One can still see marginal notes in his books in the Barneveld and Harvard libraries. He purchased, often beyond his means, good books recommended by professors and friends and started at this time the library which was to be a source of inspiration, joy and comfort throughout his life.

Francis thrived on learning and was a good student. However, during his second year his father died. This tragedy was a blow for the sensitive student away from home. In time he acquired a consoling religion, but when he lost his father his religion was inadequate. Pity for his sorrowing mother at home was added to his loss of a "tender Father and affectionate friend." Uncle Adraen, a clergyman, and Aunt Anthonia assumed his expenses at Groningen.

This loss accentuated young Francis' interest in religion. The young man added to his studies courses in ecclesiastical history, botany, and "Ecclesiastical Laws and the Laws of Nature," the latter under the respected and famous Professor Frederic Adolph van der Marck.

In a sketch of this "master" written in 1812 to John Adams, Van der Kemp recalled,

> He did resemble my Honoured friend at Quincy in many respects—in mind—in stature—in an ardent love of truth and Liberty—in hatred against Despotism— Civil or religious; tho a man of eminent talents, he was amiable in society—pleasing to his friends—

Van der Marck was a successful lawyer in Arnhem before teaching at Groningen. He was popular with the students, attracting youths from every province to his crowded lectures. Seventeen prominent lawyers and judges came regularly to hear the master.[6] Van der Kemp was irresistibly drawn to this teacher during the years he was most doubtful about the religion he had learned as a boy. The thinking of popular deists such as Voltaire, Rousseau, and D'Alembert, seemed valid to the young man, especially their criticisms which applied to the orthodox, dogmatic clergy of Groningen. His study of history supported his growing doubts. Professor Van der Marck was soon to inspire open rebellion in his young admirer.

❧ II ❧

Champion of Academic
and Religious Freedom

"YOU suspect me Madam! of having in my youth been an
Enthusiast. . . . I am it yet, and would not change." [1]
Van der Kemp wrote this to Abigail Adams when he was
sixty-five years old. She had written of her interest in his
autobiography, especially the stories of his courageous
conflicts for freedom of thought back in his native country.
The old Patriot at sixty-five still had some of the fire that
burned so fiercely when he was a university student.

The Dutch Reformed Church, the church of the Van
der Kemp family, had difficulties not only in keeping
Roman Catholicism and Jewry in a subdued, carefully
circumscribed position, but also had troubles with heresies.
The Dutch Church had originated during the struggles for
independence against Spain. William of Orange, the early
leader of the revolutionary movement, established the Reformed Church as the national religion. It was Calvinistic
in doctrine and presbyterian in organization. Other sects
were tolerated as long as their activities represented no
danger to the established church. Under these conditions
the dissenting Anabaptists organized in the Netherlands,
with Menno Simons as their most noted leader. The Ar-
minians also rose to plague Dutch orthodox believers. The
Dutch Church could and did expel those influenced by
these or any other free thinking sects.

In addition to religious thinkers such as Menno and Arminius, free thinking philosophers also contributed to the Age of the Enlightenment. The Netherlands had Spinoza in the seventeenth century and in the eighteenth knew also the political and social philosophy of the rest of Europe, especially France and England. As the middle classes were educated, they were exposed to enlightened thought. No doubt the Van der Kemps, either directly or indirectly, knew some of the works of such men as Hobbes and Bayle, Hume and Voltaire.

Bayle particularly impressed Francis Van der Kemp. In the late 1600's when France became unsafe for Protestants, Bayle settled at Rotterdam and ultimately published his *Dictionary*. He included topics on nearly all of the current religious questions, forming his work into a "virtual encyclopedia for Freethinkers," and made the book relatively safe and attractive by treating controversies with a clever disarming impartiality.[2] Among English thinkers Hume probably influenced Van der Kemp the most. As a participant in the deist movement Hume had produced his greatest writings at about the time of Van der Kemp's birth. He questioned miracles and opposed supernaturalism in his *Natural History of Religion*. Voltaire, Rousseau and Locke were probably the most influential of the French writers for the Dutch middle classes. Voltaire's *Treatise on Tolerance* had been translated into Dutch in 1796 and Rousseau's *Social Contract* was known soon after its appearance in 1762. The established church was disturbed by the popularity of these writings and secured a ban on Voltaire's work. It immediately became better known.

In the late 1760's and early 1770's another controversy arose in the Netherlands over Jean François Marmontel's *Bélisaire*. The treatise dealt with natural religion, praised toleration and even admitted the possibility of virtue among heathens. It was attacked and defended with vigor, freethinkers on one side and conservatives on the other.[3]

The university provided fertile ground for all intellectual considerations when Van der Kemp was a student. In the earlier years of the century the great professors in the Netherlands had particularly stimulated their students and had attracted many foreigners to their lectures. Willem Jacob Van s'Gravesand at the University of Leyden and Professor Petrus van Musschenbroek at Utrecht and Leyden pushed forward the study of mathematics and science, the former carrying on Newton's principles as part of his work, the latter going into magnetic and meteorological studies (background of electricity). Abraham Schultens advanced the study of oriental (Middle East) languages. Other professors and scholars, native or foreign, added to the attractions of higher education and laid a good foundation for the latter part of the century.[4]

After 1750 came Frans Hemsterhuis to stimulate the teaching of the classics through his own study of Socrates and Plato. David Ruhnken and Daniel Wyttenbach [5] in the 1760's and 1770's broadened the concepts of classical studies with a "historico-philosophical method." Petrus Camper, the friendly professor who advised Van der Kemp about his health, led the way in the study of anatomy and was a philosopher of note. Furthermore, the masters of higher education were going out from the ivory towers to share their ideas with greater numbers by lectures, writings and social contacts. The study of theology picked up the new spirit also, but not without accusations of heresy. A new national synod was proposed to settle some of the religious differences, but the provincial estates (legislative bodies) opposed it and even went so far as to suppress discussion of some religious questions.[6]

In the world of higher education, Francis Van der Kemp was thrown among other students with religious doubts. They talked his language. Neither students nor professors condemned him for his opinions. For the first time in his life Francis had freedom of thought and speech in religious matters. During his years at the university, young Van der Kemp took a position for religious freedom which he maintained with vigor throughout his life. Over coffee cups or beer mugs the students exercised their freedom in an atmosphere of respectful equality even when lightened by youthful hilarity and good-natured bantering. Over the mugs no sternfaced father appeared, no tearful mother, no pompous churchman. A boy could think out loud without evoking shock. He need not fear loss of family love nor of status because of his questions. If anything, in the university atmosphere he gained status and respect with his mug-skepticism. Francis adopted this life with spirit and vigor. This unplanned, uncataloged part of his education gave force to his pursuit of learning and gave him freedom to reach his own conclusions. Francis took it in stride. He was unafraid of knowledge, unafraid of thought.

At this time, the deists were the popular writers on religion. They were witty. They were fearless. They had questions. They were risqué. They appealed to youthful people. They were the Kerouacs of their day. Voltaire, the greatest of all, became the stimulater of Van der Kemp's religious thought. Voltaire wrote "It was only a long time after [Christ] that men took it into their heads . . . to usurp impertinent titles of grandeur, eminence, holiness and even divinity, which earthworms give to other earthworms. . . ." [7] Van der Kemp wrote in his autobiography that it was during this period he acquired a "deep hatred of the clerical hierarchy and their continued usurpations."

And he came to fit Voltaire's description of a theist:

The theist is a man firmly persuaded of the existence of a Supreme Being both good and powerful, who has created all life that is growing, thinking and reflecting; who perpetuates their species, who punishes crimes without cruelty and rewards virtuous actions with goodness.

The theist does not know how God punishes, how he gives favors, how he pardons, for he does not presume to know how God acts, but only that God does act and with justice. . . .

. . . He has brothers from Pekin to Cayenne and he counts all wise men as his brothers. He believes that religion is neither the opinions of an unintelligible meta-

physic nor vain display but that it is adoration and
justice. To do good—there is his worship; to be submis-
sive to God—there his doctrine. . . . He laughs at pil-
grimages but aids the needy and defends the oppressed.[8]

Van der Kemp acknowledged his keen interest in the
deists, shared by his fellow students, and acquired an extensive collection of deist books.

Van der Kemp's growing belief in opposition to the
clerics of his ancestral religion required the rejection of
much ritual and dogma. Francis hoped to eliminate clerical
authoritarianism with the aid of the deists. He read, "An
Englishman, as a free man, goes to heaven any way he
pleases." He applied the quip to free himself of intermediaries. Again he read how dissolute young French priests
amused themselves nightly in splendid amorous parties
and afterwards withdrew "to pray for the assistance of the
Holy Spirit and boldly call themselves successors of the
Apostles." [9] It is doubtful that young Van der Kemp knew
any profligate clerics, but he could see religious leaders
around him exercising divine authority with great human
error. In the free university atmosphere, he cast off the
worldly cloak from his personal religion.

He believed that good deeds were rewarded in heaven,
and bad deeds punished by withholding of favor. He considered brotherly love and tolerance highest virtues. He
felt the clergy should occupy positions of leadership but
not of authority, that power corrupted, "much more so—
when it presumes to be invested with the prerogative of
opening the gates of heaven to a favorite, or kicking a
damned one in the abyss." He wrote in 1813 that he had
known only two clergymen with brotherly love, one a professor of divinity who recommended a Socinian heretic "to
God's mercy, as he did see no means to save him," and the
other a Calvinist who considered Van der Kemp a heretic,
yet kept up an affectionate correspondence.[10] "If Christianity, my Dear Sir!" Van der Kemp wrote to Adams, "could
be induced to discard theology and adopt nothing but the

plain doctrine of our Divine Master . . . we all should soon be in unison of faith." [11] Van der Kemp wrote forty years later that he had formed his faith at the time of his university life and it had not been changed thereafter.[12]

He studied his Bible, particularly the Gospels, with a humble realization that much of it was not immediately understandable to him. Theology lectures were not enough. He did not understand thoroughly but he would not return to the intermediaries. At this point his religion approached simplicity of doctrine with no set creed and no difficult mysticism. He believed in God, he believed in an afterlife, he believed that Jesus came to lead the way to salvation, and he was convinced that all good believers in God would be saved. He no longer needed the orthodox clergy.

With other young university students, sons of the nobility as well as the gentry, he argued in public against the rule of the clergy. The debates were soon noted and Van der Kemp was singled out by the clerics as the chief culprit. Some of the boy's friends and patrons were grieved by his "waywardness." It was hard for them to understand his lack of respect for the clergy who represented the religion of his parents and of most of the Dutch for many generations. In efforts to help, they invited him to their homes and tried to sway him with good food followed by good arguments. His older friends argued reasonably that it was unnecessary and unwise to openly attack a whole system because of a few weaknesses. They counseled the youth to confine his liberal ideas to the classroom or tavern. Though Van der Kemp respected his friends as they respected him, he could not compromise. He was youthfully violent in his attitudes, and determined to oppose wrong openly.

Although he knew that Diderot and Rousseau had suffered for defending truth, Van der Kemp was unafraid. He was eager to join the campaign for freedom of the mind. He too opposed prejudice and ignorance in religion. He too supported the individual in the struggle against the shackles of ancient creeds and the hypocrisy of many religious rules. He intended to speak out against the forces of stagnation where he found them. He intended to write for freedom and progress.

The conservatives of the university faculty and like-minded citizens considered the defiant lad a product of the evil counsel of the eminent Professor Frederick Adolph Van der Marck. The student must be pulled away in an effort to save him. First, complaints were registered with the uncle who supported Van der Kemp. Next, the boy was brought before a council of faculty and clergy. He was warned he would soon be expelled from both the university and church if he continued his errant ways. He was advised to abandon the lectures of Van der Marck, drop his associations with other nonconforming students, "purify" his library by eliminating the deistical writings, and resume the former course of studies approved by his relatives. If he did these things, his youthful transgressions would be forgiven and he would be favored by official protection and good will.

Van der Kemp refused to surrender his principles and betray his schoolmaster, even though Van der Marck urged his spirited pupil to comply. The boy rejected the proposals "with disdain." His rebellion was now official. The idealistic lad was fighting for religious and academic freedom. However, his first freedom was economic, as conservative Uncle Adraen withdrew his financial support.

Van der Kemp's one financial asset was his fine collection of books. He prepared a catalog of a part of his library and held a public sale to pay his small debts and to sustain himself "in independence a while longer." A faculty friend bought his French deistical books privately, avoiding the scandal sure to arise from their public sale. Other sympathetic friends aided Van der Kemp in many ways.

With funds from the sale, the free student continued his work at Groningen, giving particular attention to "*Jus Publicum* [Public Law], its customs, usages and form of government." Careful management of his finances was necessary—including the elimination of the evening meal at the tavern with his fellow students. They invited him to continue at their expense but Van der Kemp declined. Instead, for dinner he reduced himself to bread, butter and cheese with one glass of wine. Friendly professors and townspeople sometimes invited him to more ample meals, and at least one patroness, Madame Mancel van Birum, opened "liberally her purse." In his autobiography, Van der Kemp described his behavior during these days:

> . . . I need not to insinuate that I was impeccable . . . my passions were violent and too often indulged, but more than once I was wonderfully spared. I owed . . . good will chiefly to . . . noble and generous minds, and in some respects to my unrelenting endeavours to save an outward decorum, to be courteous and condescending towards superiors, more so toward the females, firm and daring among my equals, kind to servants, and devoting nights and days, when not given to pleasure, to my studies.

His studies continued to include the stimulating lectures of Van der Marck.

At this time the professor published at Groningen his opinions on canon law. The clergy attacked the theses, and were enraged when Van der Marck was publicly defended by respected students and supported by important members of the church. Spies enrolled in his classes, took part in the discussions, then reported against him. Van der Marck also became the defendant in a notorious lawsuit resulting from his ridicule and condemnation of the clergy.

The final stroke was the publication of his lectures on the *Law of Nature and of Nations.* In this work he attempted to explain away many of the harsh tenets of the Calvinistic creed. The Dutch people were inflamed with rage against Van der Marck and he was accused of heresy at a special meeting of faculty and officials. The call of their church in danger aroused the "bigotted populace."

Van der Marck was tried before the Academic Senate. This court, composed of university officials and town representatives, judged students, graduates, and faculty members accused of serious offenses against university principles. Appeal could be made only to the Estates General, governing body of the Netherlands.

Weak followers deserted Van der Marck, as did many friends who were afraid. He insisted the creed he lived by was more truly orthodox than that of the Calvinists.[13] Because of the church-state relationship, politics were an inevitable part of the controversy. The case was discussed and argued throughout the country.

The national champion of orthodoxy, Petrus Hofstede, a Rotterdam preacher and professor, prevailed upon Stadholder William V, a curator of Groningen University, to support the churchmen. William's many opponents rallied to Van der Marck's defense, but to no avail. He was forced to resign and forbidden to partake of Holy Communion. Vindictive orthodox citizens made threats against the ousted professor when he attended church services.[14]

Van der Kemp was keenly moved by what he regarded as gross injustice. Though silence would have been to his advantage, he wrote and published a defense of his professor, *My Amusements*. University disapproval of this act and the vocal condemnation of the clergy forced Van der Kemp and about thirty other students to leave the University of Groningen. The master found a position of honor elsewhere and was returned to his chair at Groningen some twenty years later.[15] Van der Kemp, having already recognized that he must make his future beyond Groningen, was as ready to move as was the master.

Three opportunities were open to the young man. He numbered among his friends several prominent Remonstrants. These Protestants who had followed a path away from Calvinism offered him a full scholarship to their Amsterdam seminary. Many of his friends advised acceptance of this attractive offer, but Van der Kemp rejected it. How could he honorably accept an invitation implying he was an Arminian? How could he then convince anyone that Van der Marck was not guilty of the Arminian accusations made against him? Acceptance of the scholarship would have been a grievous blow to Van der Marck's case, and his pupil willingly made the sacrifice.

Two other possibilities remained. A position in the West Indies as tutor to the son of a Dutch gentleman was rejected as too big a responsibility. Van der Kemp wrote, "I knew myself too well to accept the guidance of a youth, when I was scarce to be trusted to regulate my own conduct." The third offer came through the influence of Van der Marck. It was a governmental position at Saint George Delmina on the African coast. Though both the position and its location were unattractive to Van der Kemp, he seriously considered accepting it, when it suddenly "struck his mind" that the Baptists and Mennonites of the Amsterdam region were liberal in principle. He had intimate friends among them, particularly Professor Oosterbaen of Amsterdam and the Reverend John Stinstra of Harlingen.

Van der Kemp wrote to Professor Oosterbaen asking for support to complete his studies at the Baptist Seminary in Amsterdam. The spirited youth included the proviso "*if* I could be admitted without compromising myself in any manner, without constraint to any religious opinions I might foster or adopt in future, and with a full assurance, that I should be decently supported." The Baptists accepted him and his conditions, with Professor Oosterbaen as Van der Kemp's champion.

At twenty-one, Van der Kemp had found a group who had full confidence in his ability and integrity. At last he had academic freedom to pursue the study of religion without restraint.

❧ III ❧

The Independent Ministry

At the age of twenty-one the mentally vigorous Van der Kemp left the university that had condemned him. What appeared to the Groningen administrators as a program of development appeared to Van der Kemp as intellectual confinement. During the summer before his entry into the Amsterdam Baptist seminary, he stayed in Franeker, where a vacationing friend had offered Van der Kemp the use of his apartment and library. The young booklover surveyed with great anticipation the numerous paths of knowledge represented by the variety of his friend's books. He spent the summer in the true scholar's solitary pleasure. He selected and read, pondered and took notes, and forgot the time of day or night.

In September he found that rooms had been engaged for him in Amsterdam by Professor Oosterbaen, "a friend and benefactor, a guide and father." Van der Kemp set up the remnants of his own library and immediately added some "indispensably required" books. Now he was ready and determined to make an inquiry into "the truth and nature of the Christian Revelation." He attended lectures in theology by Professors Oosterbaen and Van der Hersch, and in the Greek language by Professor Daniel Wyttenbach. He begrudged a small portion of time to mathematics and later acknowledged his study had been insufficient for worthwhile accomplishment. With this program of home study and lectures, "armed with the necessary knowledge of ancient and modern history, civil and ecclesiastical, with church antiquities and a tolerable supply of classic literature," Van der Kemp "endeavored to lay aside all preconceived prejudices, and desired with sincerity to discover the truth."

In the academic and religious community of the Dutch Baptists Van der Kemp applied himself diligently to the question of the historical authenticity of Christianity. He examined and studied arguments, called to mind the doubts of the deists, and finally settled the question for himself once and for all. First he examined the faults and weaknesses in the arguments of both deists and atheists. Probably his later comment in regard to Voltaire was conceived in his thinking now. "Voltaire, I am confident, did often not believe what he wrote." [1] In later years he also stated that his study of most "French unbelievers" before 1788 had left him with a low opinion of them "in regard to candour and sincerity." He felt that they were attacking practices which were not the ways of Jesus and therefore the attacks were "unfair dealing." Most of the deists he now considered to be pantheists.[2]

Next he approached the more difficult question, "What is Christianity?" He considered whether or not he could learn the answer from the lectures of Professor Oosterbaen, though he was a man of noted piety and learning and a valued friend to Van der Kemp. Could he become a preacher and merely repeat Oosterbaen's explanations? His "heart revolted at the idea of such a slavery." He could not accept on faith from any man the meaning of Christianity. He must find it for himself. His first assumption in the search was that it was possible for a man to discover this true meaning. He "took it for a truth, that if the Christian Revelation is from God, then any one, even of the meanest understanding, with a sincere heart, *may, must* be able to discover God's will, viz. what he is to do and to believe for his salvation."

Van der Kemp embarked upon the exercise with vigor and conviction. He studied the Greek New Testament, re-reading parts of the Four Gospels and the Book of Acts many times. Sections he did not understand were passed over at first on the basis that what a man could understand would be sufficient. He reached the conclusion in time that reason alone was not enough to explain life and immortality. He believed Jesus came into the world to enlighten through both reason and faith. He became convinced that God was a merciful being rather than an angry, jealous, capricious, selective deity. He believed God expected his creatures to have "sincerity of heart and genuine repentance" so that all His children might be saved. He believed man should love God and also love his neighbor.

Van der Kemp was through with the Dutch Reformed Church and Calvinism. When his cousin, Professor Didericus Van der Kemp, wrote a defense of Calvinism and the Calvinist deity, Francis shuddered "at the idea of such a God," and said he could not be converted by his good cousin's "Supralapsarian Doctrine." [3] The supralapsarian doctrine stated that God's elections were made before the fall of Adam. The infralapsarians believed the election came after the fall.

Van der Kemp continued to search for the answer to "What is Christianity?" In his autobiography Van der Kemp said that as he studied, he neither discovered nor searched for the dogmas of Calvin, Socinus, Menno, or Arminius. (He had already been accused of Arminianism because of his association with Van der Marck.) He considered the viewpoints of these four chiefly from literary or historical aspects. He intended to be free.

He was already prejudiced against Calvin as most responsible for the unreasonable strictness of the Dutch Reformed Church. Van der Kemp ultimately criticized Calvin in print through a defense of Michael Servetus.

The Spaniard Servetus had become a free thinking reformer at the age of twenty. He questioned infant baptism, the doctrines of the Trinity and predestination, and was

burned at the stake in Geneva by the Calvinists at the age
of forty-two.

Socinus was the Latinized name of Lelio Sozzini and his
nephew, Fausto. These Italian reformers planted the idea
of anti-Trinitarianism widely in North Europe, especially
Poland, where the nephew lived for a quarter of a century.
Fausto considered Christ the teacher of salvation rather
than the member of the Trinity who had sacrificed himself
for sinful man. Van der Kemp was puzzled by the Trinity
throughout his life and sometimes considered Socinianism
as a reasonable solution.

Jacobus Arminius, a former professor at Leyden, was the
recognized founder of the Remonstrants. He proclaimed
that Christ sacrificed himself for all men, that none are
elected, that believers are saved and unbelievers lost. Arminius rejected the supralapsarian and the infralapsarian
views as did Van der Kemp. However, Van der Kemp came
to emphasize good works at least as much as he did faith.

Menno Simons was also a Dutch reformer. He was opposed to infant baptism, and was a pacifist. He and his
followers insisted on good works through the threat of ex-
communication. Van der Kemp was never a pacifist but he
puzzled over baptism and fully agreed with the Mennonites
on the necessity for good works.

Actually Van der Kemp at this period attempted to do
for himself what the Dutch thinker Dirk Koornhert had
proposed in the 1500's as a general system. Koornhert had
suggested that the clergy be forbidden to say anything except the exact words of the Bible and that all treatises on
theology be eliminated. Van der Kemp proposed to search
out a true religion by personal use of this system. However,
his wide reading had already provided a background for
his interpretation. By November of 1773 his explanations
of his conclusions and beliefs to Oosterbaen led to his baptism at the "Tower and Lamb," [4] the familiar name of the
Amsterdam church where the service was performed.

For another two years the young man continued his
studies profitably and attended lectures faithfully. In addi-

tion, he made friends in Amsterdam. He grew to love Cornelis de Gyzelaer, about whom he later wrote, "Our intimacy began in 1774 at the University [Seminary], and was as ardent in our declining years as in the days of our youths." [5] He also extended his correspondence, an education in itself that Van der Kemp nourished and cherished as long as he lived. Among the new correspondents were learned men of Germany, Switzerland and Transylvania. On December 18, 1775, he was graduated and admitted as a candidate for the Baptist ministry.

The fledgling minister declined several unpromising calls in the spring and early summer. He accepted his first pastorate in August at the fishing village of Huyzen, near Amsterdam. The members of his consistory, the church's governing body, were "well instructed" men, an attraction to Van der Kemp, and community leaders were eager and energetic in making his life there comfortable and successful. His parishioners were either farmers or fishermen, living in relative ease but not quite in the main stream of Dutch life. Here he began his ministry in August of 1776 with a sermon based on I Corinthians, X, 15, "I speak as to wise men; judge ye what I say." This text exemplified his own long-held conviction that the clergy, including himself, were not infallible. The text also fitted the Baptist practice in regarding the minister merely as a spiritual leader. Van der Kemp always encouraged open and positive reactions to religious and political questions. He sincerely wanted people to judge what he said, then to act according to their judgments. Passive parishioners must have annoyed him.

While at Huyzen, Van der Kemp retained his connection with the seminary and Professor Oosterbaen. At the professor's suggestion he began the translation of some letters of Ganganelli (who became Pope Clement XIV), a project probably designed to keep Van der Kemp's scholarly interests alive. He began the work with enthusiasm but Oosterbaen frequently had to lend a hand, apparently even had to finish the work, saying, "Although you cannot submit to the drudgery, you shall not destroy my good intention."

Within a few months the young minister was offered a pastorate in Flanders but declined. The following summer he preached single sermons at Leyden and at Middelburg. In November, 1777, he took the pastorate of the Leyden church. This stimulating position established Van der Kemp in a center of Dutch religious and political thought where he was readily drawn into various political and religious controversies. The Leyden congregation had engaged a lively preacher who proceeded to lead his parishioners into spirited action.

His inaugural sermon was based on Paul's Letter to the Romans, I, 20:

> For the invisible things of him from the creation of the world are clearly seen, being understood by the things that are made, even his eternal power and Godhead; so that they are without excuse.

His studies of botany and chemistry had sparked a keen interest in God's creation which never waned. This text became a favorite theme and firm belief, that man could understand the world around him—even the universe. His sermon ended with emphasis on the last clause. He exhorted his parishioners to pursue knowledge "without excuse." The sermon was delivered to a large congregation, and Van der Kemp thought it successful. He did not give offense, he wrote, "except that a few old members of my congregation shuddered, when I told them that my father followed the army, and that I served in it during five years." The Baptists were pacifists and probably more than a few were uneasy.

In 1778 Van der Kemp preached a sermon on the Lord's Supper. The manuscript copy in his handwriting still exists. Years later (perhaps 1812–13) in America he translated and revised this sermon as one in a series, "The Scripture Doctrine of Baptism with three preliminary lectures on the use of the S.S. [Sacred Scriptures] and one on the Duties of a Religious Life." He began the Dutch sermon with a veiled attack on churches with a firm dogma. He then said two forces had disfigured the Christian religion, the educated and class-conscious clerics with a vested interest in controlling religious practices, and clerics uneducated in theology but ambitious for power. He said these two groups had changed "the simple and pure Gospel of Jesus" over the centuries into an "absurd system of human inventions," and that these changes had been largely responsible for the division of Christianity. The young minister suggested that his parishioners search the Scriptures for the path to salvation, as he had done. His text was taken from I Corinthians, X, 17, "For we being many are one bread, and one body: for we are all partakers of that one bread." He explained that he believed sincerely in Christianity.[6] His parishioners agreed with this interpretation and the idea of salvation through study, though these views were generally unacceptable beyond his own sect.

Some of his other surviving sermons are concerned with the excellency of God's law and natural consequences of virtue and vice. He frequently applied the words "natural" or "rational" to God's system and to man's ideal reaction to it. He also preached on subjects such as the Holy Ghost and the sins of pride. Psalm XIX was one of his favorite Bible passages, frequently used in whole or in part. "The Heavens declare the glory of God and the firmament sheweth his handiwork" became a guide to his religious philosophy and a challenge for him to learn ever more about the heavens and the firmament. A few of the sermons are dated at Leyden between 1778 and 1787. One with two dates was apparently delivered twice.[7]

In running conflicts between the Dutch Reformed Church and the liberal Van der Kemp, the Baptists were on his side. Arguments gradually became more political than religious. The conservatives generally supported the stadholder and his advisers. Van der Kemp was accused anew of being an Arminian because of the teaching of Van der Marck. Again, one of his critics was his cousin, conserva-

tive Professor Didericus Van der Kemp, who was eager
to destroy "tolerantism" within the Dutch Church. He
was "affable and courteous" but would not "commune with
a doubtful brother." He "approved the sincerity" of Francis but "lamented his errors."

An early struggle within the congregation at Leyden
concerned the freedom and autonomy of the local church.
The church had set up a fund for the poor at a time long
past but somehow the management and distribution had
been taken by a civil magistrate. Van der Kemp was determined to regain control for the church but found his tradi-
tion-bound consistory unwilling to support him. Over a
period of months he tried to talk them into action as they
tried to talk him out of it. He finally regained the fund for
his church. The consistory was not convinced that the campaign was proper but thanked their pastor.

Probably this episode of disagreement led to another of
greater personal import to Van der Kemp. Some one or
more members of the consistory now decided the present
pastor should subscribe to the formularies and creed of the
church as had previous ministers, and all but two supported
the request. These two board members supported Van der
Kemp in his refusal. His original expression of faith had
been accepted by the Baptists and he stoutly objected to
another imposed by the local church. The tyranny of a
consistory seemed just as dangerous to the understanding
and practice of Christianity as had the rules imposed by
leaders of the Dutch Church in Groningen. He refused to
comply and once again took a stand for religious freedom.
He held fast to this principle all his life.

Many sessions of the consistory were held to argue the
matter. Numerous discussions took place between the pastor
and individuals on the board.

Reasoning, ridicule, all was employed, long in vain,
till at length having exhausted their patience, and convince[d] of my unwillingness to give way one single hair-
breadth, one and another from time to time leaving their

side, all submitted to annul forever the articles of subscription.

In later years Van der Kemp said that Adams could have
been a member of the Leyden church even though his beliefs differed from those of the pastor. He wrote:

> We had no shackles whatever—I broke the last Cob-
> webs by a *minority* of three against twenty odd—say 24
> or 25—headed by my colleague. It was a truly popular or
> clerical assembly—and not the first, nor the last, where
> few daring individuals dictate. In that state the Church
> continued till my resignation—and then upon the same
> plan of Christian liberty a call was given to my successor
> —so it was my fate to oppose domineering power in
> church as well as state—and I yet feel some pride that
> all my labour was not in vain.[8]

This was Van der Kemp's last fight within the Leyden
church. He was given freedom of the pulpit and used it
to preach a live religion, often in sermons dealing with the
political questions of the day. Van der Kemp and the liberal Baptists were opposed to the stadholder and his party,
who supported and were supported by the Dutch Church.
Yet his parishioners may sometimes have questioned the
wisdom of their pastor's sermons or the expediency of his
recommendations for action. They may even have condemned his political activities as foolhardy. Many must
have disapproved when he appeared in the pulpit in the
uniform of the Free Corps, a citizen volunteer military
organization of the liberals. Some may have doubted the
wisdom of implying from the pulpit that the stadholder
tyrannized the Dutch in the way Samuel warned the children of Israel against in I Samuel, VIII, even as they
agreed with Van der Kemp's use of the 109th Psalm to
show the need for vigilance and positive action to maintain
the Baptists and liberals against their enemies.

Whatever faults his parishioners may have found, their
affection was sincere. The congregation's general apprecia-

tion and support was demonstrated when Van der Kemp became ill. The church held his place for six weeks until he recovered. When he went to Wyk am Dursted in 1787 to lead the Free Corps, his place was kept until he resigned it a few months later. The resignation was regretfully accepted with a resolution of commendation which Van der Kemp considered most flattering and honorable.

Van der Kemp never took another congregation. He had won the battles for freedom and righteousness in his church. At Groningen he had come out honorably in the struggle for academic freedom. In both situations politics were involved and Van der Kemp found that he had been inexorably drawn into the struggle for political freedom. He accepted the challenge while still at Leyden.

❦ IV ❧

The Sacred Fire of Patriotism

VAN DER KEMP was twenty-five years old when he became the pastor of the Leyden church in 1777. For the ten years that he served his congregation, his life was a continual, feverish drive for service. He served his God and his fellow men with enthusiasm, eager to identify and carry out his civic responsibilities along with his professional duties.

All the time which I now could spare, I devoted to becoming thoroughly acquainted not only with the history and antiquities, but principally with the laws and constitution of my country. My bosom glowed with the sacred fire of patriotism, and it seemed to me the period was fast approaching, if not already there, in which these sacred rights—long lost or neglected or made doubtful—for which the blood of our ancestors had been shed with such a profusion, might be recovered.

Van der Kemp had been a child of the Enlightenment. Now he was to become a man of the Age of Revolution.

Already the American Revolution was being fought and Dutch interests were involved. Would the Netherlands support the English as the stadholder and his party wished, or would it try to advance Dutch trade and lend money to the Americans in a policy of pulling away from the old ties

30

with England? Most Dutchmen took a position consistent
with their support of, or opposition to, the stadholder's
policies. Van der Kemp, one of those who opposed, had
an emotional as well as an intellectual interest in the American struggle. He had become a liberal through his experiences and his learning. He was determined to live his lib-
eralism.

The stadholder's position was hereditary, but only with
the approval of the people by election. Though he was not
a king, many of his supporters treated him like one and
called him "the Prince." The Estates General, the Dutch
national congress, had evolved into a legislative body still
representing the provinces but dominated by commercial
interests. Most of the aristocracy, other than the stadholder,
were prominent people who had become wealthy through
commercial undertakings. For a century they had kept
the stadholder in a limited executive position, with the
ultimate decision-making in the Estates General. However,
control wavered according to the national and international
situation and according to the problem at hand.

Each province of the Dutch union had a parliamentary
body with party lines drawn in similar fashion. Belief in
states' rights was generally prevalent and the provincial
leaders considered their territories to be sovereign, acting
outside the union on some occasions. The stadholder was
looked upon by the liberals as a convenience that could
be dispensed with at will. The conservatives in the provinces
were apt to support the stadholder as the dependable
head of the Dutch nation in opposition to the lesser folk
who appeared to be striving for power. In the provincial
legislatures questions of policy might be decided with little
concern for international consequences, perhaps even in an
isolationist spirit. The local governments in the towns and
cities were important chiefly in local affairs, but the larger
cities sent representatives to the Estates General.

Only members of the Dutch Reformed Church could
serve in governmental positions and as officers in the army.
The established church could thereby wield a strong power

in national and local politics. The church also exercised great influence upon and some control over the universities and education in general. However, dissenters from the Dutch Church had freedom of worship and were not prevented from gaining a livelihood in commerce, agriculture, or other pursuits outside of civil service. These dissenters were frequently leaders of thought and were respected if not honored.

In the over-all development of European ideas during the Enlightenment the Dutch did not contribute significantly but they did participate and were greatly influenced by popular literature. Some of the more important writings were banned by various provinces, complete freedom of the press being considered undesirable. However, the publishing business was active. Many books, pamphlets and periodicals flowed from the presses, mostly in Dutch or French. Thus most of the literature that preceded the Age of Revolution was available in the Netherlands. Van der Kemp was one of those who read avidly and tried to apply enlightened ideas to the Dutch nation.

Two important people of character and merit aided the young minister in his quest for political righteousness. Johan Derk Van der Capellen and Peter Paulus became his friends and political tutors. Baron Van der Capellen of Pol was a member of the provincial legislature of Overyssel, Van der Kemp's home province. He was only eleven years older than his new friend and had made his way into Dutch politics just a few years before. He first gained prominence in 1775 by speaking in the provincial legislature against sending a brigade of Scottish mercenaries to help England subdue her American colonies. The occasion called for vigorous counteraction, as the well-trained brigade was already in service in the Netherlands, apparently available and ready to leave for America.

Van der Capellen was not content with blocking the measure only in Overyssel, but spoke outside the legislative hall against the proposal. This action was seized upon by the stadholder's partisans as contrary to the established precedent of secrecy of discussion. He was expelled from the legislature.

In the considerable period of time before his reinstatement, Van der Capellen continued to be active. The courageous baron was engaged in a prolonged campaign to abolish the *corvées* in his province. He opposed this rem-nant of the feudal age whereby small farmers had to give two days of service per year to the province.

Robert Jaspar Van der Capellen of Marsch, a cousin, was also a leading Patriot and later became a close friend of Van der Kemp.

In 1776 the established order was further alarmed by Van der Capellen of Pol's publication of his Dutch translation of Richard Price's *Essay on Civil Liberty*. By this time Paulus had become a close friend to both Van der Kemp and Van der Capellen. At about the same time that the baron's translation appeared, Paulus wrote and published an *Essay on the Usefulness of the Stadholderate, as it Ought to Have Been,* a criticism of the current operation of the Dutch government. He followed this by other essays attacking the stadholder's lack of adherence to the Union of Utrecht, the constitutional arrangement established in 1579 by which the provinces were bound together. Van der Kemp, inspired by the work of his compatriots, was determined to assist in righting the wrongs of his political world.

After careful consultations with his friends, Van der Kemp published in the form of five letters his *Observations on the Union of Utrecht,* first anonymously but later reprinted under his name. In these letters he commented on issues such as military jurisdiction, army quotas, and the settlement of disputes within the union. These *Observations,* along with the writings of Paulus, were a first step toward public action. It was necessary at the outset to impress upon the Dutch populace the point that the system of the union and the stadholderate should and could be reevaluated and examined for weaknesses. If patriotic citizens could be convinced they had a right and obligation to criticize their government, serious faults might be corrected. Van der Kemp continued the examination by a great research task of finding and collecting as many documents as possible bearing on the Dutch government— from archives, from libraries, from private papers. In regard to the research, he wrote:

> I perceived the forged chains which were to be riveted on the necks of my countrymen, and deemed it a feasible thing to break these. I perceived their insensibility and indolence, and would rouse them to vigorous unrelenting action; I glowed with indignation when I became convinced that in the fetters prepared for the Americans, the slavery of my own country was a chief ingredient.

Encouraged by other incensed citizens such as Peter Vreede, Cornelis de Gyselaer and John Luzac as well as Van der Capellen and Paulus, Van der Kemp not only preached reform in his church but wrote about it for the "larger parish."

In a continuation of the efforts begun by Van der Capellen to abolish the *corvées,* Van der Kemp wrote a series of essays with documentary support. He felt the work levies were retained only to keep the people in subjection. He published his attack anonymously, for the official party was already alarmed. A reward was offered for either the printer or author, but the officials were out of tune with the times. Not only did they fail to locate the culprit, but they received petitions from every section of the province for discontinuance of *corvée* slavery. The provincial government yielded to the pressure and abolished the work days.

A follow-up of this victory was the publication of papers objecting to the expulsion of Van der Capellen of Pol from his seat in the legislature of Overyssel. Van der Kemp's research and editing in *Capellen Regent* persuaded the people but not the authorities. It was not until 1782 that Van der Capellen was restored to his legislative seat.

In the meantime the liberals—Patriots, as they soon called themselves—became more interested in the American Revolution. Already the *Gazette de Leyde,* edited by John and

Etienne Luzac and boasting an international circulation, had been reporting the news from America as well as that from Europe. Now the editors began to advocate Dutch support of the American Congress. The British request for the Scottish brigade had caused contention and the problems facing Dutch commerce, particularly privateers, drew attention to the American war. In September, 1779, John Paul Jones, arriving victoriously in the Zuider Zee with his prize, the *Serapis,* was honored with ballads and toasts in Amsterdam, the Hague, and many towns and cities.[1] Jones' triumphal visit increased reader interest in Van der Kemp's *Collection of State Papers on Unlimited Convoys,* which supported the popular view of convoying that would aid Dutch commerce and at the same time aid the American cause. In the war the stadholder was favorable to England in spite of the privateers preying on Dutch merchantmen and warships stopping the Dutch for search. The unlimited convoy would furnish the protection of the Dutch navy for a great many more ships, but would be contrary to the stadholder's wishes.

Early in 1780 John Adams came to the Netherlands to win support for his country. He called upon friendly noblemen, merchants, and other influential people for loans and recognition of the United States. Since the stadholder's supporters were largely pro-British, Adams came to be associated more and more with the Patriots. However, his duty was to gain favor from all. At Leyden, where his sons, John Quincy and Thomas, were at the university, Adams composed a pamphlet on the resources and prospects of his country which gained wide circulation in Dutch translations. It was a good beginning.

The worthiness of Adams' cause impressed Patriot Van der Capellen. The baron loaned to the Americans a goodly portion of an inheritance he had just received.

And it was Van der Capellen who brought John Adams and Francis Van der Kemp together. As Van der Kemp put it, ". . . My confidential friend inspired me with an irresistible desire to see and know that man, on whom he bestowed with profusion his enthusiastic encomiums, . . ."[2]

In writing to Adams in October 1780, Van der Capellen asserted that his good friend Van der Kemp could be of great help to the American cause inasmuch as he had a great deal of learning, intense loyalty, and fearlessness not ordinarily found in a Mennonite preacher.[3] On February 24, 1781, Adams met Van der Kemp at Leyden and in April invited him to a meeting.

> Mr. Adam's Compliments to Mr Van der Kemp and asks the favour of his Company this Evening at the golden Lyon, to spend the Evening and Sup with a chosen few of honest Americans.[4]

In later years Van der Kemp recalled with pleasure the meetings with Adams and various Dutch Patriots at the Golden Lyon and elsewhere. Adams, too, wrote of these meetings, giving the following particulars:

> Capellen was frequently puzzled with the Reports fabricated by the Anglomanes, representing the affairs of America to be in a desperate situation. I recollect some instances, when he seemed to be in a state of despondency. Upon these occasions I made very light of his fears, contradicted the facts he had heard and denied the inferences he drew; which sometimes brought on spirited argument between us, but never any coolness. Time always justified me and confuted him, and he was always ready to acknowledge when he was convinced.[5]

Van der Kemp was strongly impressed with Adams' arguments, being more than confirmed in his already favorable opinion of American political leaders. His interest turned from Dutch documents to American papers. He published a *Collection of Tracts Relative to the United States of North America,* including letters of Governor Jonathan Trumbull of Connecticut and Governor William Livingston of New Jersey in defense and explanation of the American system, along with a sermon of Dr. Myles Cooper, formerly president of King's College (Columbia University). Van der Kemp's preface described the new nation and compared it to the Dutch union. The collection was dedicated to the American republic and published under the pseudonym of Junius Brutus.

On June 5, 1781, Van der Kemp informed Adams of his work as follows:

> The letter of Governor Trumbull is at the printer's. I have finished the translation of the Articles of Confederation of the United States in 1778 and also the sermon of Dr. Cooper and the article of the heads of enquiry with the answer to it printed at Boston, all as one piece relative to the letter of the Governor. One of my friends is translating the other pieces and speeches relative to the Constitution of Massachusetts Bay, and after my return to Leyden I shall give all these papers to the public with a preface, which I shall write in the free air of Appeltern.[6]

John Luzac, the friend who was aiding in the translation had been in communication with Adams about American affairs for more than a year.[7] When Van der Kemp presented a copy to the New-York Historical Society in 1818 through De Witt Clinton, he wrote, "I defended the American cause with my pen and purse, when no distant thought beat in my breast of visiting this country, when it required some courage to take its side against a powerful Court-Party." [8]

In November of 1781 he wrote to Adams in imperfect English congratulating him on "the complete victory of your arms in the Chesapeake-bay and the Burgoynishing of that mighty Lord [Cornwallis] with his many thousand slaves." He believed that the corrupt British ministry would now learn that despotism "must be vanquished by the soldiers of Liberty." He thanked God for the success in America and wished his own countrymen would awake from their lethargy and "oppose the measures of a profligate court with vigour and rather die gallantly in the battle than to bow their knee for a man." Yet he feared both barons Van der Capellen might be persecuted for their activities and that he himself might be in jeopardy for his recent publications.[9] He hoped the American republic, an ideal to Dutch reformers, would be an example for stirring up all people deprived of their rights.[10]

Overworked by his vigorous preaching of political reform, his frequent meetings with other Patriots, and his extensive research and writing, Van der Kemp became sick in the winter of 1779–80. He narrated the interlude of suffering and threat of death with great feeling.

On Friday evening when returning from my literary club earlier than usual, a violent headache compelling me to retreat, I went to bed, passed a restless night, awoke with increased pain, which compelled me to go again to bed in the afternoon, giving orders to my servant to awake me at three in the morning, as my sermon was yet unfinished. I executed my task above my expectation, preached with an increasing headache from instant to instant, laid down as soon as I reached home, and was on Monday morning so much exhausted that writing three lines to my friend P. Vreede, they were illegible. My strength gradually diminished and I was reduced that day to a state of stupid lethargy; all my faculties were benumbed; pain had left me; time seemed not to exist. My physician was perplexed, and apprehensive that the vital powers were so far absorbed that I must ere long sink under it. What was remarkable, the moment I shut my eyes I had a MS. leaf, then on the press, in my hand, read it till I arrived at an erasure, and then I awoke; this sensation continued a fortnight. My physician had ordered me the use of Peruvian bark [quinine, used for fevers], and recommended the country air. I was carried to the seacoast, and received at my former residence [Huyzen] with kindness, mingled with deep distress at my situation. Not one but despaired of my recovery. I took every hour a teaspoonful of bark in powder, made to a palatable conserve by syrup of roses. Within a fort-

night after my arrival I began to revive, and moved
through the room; my appetite returned; with this I
joined sea bathing, increased my bodily exercise with my
renewed devouring appetite, lessened gradually the use
of the bark, and continued my exercises, amusing myself
in the society of my surrounding friends, without so
much as looking at a book, and within six weeks I returned in the full bloom of youth and muscular strength
to Leyden, so that every one was astonished in witnessing
this surprising recovery. Thus was my usefulness restored.

These six weeks probably comprise one of the longest
periods of time in Van der Kemp's adult life spent "without so much as looking at a book."

Instead of moderating his strenuous program of research,
writing and preaching, Van der Kemp, with the sacred fire
of youth and patriotism, increased it. Before his illness he
had outlined a series of documents illustrating the encroachments of military courts on the rights of Dutch
citizens. He now embarked upon the necessary research
with vigor. He collected documents and records from obscure places, and searched out copies of papers which had
been maliciously destroyed. Editing and arranging the vast
amount of material was a monumental project.

He first interrupted this work to strike off a "cutting
philippic," *A Laurel Wreath for a Few Nobles,* an attack
on a segment of the Court party. Though Van der Kemp
considered it of little value, the short essay reached more
readers than the eleven-volume collection of documents on
which he worked for several years.

Now Van der Kemp, with the support of his friends,
faced a critical court action involving freedom of speech
and of the press, and the right of citizens to criticize the
government. On January 1, 1780, Van der Kemp published
a lyric poem written by Peter Vreede in praise of the active
Friesland opposition to the Court party.

When John Adams came to the Netherlands seeking
recognition, Friesland was the first province to act favorably

in its legislature, sending a petition to the Estates General for recognition. The provinces of Zeeland and Overyssel soon followed. This Frisian Act had been foreshadowed by a lesser act of opposition to the stadholder in behalf of unlimited convoys, and the poem praised the Frisian democratic spirit. The printer was arrested and immediately asked Van der Kemp to accept full responsibility. Van der Kemp felt obliged not only to protect the printer but, being single, was willing to take the blame to protect Vreede, married and father of two children. The accused man was summoned to appear on April 10, 1780, for criminal process. The Patriots were alarmed. Was Van der Kemp being prosecuted because of his other writings, especially the *State Papers* by Junius Brutus? They urged him to flee the country, arranged a place in Brussels, and secured the protection of the French government for his safety. Even Van der Capellen thought Van der Kemp would be a useless sacrifice if he stood trial. Only John Luzac, a lawyer as well as editor, saw the possibilities of a great victory against tyranny, a strike against unjust prosecution. He and Van der Kemp had a long discussion.[11] Luzac not only agreed to defend Van der Kemp but secured the assistance of the eminent lawyer Van Zelderen who was an Orangist but had the courage and independence to stand for justice. Although Van der Kemp and Luzac differed at this time over political theory, they respected and supported each other with zeal.[12] Van der Kemp stayed.

The first hearing of the prominent clergyman from Leyden was held on May 1 before the High Academic Tribunal, composed of the rector of the University of Leyden, four professors, four burgomasters and two *échevins* or magistrates of the city. Procedure required withdrawal of the defendant's lawyers while the prosecutor questioned the defendant before the tribunal behind closed doors. Standing before the court from one o'clock in the afternoon until ten o'clock that night Van der Kemp faced 94 major questions, "some very intricate and ambiguously expressed." His ardent study of the law stood him in good stead. He answered fearlessly many of the leading questions. He declined to answer those he knew he was entitled by law to refuse. He was spirited in his answers regarding religious issues brought into the case, and was told secretly that various members of the tribunal sided with him in this matter against the prosecutor. He was released that night on solemn promise to reappear when summoned. After several postponements had been granted to the prosecutor, he appealed to the Committee of State for permission to prosecute Van der Kemp as author of the Junius Brutus writings. This was referred back to the Academic Tribunal, as was an appeal to the provincial legislature for more time. Two outstanding law professors now prepared a remonstrance, accepted by the tribunal and sent on to the legislature. Nothing happened. The tribunal in forceful language demanded that the case be completed and justice rendered. The tribunal suspected that by avoiding a decision, the prosecution intended to leave Van der Kemp permanently damaged through their strong accusations. The tribunal was against this injustice and advised Van der Kemp to appeal in person directly to the legislature at the Hague. He did so, "claiming loudly for justice, either by absolution or condemnation." Additional insistent requests from the tribunal brought orders to the prosecutor from the legislature to terminate the trial. A new prosecutor was in office and appeared with a declaration that he had no grounds for continuing. Van der Kemp was acquitted on January 28, 1782.

The nature of this lengthy court action would have ruined the career of a lesser man. Though it had disturbed many of his parishioners, Van der Kemp was rightfully proud of the victory. Peter Vreede paid the full expenses.

Victory for freedom of the press was heralded by Van der Kemp's publication of a full account of the court procedures together with Vreede's ode. To please his congregation he also published a volume of sermons, but his more timid parishioners were unable to rejoice long. Their pastor soon wrote a forceful sermon, *A Delineation of the Conduct of Israel and Rehoboam* "as a mirror for the Prince and the Nation."

> And Jereboam and all the congregation of Israel came, and spoke unto Rehoboam, saying: Thy father made our yoke grievous: now therefore make thou the grievous service of thy father, and his heavy yoke which he put upon us, lighter, and we will serve thee. . . . And the king answered the people roughly, and forsook the old men's counsel that they gave him; and spoke to them after the counsel of the young men, saying, My father made your yoke heavy, and I will add to your yoke: my father also chastised you with whips, but I will chastise you with scorpions. . . . Then king Rehoboam sent Adoram, who was over the tribute; and all Israel stoned him with stones, that he died. Therefore king Rehoboam made speed to get him up to his chariot, to flee to Jerusalem. So Israel rebelled against the house of David. . . .

The fiery sermon, a threat to the stadholder and the House of Orange, soon became famous. Van der Kemp was requested to deliver it three times, and it was twice published.

The 109th Psalm, invoking God's wrath upon the enemy who "persecuted the poor and needy" was used as a favorite hymn. Samuel's account of the ills that befell Israel under evil kings furnished texts for sermons delivered with great ardor.[13] Van der Kemp criticized not only the prince, but demanded right action from all in authority. He held up revolutionary America as a beacon for the Netherlands. On February 27, 1782, shortly after his acquittal, he delivered an oration in which he declared his hope.

> In America the sun has risen brightly, a promise to us if we will it. America alone can make our commerce and shipping revive. America alone can make our factories blossom again and restore Leyden to its former luster. America can lift us up, if we dare look up. It is a land of justice, we are a land of sin. America can teach us to reverse the degeneration of the national character, check

the corruption of morals, stop bribery, smother the beginnings of tyranny, and dying freedom restore to health. America has been ordained to heal the wounds of the Netherlands people, if we will follow her footsteps, if we will rise up and build anew.[14]

The Leyden congregation had an agitator for a minister, but they respected his ideals and his sincerity. They did not reject him.

❧ V ❧

The Shadow of Liberty

THE revolution in the English colonies in America had broadened into an international war. France allied herself with the revolutionists in 1778 and Spain followed in 1779. France's entry into the war affected the Netherlands because of French influence on the anti-English party, the Patriots. In spite of British interference, Dutch trade with the colonies continued to flourish, mostly through the Dutch island of St. Eustatius in the West Indies. Hoping to stop this trade and the growing friendliness between the nations, Great Britain declared war on the Netherlands in December, 1780.

Amsterdam had led the way in the expansion of the lucrative trade with America, going so far as to make a secret treaty with the United States in 1778. Cordial feelings toward America prevailed in this city led by the Regents (the commercial nobility), who were in loose alliance with the Patriots. When Great Britain declared war, the stadholder and the Orange Party accused the commercial group of stirring up an unnecessary war with the "friendly" British.

Two famous pamphlets, published in 1781, solidified the political division. R. M. van Goens wrote *A Political Remonstrance Against the True System of Amsterdam* in which he exposed the "evil" acts of the commercial interests since 1581, particularly Amsterdam's secret agreement with the American colonies.[1] Van der Kemp was visiting

44

his friend Van der Capellen at Appeltern when the latter wrote a powerful counter to Van Goens, with Van der Kemp's hearty approval, entitled *An Address to the Netherlands People.* Van der Kemp said, "Seldom had use been made of bolder language; the alleged facts were stubborn, and truth appeared in all its awful solemnity." The pamphlet pointed out schemes of the Orange followers over the past two hundred years designed to put a hereditary yoke on the Dutch. The princes of the House of Orange were described as tyrants, with the present William pictured as courting and conspiring with England against Amsterdam, building up the army and neglecting the navy, and seeking trouble with France. The Duke of Brunswick, in charge of military affairs, was absolved of guilt. The pamphlet called for change, charging that encroachments had been made on the rights of the people by the princes and their followers for two centuries. Van der Capellen proclaimed that the Dutch people owned the Netherlands in the same way that shareholders own a commercial enterprise. He claimed the officials were only employees and should be controlled through elections, as in America. The prince was denounced for filling the town councils, the provincial legislatures and the Estates General with sycophants.[2] The essay exhorted the Dutch to action:

> Assemble in your towns and villages. Meet peaceably, and elect from among yourselves a moderate number of courageous, virtuous and pious men; choose good Patriots that you can trust. Send these as your deputies to the places of assembly of your several provincial estates, and order them in the name and by the authority of this nation, to make an inquiry, by and with the estates of the other provinces, into the reasons for the extraordinary inertia with which the arming of the country against a formidable and active enemy is being handled. Order them also . . . to choose a council for His Highness . . .
>
> Provide for the freedom of the press, the one support of your national liberty. . . .

Arm yourselves, elect those who must command you
. . . and in all things proceed like the people of America,
with modesty and composure.[3]

This revolutionary writing advocated force only if necessary, following the typical Dutch philosophy of seeking
freedom by lawful means, with no desire for the violence
soon to come in the French Revolution. Nevertheless, it
clearly called for open defiance. Van der Kemp had been
considered a dangerous foe to the established government
for merely publishing an ode of criticism, so both he and
Van der Capellen were fully aware that the author of this
rebellious pamphlet would be even more severely prosecuted.

Van der Kemp arranged for the booklet's secret printing,
then its secret distribution in both cities and countryside
on the night of September 25–26, 1781. He chose his con-
spirators well, as neither author nor distributors became
known. Several provinces offered rewards for information
leading to the author or printer. Banishment and heavy
fines were threatened if anyone should print, publish or
distribute the pamphlet in the future.[4] But suppression of
the work was impossible. It was widely read in the Netherlands, soon appeared beyond its borders, and within a
month was translated into English.

After the English declared war against the Dutch, the
Patriots' sympathy for the American revolutionists increased. However, documents and articles about American
ideals and principles seldom appealed to members of the
mercantile aristocracy, even if they were opposed to the
stadholder. In his correspondence with Van der Kemp,
John Adams asked in June of 1781 "What say the People
of the Country? It is among the Yeomenry of every country that we are to expect to find the Supporters of Liberty." [5] In another letter of November, Adams further advised his friend, the Dutch preacher-agitator:

[I]t is necessary for Some Individuals in critical Seasons
to run great Risques Submit to great Sacrifice and en-

dure severe Sufferings. National Characters are not
formed nor great publick Blessings, especially that greatest of all Liberty but by the Patience and Steadiness of
Individuals. A Man must be possessed of Benevolence to
his fellow Men, stronger than any of his Passions,
stronger than death, before he is qualified to Stem the
Torrent of Venality, and Servility, which opposes the
Introduction of Liberty in some Countries and which
tends to expell it from others.

Adams indicated a desire to see Van der Kemp at Amsterdam where he could express in person his respect for "so
able and intrepid an Advocate for Liberty." [6]

From time to time Van der Kemp worked on his *Magazine of Authentic Documents on the Military Jurisdiction*
and by the end of 1781 four volumes were finished. The
editor's contention, and that of his friends, was that military
men should be tried in regular courts for both military
and civil actions except where the Estates General called
for a military trial.[7] The subject had been taken up by
various provincial legislatures, the Orangists not opposing.
Van der Kemp made his volumes available to all these
bodies. They were appreciatively received by most, rejected
by some.[8] The popularity of the cause grew until all
provinces annulled the jurisdiction of the High Military
Court. Soon thereafter the national legislature and the
stadholder gave their approval. Four more volumes were
published in the course of the arguments and a final three
after the decision as "warnings to posterity, how usurpa-
tion, slowly creeping forward, at length takes hold with a
thousand roots, not to be eradicated without a great struggle."

How Van der Kemp found time to do other things is
difficult to understand. In the summer of 1781 he attempted
to arrange passage as chaplain on Commodore Alexander
Gillon's American ship for a clergyman friend.[9] Some time
later Commodore Gillon invited Van der Kemp to dine on
board his ship, the *South Carolina*.[10]

On May 20, 1782, Van der Kemp married Reinira Engelbartha Johanna Vos, a descendant of the Beekman family, some of whom had emigrated to America and become prominent on the lower Hudson. Van der Kemp probably met her through John Luzac, a close friend of the Vos family for many years. However, the family was not of the Patriot persuasion. Engelbartha's father had been a burgomaster of Nymegen and her brother was a partisan for the stadholder. Her mother reluctantly consented to the marriage but in time developed a great affection for her son-in-law.

If one judged by a letter Van der Kemp wrote in April, one might humorously think he was contracting marriage in the way he might contract a small business matter. In one sentence he offered his services to Adams to influence the Regents of Leyden for a treaty of commerce. In the next he said he was going to Nymegen on Monday to complete arrangements for his marriage and expected to be in Friesland in June—these details so that Adams would know where to reach him.[11] The fact of the matter seems to be that he separated his private life and his public life. At this time he was not a close enough friend to Adams to discuss his private life. Such closeness developed slowly.

They were married when Engelbartha was thirty-six and Francis was thirty. Each had waited long enough for a good match and this was it. Their first son, John Jacob, was born on April 22, 1783, their daughter, Cuneira Engelbartha, on February 17, 1785. The third and last child, Peter Anthony, was born in America in 1789.[12]

With a wife and family to share his life, Van der Kemp's personal fortune was much to his liking. But the prospects for the future of his country were far less promising, and he continued his political activity. The Patriots, meeting first in secret, came together openly in Amsterdam beginning in April, 1783. Other meetings followed in August and October and came to be looked upon as the "party assemblies of the democrats over the whole republic." Van der Kemp and Peter Vreede were among the most outspoken and demonstrative Patriots at the assemblies.

The Patriot cause of reform in government, including the curtailment of the stadholder's power, was not as strong as the Patriots desired. France apparently expected the Patriots to succeed with little assistance, while England was beginning to support and urge action of the House of Orange against them. Prussia also indicated strong support of the stadholder and his Prussian wife. The Regents were having doubts about their tentative collaboration with the Patriots because they merely wanted to curb the stadholder, not raise up democracy.

Through all the maneuverings, one province could hardly depend on another, and the rural people throughout the Netherlands stood firm for their Prince. Every action seemed a crisis.

A central office was set up at the Hague to preserve unity. The national militia, almost entirely under the control of the Orangists, did not always respect the rights of the common man. Therefore, the organization of new military companies was urged. This Free Corps proposed to share the duties of preventing violence, external or internal, a function long thought of as belonging only to the established government.[13] The Patriots felt that through the Free Corps they could participate more fully in government, bear a greater responsibility, and help to promote the cause of liberty. In Leyden the corps to which Van der Kemp belonged was called the Society of Manual Exercise for Freedom and Fatherland.[14] The new militia was open to all, regardless of religion, and Van der Kemp with his cadet training was a valuable corpsman. The companies multiplied with rapidity and by the end of 1783 had secured provincial unity, in another year national unity. At Utrecht the Free Corps, led by Philip Jurian Ondaatje, a university student, proposed that the stadholder's power to name members of the provincial legislature be abolished. Another proposal called for the election of representatives to sit with the Utrecht Provincial Council to discuss taxation and appointments. The first proposal failed to win approval, but the second met with success. Twelve companies in the city chose two representatives each. The council accepted these consultants but hesitated when a further request was made for popular election of burgomasters.[15] With its effective leadership, Utrecht became the center for national Free Corps activity, with its successes and failures of great interest to Dutch citizens. With the shaky alliance between Regents and Democrats about to break up, and the House of Orange ever more determined not to give up any of its powers, internal trouble was inevitable.

In Leyden the Free Corps under the leadership of Van der Kemp asked for consideration and a redress of grievances. The requests were refused and Van der Kemp resigned as being of no further value. Shortly he left Leyden to go to Wyk where he gave all his energies to writing and to political and military organization.

During this time, Van der Kemp produced unsigned articles for the *Amsterdam Political Courier,* the principal organ of the rebels, edited by Jan Christiann Hespe. Van der Kemp also wrote for the *Post of the Lower Rhine* and *The French Observer.* In 1785 editor Hespe was prosecuted and imprisoned for his printing. Van der Kemp wrote an article in his behalf. A prominent citizen answered and a series of arguments and rebuttals followed. The trial became another national issue, with public opinion favoring the oppressed editor. Hespe's acquittal was a significant victory for freedom of the press. Hespe and Van der Kemp, perhaps others, "wrote then with greater ease and more liberty than ever before." Further writings included sequels to his Van der Capellen defense, *History of the Admission of Johan Derk, Baron van der Capellen of Pol, into the Equestrian Order of Overyssel; and Defence of Colonel Alexander Baron van der Capellen* (formerly chamberlain to the stadholder). In collaboration with Peter Vreede, "the friend of my bosom," and P. van Schelle, he produced biting and witty sketches of prominent Orange partisans, *Catalogue raisonné des tableaux,* in answer to unfriendly sketches of Patriot leaders. He "was day by day deeper entangled in the political labyrinth, till at length it became utterly impossible to extricate" himself. Once he tried in earnest to withdraw but could not.

The French and British governments were supporting the two parties with funds by 1785. Van der Kemp "hated the British influence then so predominant at the Court, but could not bear that of France." He warned his Patriot friends against the soft pledges of France and predicted a betrayal. They did not listen. He and Luzac were too well acquainted with the history of the French Court and nation to be duped and betrayed by French promises. The two Patriots admired, yet hated the British for their domineering spirit and their support of the stadholder. With a British alliance the Dutch had been subject to the tyranny of the House of Orange. Without the alliance France was needed.[16] Van der Kemp joined openly the Democratic party of Utrecht but hoped somehow "to save the whole by a timely reconciliation of all the dissenting parts." He wanted good government with real liberty. In 1814 he wrote:

> You know that under the ancient form of Republican government—I speak of the times before 1787—it was only a shadow of Liberty which was enjoyed by the mass of the Nation. The Magistracy of the voting cities might be called free, but besides these few distinguished families, besides the safety of property and persons, all the remaining parts had no more share in their government as an American or Asiatic could have claimed in it. Also the ancient forms, marks, &c were abolished. . . . I was not afraid of a constitutional king but would not bear the countroul of an unlimited arbitrary master.[17]

On another occasion he had written that the Dutch

had contented themselves with a shadow—the name of Liberty—while they had it in their power to consolidate all the blessings to their posterity, had they dared to make a sacrifice of their prejudices, limited the executive powers [but] with increased splendour in the House of

Orange, and allowed the people at large an equal representation. This with an armed well-disciplined militia and a sufficient navy might have construed their Republick till this day. . . .[18]

He zealously attempted to organize this needed "armed well disciplined militia" even though he suspected it was too late. He had misgivings about the possibilities of establishing a democratic form of government in the Netherlands at this time. In a letter to Adams on December 11, 1785, he asked for letters of recommendation to America, saying he would leave as soon as he could persuade his wife. He would not, he could not with safety, linger beyond the time when all hope of re-establishing liberty was gone.[19]

In the meantime, Van der Kemp joined Philip Jurian Ondaatje and Peter Vreede in attempts to unify the Free Corps. Otto Derck Gordon and Adam G. Mappa soon joined the effort, the latter with his great military knowledge and skill taking charge of a small Patriot army. Van der Kemp himself was unanimously elected captain of the Wyk Corps, *Pro Pace et Bello,* on August 1, 1785.[20] His critic, Nicolas Calkoen, said that in Wyk "Nothing was done, or all was done, Van der Kemp *unico consule.*"

In 1786 the Free Corps gained control of the provinces of Holland, Groningen and Overyssel. Holland Province deprived William V of his offices of Stadholder and Captain General. In a meeting at Leyden the Corps resolved, "Freedom is an inalienable right belonging to all citizens of the Netherlands confederation." They further declared, "This liberty would be a deceptive shadow if representatives were to be independent of those whom they represent; and their appointment by the people, by a firmly settled plan, is the most appropriate way to prevent this independence." In 1786 Utrecht abolished the old council and got a new one by election.[21] Van der Kemp described this series of events as "a revolution constitutionally begun and finished without a shadow of disorder, without injuring

any individual's property, without spilling one single drop
of blood."

The National Assembly of the Free Corps at Utrecht
sent Van der Kemp to the meeting of Patriot Regents at
Amsterdam. A joint declaration was agreed upon and published calling for a true republican form of government
with a subordinate stadholder and opposing any government by one man or by one family.[22]

In October and again in December of 1786 Van der
Kemp wrote to Adams for letters of recommendation and
for advice regarding settlement in America. He asked for
some detailed information about living in the new country, particularly New York and New Hampshire. For four
years he had wanted to come to America. Now he hoped to
embark in May or June of 1787. He wrote that public affairs had taken a bad turn. The aristocracy and their blind
followers were rejoicing. A number of people of eminence
and promise, convinced that the stadholder's powers were
weakened, now connived to further their own causes. The
Regents party of the province of Holland were appeasing
the stadholder in other provinces while trying to maintain
the independence of their own province. Utrecht and Wyk
were uncertain, grievances were unredressed, and potential
enemies were all around. Van der Kemp feared that secret
compacts were being made, one perhaps by Amsterdam,
whereby William V would regain his power over his
"slaves." [23]

The prophet of doom was neither heeded nor honored.
Unable to convince his friends of the inevitable dissolution
of the Patriot party, Van der Kemp nevertheless chose to
work with them to the last. He expressed in letters to Adams
his hopelessness for the Patriot cause in 1785 and 1786.
Success of the French diplomat La Vauguyon in securing
guns and money for the Patriots was more than offset by
English support of the Orange aristocracy. The French
were not ready to threaten England with force. The Austrians had been discouraged from warring against the Dutch
but Prussia was a danger to the Dutch rebels because the

wife of William V was the daughter of the Prussian king. And formidable support for the stadholder remained among the Regents and was increasing among the peasantry and aristocracy.

In September of 1786 in Gelderland a force sent by the stadholder overawed a force of the Free Corps. Lack of leadership resulted in confusion, then panic and flight in spite of the Free Corps' watchwords, "Dead or free." The historian Blok gave the cynical summary, "Thousands of tears were shed, not a drop of blood." [24] In the province of Holland the Patriots took vigorous action but had little reliable force in their Free Corps. The Patriot Regents met in Utrecht in October and the assembly of the Free Corps met there in November. They anticipated civil war. Utrecht Province vainly expected aid from its neighbor Holland where a number of regular army units were operating under Patriot orders, and the actions of the stadholder's forces became stronger in 1787. On May 26 the Prince issued a declaration forbidding compromise. In early June the British minister to the Netherlands, Sir James Harris, demanded more energetic action against Utrecht. Some of the army regiments under the control of Patriots in Holland Province went over to the Orange and had to be replaced by inadequate Free Corps. The wife of the stadholder, Princess Wilhelmina, now endeavored to go from their seat at Nymwegen to the Hague to arouse the Estates General for the princes.[25] She was stopped and forced to turn back by provincial troops, but aroused public sympathy because of the troops' high-handed methods. Furthermore, the ire of the king of Prussia was roused at this insult to his daughter. With these discouraging episodes, it was little wonder that Van der Kemp prophesied doom for the Patriot cause.

However, the Free Corps captain did his best at Wyk. When military action threatened in the Province of Utrecht Van der Kemp was sent as a delegate to a compromise conference. A truce was agreed upon. The Patriots promised not to break the dikes in exchange for an assurance that the stadholder's troops would not "commit any hostilities" for the duration of the truce. The truce was dishonorably broken three days after the conference when Van der Kemp's forces were surrounded at Wyk by an aristocratic segment of the provincial militia numbering some 1500 men, with six pieces of artillery and two mortars. Van der Kemp commanded less than a hundred men in his Free Corps, with Adrian de Nys as commander of the village. The officer of the opposing force declared formally that he came by order of the prince to garrison the city and nothing more. He promised solemnly neither persons nor property would be molested if there was no resistance. The magistrates of Wyk repeatedly asked that the force be admitted to avoid sacrifice of women and children. But this military action was a betrayal of the recent conference truce agreement. Van der Kemp wrote:

> I tried in vain to raise their spirits; in vain I called duty and honour to my aid; they vociferated louder and more and more; the confusion increased; nothing was heard but "Open the gates"; so that even my friend de Nys, the first in command, would have given way. I then took boldly the lead, and told the Magistrates that they were in office and should be obeyed, but only on written orders duly signed by their Secretary; and that if they hesitated one moment longer to give my friend that pledge that they commanded the surrender, I should without any further delay, command to fire. . . . My friend received their orders and while he made the preparations to open the gates, I led the whole of our armed force, in number about ninety men, through the gate which was not occupied; . . .

Thus on the fourth of July the surrender was agreed upon and was carried out on the fifth. Van der Kemp and De Nys changed to civilian clothing and awaited to see if there would be further action by the force which had promised they would suffer no reprisals following their un-resisting surrender. They were arrested the next day.

They were first held in informal custody, but two days later were taken to Amersfoort, stronghold of the prince.

Here Van der Kemp was kept under close guard in a public building, though not behind bars. His mail was examined and he was not permitted to see members of his family. The people of the vicinity of Amersfoort saw him as a spectacle either when he was allowed to exercise or by entering the building where he was confined. The old partisans of the stadholder treated him "with great courtesy, the mob with insolence, and they who had become renegades of the Patriot party with a rancorous malice."

After the province of Utrecht was taken over by the Prussians for the stadholder, Van der Kemp and De Nys were moved to a building in the city of Utrecht, and again were put under heavy guard. However, various officials had conferences with them and, when the Patriot cause was no more, other Patriots visited Van der Kemp. At this time, they arranged for the painting of his portrait, the one good picture which remains. Van der Kemp was free enough to have books in prison and he probably played chess or whist.

Van der Kemp was held prisoner until December, under no clear accusation. However, the confinement was obviously because of his writings, his preaching, and his organization work among the Patriots and in the Free Corps. His country had fallen "in the flames" and the "most honest people had been the victims." When the Prussian army came, the Free Corps everywhere disbanded and tens of thousands of Patriots fled, with the majority seeking refuge in Belgium.

From Amsterdam in 1788 John Adams summarized the situation for Abigail:

> The rich complain, at present in Holland that the poor are set over them in the Regencies and the Old Families that they are set aside by new ones. Discontent rankles deep in some places, and among some sorts of men: but the Common People appear to be much pleased.
>
> The Patriots in this country were little read in History less in Government: knew little of the human heart and still less of the World. They have therefore been the

Dupes of Foreign Politicks, and their own undigested systems.

Changes may happen and disorders may break out, tho at present there is no apparent Probability of either.[26]

Van der Kemp had fallen an early victim to counter-revolution and the aristocracy steadily became stronger and his imprisonment continued.

Recognizing Van der Kemp's considerable influence on his countrymen, a faction of the stadholder's supporters endeavored to win him over to their cause. In the Netherlands there had long been a middle group critical of and often antagonistic to the House of Orange—"A sort of Whiggery in which the people had no concern." [27] In times past this group was the only opposition but now found themselves between democracy and aristocracy. The Dutch called this loyal opposition group Loevestein. When Van der Kemp was released it was rumored that he intended to support the Loevestein group. During his imprisonment pressure had been applied to his wife to persuade Van der Kemp to accept a respectable compromise position. In addition, Van Loon, a prominent civilian Orangist, had visited the prisoner and promised to make arrangements for Van der Kemp's further service to his country in an honorable capacity with those who had been his opponents. Van der Kemp could not compromise his strong stand against a tyranny which usurped the liberty of his people. He resolved to go to a new land. The treachery of those in power and the desertion of those to whom he looked for support had made the cause of freedom hopeless. The bitterness of being unable to serve and help save the cause of freedom in his native land was revealed when he said some fifteen years later, "I swore when I was sacrificed in Holland that I never if my life was preserved again would step forward [for a hopeless cause] never without any exception . . ." [28] He had been sacrificed to "the shadow of Liberty" and he never forgot. Throughout his life he continued to warn the people how easily their liberties could be lost and how hard they were to regain.

❧ VI ❧

New Home,
New Allegiance

Van der Kemp's published essays revealed his increasing admiration for America, while his visits to the Golden Lyon and to Gillon's ship increased his admiration for Americans. He especially admired John Adams and Josiah Quincy for their impartial and skillful defense of the unpopular Captain Preston in the Boston Massacre case.[1] The British captain was acquitted. Van der Kemp's correspondence with Adams discloses an emerging idea and growing plan of going to the land of the Americans.

The advice given to a friend who wished to emigrate must have shaped some of his thinking. On June 5, 1781, Van der Kemp asked Adams if a clergyman friend might go to America. The friend had great talent, profound judgment, much learning, a brilliant character, and was a lover of liberty. A resident of Middelburg in Zeeland, he was discouraged at the course of events in the Netherlands. He hoped to be able to preach in America as soon as he improved his English. Adams was asked for letters of recommendation and also if passage could be obtained as chaplain on board an American vessel.[2] Adams replied promptly that he would speak to Commodore Gillon. He added, "There are in America so many clergymen, that I cannot give your Friend any Encouragement of Success: but if he persists in his Resolution to go I will give him a Letter of Introduction to Some Friends." [3]

A few months later Van der Kemp was jubilant upon hearing of the surrender of Cornwallis. He congratulated Adams in spirited but poor English: "If any man rejoice in the prosperity of the United States i wil hope that me shal not be denied a place amongst them. . . ." He told of the possibility of being prosecuted for his writings on America and said with certainty that America would be his asylum if he had to leave his native land. The letter concluded with his plans for further writing.[4] Adams replied that he would be happy to see the proposed publication and added the compliment, "I shall be very happy to see you at Amsterdam, and the sooner the better, that I may have an opportunity to express in Person the high Esteem and Respect for so able and intrepid an Advocate for Liberty. . . ." [5]

In April of 1782 Van der Kemp wrote that not one of his countrymen was more addicted to the cause of America and more attached to Adams than he, and offered his services.[6] Some months later Adams wrote from Paris that Dr. John Wheelock, president of Dartmouth College, was coming to the Netherlands to seek subscriptions for the college. He asked Van der Kemp to advise Wheelock.[7] The two learned scholars enjoyed several interesting conversations about America and American education. Van der Kemp repeatedly displayed eagerness for news and information regarding almost every aspect of American life.

When the American war was over and the British also made peace with the other countries which had been involved, the cause of the Dutch Patriots became less promising. Van der Kemp wrote that as soon as he could persuade his wife to leave, he would ask for letters of recommendation to be used in America although he was not sure that political affairs would allow him to remain alive in the Netherlands for long.[8] On October 31, 1786, he wrote again of his fears for freedom and his desires for the past four years to go to America. His fortune had recently improved; now his funds might suffice to support himself and family in a new land. He had investigated briefly the states of New Hampshire and New York, especially the less expensive rural areas. Were these places pleasant and fertile? Could he live with "ease, dignity and reputation" with sixteen or seventeen thousand florins? Could he hope to provide an inheritance for his children? He asked Adams to send enough details to persuade his "respectable wife to quit this place." He hoped to leave the Netherlands in the spring of 1787 and thought some other families might accompany them. If others were willing, it would help to convince Mrs. Van der Kemp.[9]

Adams did not answer the letter until December 1, probably because of mail delays between Leyden and London. Before Van der Kemp received the reply, he impatiently wrote again, wondering if his first letter had not arrived. This time he specified the area around Albany as his choice and asked if there were a better atlas of America than Jeffreys, which he already had.[10] Adams replied:

. . . The questions you do me the Honour to propose to me, are very difficult to Answer. I have ever been Scrupulous of advising Strangers to emigrate to America. There are difficulties to be encountered in every Exchange of Country, Arising from the Climate Soil, Air, manner of Living &c, and Accident may always happen.

With the sum of Money you mention, a Man and a Family may live in America: but it must be in a frugal manner—with a taste for Rural Life, by the Purchase of a Farm, and diligent Attention to it, a Man might live very comfortably. You may have views of Commerce, or other occupations, which may improve the Prospect. If a Number of Friendly Families were to remove together, they would mutually assist each other and make the risk less as well as Life more agreeable.

If you determine to go, I will give you Letters of Introduction with Pleasure. . . .[11]

This reply was quite enough for Francis Van der Kemp but not encouraging enough to persuade his wife, Engelbartha. They stayed in the Netherlands, where Francis became more and more involved with the Free Corps at Wyk. The surrender on July 4 and his subsequent imprisonment awoke Engelbartha to the dangerous position of an outspoken advocate of liberty in the Netherlands. The arrival of the Prussians increased her alarm. Yet she supported Francis in his refusals to compromise his principles. Various members of the Orange party came to "lure and persuade" her to "appeal to the Prince Stadholder, and solicit his intercession." She refused to try to influence her husband to act against his principles, even when her brother, now a member of the Estates General, asked it. Other efforts were made directly to Francis but were treated by him with haughty disdain.

In early December the Orange party saw only fragments of opposition and no longer feared Van der Kemp and De Nys. It was announced they would be released upon payment of a huge sum of 45,000 florins each as surety for damages incurred by the state. Van der Kemp's penalty also specified his permanent and immediate departure from the province of Utrecht.[12] De Nys paid both sums of money. The two men were freed on December 19. They went to the home of De Nys in Wyk where they were entertained in great festivity by numerous friends and acquaintances. Van der Kemp, under orders to leave the province, prepared quickly for his journey, ate, bade his family and friends farewell and "sprang on a chariot" with a companion of Wyk, Major de Wys. A friendly and reliable Orange man accompanied them, promising Mrs. Van der Kemp he would conduct her husband safely to Belgium. The exile reached Antwerp on December 21 and planned his next step. Engelbartha was at last willing to go to America with her husband. He now wrote her at Leyden that, "if it remained her firm purpose to share my fate," she should sell their property in Leyden—house, library, statues, busts, medals, and superfluous furniture—and send the rest (including

selected books) to Amsterdam in care of the commercial
firm of Wilhelm and Willink. After that she and the children should join him at Antwerp. He found it difficult to
part with his library, and sent word to his wife to keep
much of it. By the following March the family was reunited
in Antwerp.

Van der Kemp wrote to Adams shortly after his release.
He explained his imprisonment and release, said that Van
der Capellen of Marsch and Luzac would vouch for his integrity in the Wyk affair and asked for the promised letters
of recommendation. He expected to sail for America in
March and to settle in the vicinity of Albany.[13]

Adams replied immediately that he was much relieved to
hear Van der Kemp was at liberty and safe in Belgium. He
enclosed two letters of introduction and added the cheerful
news that living had become cheaper and that Van der
Kemp should "succeed very well" in America, if not in
New York, then in Pennsylvania. However, he added the
warning, "You will be upon your guard among the Dutch
people in New York respecting religious principles, until
you have prudently informed yourself of the state of parties
there." [14]

From Antwerp the Van der Kemps went to Brussels
where they were gladly received by Baron van der Capellen
of Marsch. He provided letters of recommendation from
Lafayette and agreed to get others from Jefferson in Paris.
The baron had fled from the Netherlands along with
thousands of Patriots. Many of these Patriots knew Van
der Kemp, welcomed him, and regretted his proposed departure. Jacob Hoofman, a generous and zealous patron of
Van der Kemp in his youth, perhaps at Groningen, now
gave his protégé the generous gift of a thousand guilders.
He admired Van der Kemp and his loyal wife and wanted
to make their passage across the Atlantic as comfortable as
possible.

After a few days at Brussels the Van der Kemp family
went on to Havre de Grace where they expected to board
the packet for New York. However, the ship was under-

going repairs and had canceled the March sailing. The impatient exiles were on the point of going to England to get a sailing when an American frigate, *L'Henriette,* stopped for ballast and was recommended. Captain Benjamin Weeks was in charge of the ship, in the employ of the Rosses of Philadelphia. The Van der Kemps were delighted. They sailed on the twenty-fifth of March and had a good passage of about six weeks. The captain enjoyed his unexpected passengers and extended many favors to the Van der Kemp family. He even hired a Dutch cabin boy to serve Mrs. Van der Kemp, who spoke no English except *yes* and *no.* The captain was "pious without ostentation." "No better order could be kept in a vessel than that which was maintained with regard to every individual on that of Captain Weeks'; never could a vessel be better manned with expert sailors or have a more intelligent and prudent master, . . ."

They arrived in New York harbor on May 4, Van der Kemp's thirty-sixth birthday, and went to a respectable boarding house in Hanover Square. With their feet on American soil and a wonderfully kind feeling toward Captain Weeks, the American who had brought them safely to their new land, the Van der Kemps went about the practical matters of becoming re-established. The first consideration was the payment of their passage. The captain could not take the French coins offered but said his company would make a draft on a New York house. This was soon done with notification that no charge was made for the two children. Included was a cordial note that the company would be happy to receive a visit from their passengers. Next Van der Kemp sent his letters of recommendation and picked up the ones from Jefferson, along with other mail from Europe.

Among the letters was an offer of a position in Russia. His fine old master, Professor Oosterbaen, had secured through Prince Gregory Potemkin and the Russian ambassador to the Netherlands, Prince Dmitri Alexeievitch Gallitzin, an offer to superintend a large colony of German Baptists located in the vicinity of Kherson in the Crimea. This was an important post with great prestige. Yet Van der Kemp's arrival in America had been too pleasant for him to be tempted by the Russian offer.

In 1813 he wrote that he had rejected the offer because he "had too much the fear of Siberia in my eye and prefer yet, to be here a tenant at will—than to bathe in opulence, and watch the wink of the greatest Boyar in the world." [15] Nothing could induce him to put his "shoulders under the iron yoke of a despot, how well soever that yoke was gilded and adorned."

The immigrants arrived in New York City just a few days after the election for delegates to the convention at Poughkeepsie to determine whether the state of New York should ratify the new constitution. The party of George Clinton had won a commanding majority of the delegates, but the able politicians Hamilton, Jay, and Robert Livingston of the opposition, were wholeheartedly in favor of immediate ratification. The outcome was uncertain and there was much activity to influence doubtful delegates, both before the convention started on June 17 and while it was in session.

The Van der Kemps did not realize that much of the excitement at the time of their reception was political. A revival of commerce and industry, giving the promise of prosperity, added to the optimistic good will with which the Van der Kemps were greeted. Alexander Hamilton, Henry Knox, Governor George Clinton and Melancthon Smith received the Van der Kemps graciously and generously. To the new Americans, it almost seemed that the families were in rivalry to do the most for them. "No relatives, no parents could do more than Mr. and Mrs. Clinton; the venerable Mrs. Tappan welcomed Mrs. Van der Kemp as a daughter. Both ladies and also Mrs. Hamilton conversed with . . . [her] in Dutch."

Van der Kemp sent letters of introduction to James Madison, Jeremiah W. Wadsworth, Governor William Livingston, Benjamin Franklin and George Washington. He greatly admired both Franklin and Washington and had published a Livingston letter back in the Netherlands.

The immigrant was especially pleased at a cordial and respectful letter from Washington with an invitation to visit Mount Vernon:

> Sir: The letter which you did me the favor to address to me the 15th of this instt. from New York has been duly received, and I take the speediest occasion to well-come your arrival on the American shore.
>
> I had always hoped that this land might become a safe and agreeable Asylum to the virtuous and persecuted part of mankind, to whatever nation they might belong; but I shall be the more particularly happy, if this Country can be, by any means, useful to the Patriots of Holland, with whose situation I am peculiarly touched, and of whose public virtue I entertain a great opinion.
>
> You may rest assured, Sir, of my best and most friendly sentiments of your suffering compatriots, and that, while I deplore the calamities to which many of the most worthy members of your Community have been reduced by the late foreign interposition in the interior affairs of the United Netherlands; I shall flatter myself that many of them will be able with the wrecks of their fortunes which may have escaped the extensive devastation, to settle themselves in comfort, freedom and ease in some corner of the vast regions of America. The spirit of the Religions and the genius of the political Institutions of this Country must be an inducement. Under a good government (which I have no doubt we shall establish) this Country certainly promises greater advantages, than almost any other, to persons of moderate property, who are determined to be sober, industrious and virtuous members of Society. And it must not be concealed, that a knowledge that these are the general characteristics of your compatriots would be as favorable circumstances, as I hope will attend your first operations; I think it probable that your coming will be the harbinger for many more to adventure across the Atlantic.
>
> In the meantime give me leave to request that I may

have the pleasure to see you at my house whensoever it
can be convenient to you, and to offer whatsoever services it may ever be in my power to afford yourself, as well
as to the other Patriots and friends to the rights of Mankind of the Dutch Nation.[16]

The invitation was too great an honor to reject but first
Van der Kemp wanted to take care of his family. He, Mrs.
Van der Kemp, and their daughter, Betsy, took a five-weeks'
tour of New York State. They traveled on the Hudson to
Albany and up the Mohawk as far as Philip Schuyler's house
at the Palatine settlement. On July 15 Francis wrote to a
correspondent in Kentucky that his trip in New York had
been difficult for his wife and she was dissuaded from going far to settle. He appreciated the invitation to Kentucky
but thought he would purchase a little farm in New York.[17]
On July 25 he wrote to Adams that they had seen two farms
near Kingston that suited them and if the price were right
they would make a purchase in two or three weeks. While
he awaited developments he was going to Philadelphia and
Mount Vernon. He then congratulated the people of Massachusetts for their good sense in electing Adams to Congress and asked what the best history of the American Revolution was.[18]

Soon Van der Kemp set out to meet more of the great men
of America. He went first to Elizabethtown, New Jersey, and
spent some time agreeably with Governor Livingston. From
there he traveled to Philadelphia where he visited Benjamin Franklin, an Antwerp mercantile firm, the family of
Captain Weeks, and the house of Ross to express his appreciation for the favors on his voyage. He went on to Baltimore to see his old friend Adrian Valck who was in business
and also serving as Dutch Consul. He arrived on July 29
at Mount Vernon "where simplicity, order, unadorned
grandeur, and dignity had taken up their abode." He told
Adams "the politeness with which I was received there gives
me new pleasure by their remembrances." [19] However, in his
autobiography he said of Washington,

There seemed to me, to skulk somewhat of a repulsive coldness, not congenial with my mind, under a courteous demeanour; and I was infinitely better pleased by the unassuming, modest gentleness of the lady, than with the conscious superiority of her consort.

Later statements about Washington indicate that no harsh criticism was intended by the statement and that he always honored Washington. Washington's diary, primarily concerned with plantation supervision, nevertheless mentions Van der Kemp's visit briefly. A cordial letter written by Washington in the fall after Van der Kemp's July visit, indicates that Van der Kemp impressed him. Washington wrote that he was pleased that Van der Kemp had purchased a good farm and hoped him a happy asylum.

The trip was good for the immigrant. He had been warmly welcomed to his new country in Elizabethtown, Philadelphia and Baltimore. He had met great patriots and started firm friendships, including those with John and Abigail Adams. He had breathed the air of freedom longed for in vain in his native land. He returned from Mount Vernon to his own property, the farm in Esopus (though its title was not clear for several months), eager to take up his role as a free American.

Only one thing remained. On February 28, 1789, the legislature of New York passed a measure entitled, "An Act to naturalise the persons therein named, and to prevent the avoidance of titles in certain cases, by reason of alienism." The Van der Kemps and a number of other people had petitioned for citizenship. It was granted upon taking an oath in a court of record for a fee of nine shillings. Children were to take the oath upon reaching the age of twenty-one.[20] Van der Kemp proudly made the affirmation and became an American, eager to participate in the struggles for progress in political, social and economic life, eager to share in the dreams and promises of America.

ᛥ VII ᛥ

The Farm on the Esopus

THE Van der Kemps bought a farm northwest of Kingston
near the Saugerties road in the basin of Esopus Creek. Van
der Kemp was aware that its soil had been exhausted by
excessive cropping and little fertilizing, but was confident
he could farm it successfully and that in a half dozen years
"well employed" he would gain for himself and family "an
easy and honest subsistence," the highest reward of his desires.[1] His meager farming experience in Holland had been
greatly augmented by reading and keen observation. He
intended to apply the same intelligent scientific care that
George Washington and Robert Livingston gave to their
estates.

On February 26, 1789, he bought the farm of Sylvester
Salisbury, deceased, for £1100. The house was of blue lime-
stone, one and a half stories high,[2] similar to many other
Dutch houses along the Hudson. The roof of such a house
was of shingles, perhaps white pine, and there were two
chimneys—one for the huge fireplace in the kitchen and
the other for the parlor. Other downstairs rooms were generally not heated nor was there heat in the sleeping quarters upstairs. Family life centered around the kitchen.
Here the cooking was done in the fireplace, the spinning
wheel was often busy, the meals were eaten, and intellectual and business interests were pursued.

The Van der Kemp furnishings were better than common.
An upper middle class Dutch home usually held a highly pol-

ished dining table, good chairs, a Dutch corner cupboard for fine china, high poster beds, and a grandfather clock. Chests held clothing and bedding while open cases held the treasured books Van der Kemp brought so carefully from Holland. Probably he had a desk for writing and business affairs, with the business definitely second to the writing. Engelbartha Van der Kemp was a good Dutch *huisvrouw* and kept the house spotless—with the possible exception of the desk.

The neighbors looked at the Van der Kemp furnishings and suspected the family of being wealthy. When the prominent Clintons stopped by to visit and the wealthy Livingstons came from Claremont, the last doubt was removed. Van der Kemp, resolved to provide well for his family, spent money in farming not as a Hudson Valley tenant or yeoman but as a country squire or lord of a manor. Census figures for 1790 number seven people living on the Van der Kemp lands in addition to the immediate family.[3]

Actually Van der Kemp was short of money. His liquidation of assets in the Netherlands did not provide him with all that he hoped. When he purchased the Salisbury farm he was unable to pay for it outright and had difficulty securing money for the payment due in the following summer of 1789. He asked Governor George Clinton for advice and received it immediately. Since the farm was "considerably improved" and 25 per cent of the purchase price had been paid, Van der Kemp could either borrow money for the payment, though Clinton did not have the money to lend and it might be hard to get, or ask the creditors of the Salisbury estate to extend the due date. He assured Van der Kemp of his friendship and urged him to discuss his affair with "Mr. Tappan," (perhaps Christopher Tappan, Clinton's brother-in-law), the bearer of the letter.[4]

Clinton had just gone through a strenuous and bitter political campaign in which he had barely managed to defeat Robert Yates in the election for governor. The letter expressing concern and good wishes for Van der Kemp was written by a tired and busy man.

Van der Kemp obtained a loan from Holland, apparently from the firm represented by Nicholas Van Staphorst and Wilhelm Willink [5] who handled various loans for the United States government. With this help he continued his new life in the Hudson Valley, the life of a preacher-soldier-scholar turned farmer.

The depleted soil demanded the major portion of his time and energy. Religious activities he reduced to family devotions and friendly discussion, thereby also avoiding antagonizing his Dutch Reformed neighbors. His love of books and learning continued as much a part of his new life as it had been in the old. His military life was over but not forgotten.

Secretary of War General Henry Knox submitted a revised plan for a standing army to President Washington on January 18, 1790, and the president sent it to Congress on January 21. The secretary recognized the sentiment against a professional standing army and proposed a well-trained militia, part of which would be in the service of the national government. The proposed number of troops was 325,000, with about one-fourth to be older men, trained but in reserve. Van der Kemp wanted this militia to succeed in order to avoid a strong standing army. On November 12, 1790, he wrote to General Knox that more training in theory was necessary and should be provided in a military academy similar to those in France and Prussia. The curriculum should include geometry, algebra, trigonometry, geography, engineering, fortification and tactics. He suggested a plan for selecting cadets and outlined library needs and a testing program with medal awards.[6]

Other people, such as Alexander Hamilton and Frederick W. von Steuben, also had plans for an academy. The idea was debated in the president's cabinet in November, 1793, and Washington called for the establishment of such a school in 1796. Adams repeated the request but the act of establishment came under Jefferson in 1802.

According to the 1790 census report, the Van der Kemp neighbors were the Ten Broecks, Van Gaasbecks, De Witts,

Folands, Jansens, Salisburys and Swartzes.[7] There were Beekmans a little farther away but within easy walking or riding distance. Two of the neighbors, Jacobus Van Gaasbeck and Johannis Beekman, had served on the Kingston Committee of Safety during the Revolutionary War, and there were two Beekmans in the militia.[8] Nearby Kingston was an outstanding center of Patriot sentiment and activity, having served as the meeting place for the convention which drew up the first New York State constitution in April, 1777. Later in the year the town was burned by General John Vaughan for its activity, but the Patriots were not subdued.[9] The home and other buildings of Robert Livingston, chancellor of the state of New York, were burned at about the same time.[10] Near the close of the war, George Washington was given a fine reception in Kingston. A year later, in 1783, the citizens offered their village as the national capital.[11]

When the Van der Kemps settled in Ulster County, American Patriots with Dutch ancestry had common bonds with the Dutch Patriot from the old country. However, these neighbors in Ulster were influenced little by the Enlightenment. They farmed and lived in traditional modes, uninspired by new methods, with little interest in science and philosophy. When John Lincklaen, agent for the Holland Land Company, stopped with the Van der Kemps in 1792, he wrote in his journal,

> Mr. van der Kemp, by taking more care to cultivate & clean his grain than his neighbours, has sold it for a shilling the bushel more than his neighbours. He has sold it for 7/6 the bushel, weighing 64 pounds on the spot.[12]

Van der Kemp discussed farming with George Washington, William Livingston, governor of New Jersey, and many others. In the fall of 1789 he asked Livingston for lima pole beans and offered to send something in return. Van der Kemp happily reported that at least forty out of his sixty apple and pear trees from Europe were alive. He expected another shipment in the spring. A postscript announced the birth of his son Peter, "a part of my payment as an American Citizen." [13]

In 1793 Van der Kemp corresponded with Chancellor Robert Livingston concerning the fertilizing of lands. He recounted Schubart von Klefeld's successful experiments on crops and meadows from 1777 to 1785 through the use of Gips (gypsum) or plaster.

Van der Kemp described his own experiments:

> In 1790 I tried it upon wheat and rye, without any remarkable benefit—the same year on clover with no benefit at all—but the soil was exhausted—not manured in several years cold—wet and compacted.
>
> In 1791 I manured ½ of not quit[e] two acres with common dung the other with Plaster—sowed it with Buck-wheat—and gathered from the first part 11 Bush. from five small slu-loads—36 Bush. from six small slu-loads—from that manured with Plaster—the straw being uncommon thick—warm sandy soil.
>
> In 1792—a piece of oats of 15 Bush. a 5 part manured with Plaster—the other ⅘ with common dung—The whole piece was sowed with 55 [?] Bush.—No finer Piece of oats in the country—The part manured with Plaster was too heavy and lay down—the produce of the whole was better than 350 Bush—and two years before, this same piece could not pay the expenses when it was planted with corn, though wel[l] fallowed—being three times plowed and well manured. For this last crop it was plowed four times, once in the fall, and three times in the spring.
>
> I tried it again this season in Buckwheat—and Indian corn—had you any success with the Bromus [?] Giganteas? the mice damaged that of last year—this year I was more successful—I shall sow a part this fall on the Oneida—My Astracan Buck-wheat promises much—[14]

Chancellor Livingston was also an agricultural experimenter and welcomed new knowledge furnished by Van der Kemp's letters. The administrative position as chancellor of the state was second to the governor in New York State. Though the term of office coincided with each administration, the title of honor was retained for life, much as that of judge. Livingston was the first president of the New York Society for the Promotion of Agriculture, Arts and Manufactures. Among the early topics considered by the society were the uses of lucerne, lime and gypsum. The chancellor was a strong exponent of the virtues of these three aids to good crops.

The gentlemen farmers and learned professional men who composed the membership of the society were impressed with the vital importance of soil conservation. Livingston promoted understanding by sharing his remarkable knowledge of the chemistry of plants and soils. He contributed a great deal to the society by describing his own experiments and evaluating the experiments of others such as Van der Kemp.[15]

The owner of Mount Vernon faced similar problems and exchanged ideas with many agriculturalists, including Van der Kemp. Two weeks after the latter's visit to the general, Washington wrote to a friend about attempts to grow white wheat from England at Mount Vernon and the need for improvement of the crop rotation system. He was certain that the common rotation of corn, wheat and hay was ruinous. Instead of three fields, he was using six:

In 1788 for instance, one of them (say No. 1) is planted with Corn 8 feet by 2, single stalks; with Irish Potatoes or Carrots, or partly both between. That Corn planted in this manner will yield as much to the Acre as any other. That the quantity of Potatoes will at least quadruple the quantity of Corn, and that the Potatoes do not exhaust the Soil, are facts well established in my mind. In April 1789 it is sown with Buck Wheat for manure, which is plowed in before Harvest when the Seed begins to ripen and there is a sufficiency of it to seed the ground a second time. In July it is again plowed; which gives two dressings to the land at the expence of a bushl. of B. Wheat and the plowings which would otherwise be essential for a summer fallow. In August, after the putrefaction and fermentation is over, wheat is sown, and in 1790 harvested. In 1791 the best, and earliest kind of Indian Pease are sown broadcast, . . . [He was going to change this to a mixture of peas, buckwheat, turnips and pumpkins.] In 1792 Spring Barley or Oats, or equal quantities of each, will be sown with red clover; the latter to be fed with light Stock the first year after harvest. In 1793, the field remains in Clover for Hay, or grazing according to circumstances, and in 1794 comes into Corn again, and goes on as before.[16]

Washington's experiments sound remarkably like Van der Kemp's. On September 27 he wrote to Van der Kemp:

The Mangal Root which you saw growing in my garden is not, I believe, of the best sort, it was as you have observed red. That which is marbled, I am told, is the best. If of this kind the Revd. Dr. Doll could spare a little seed it would oblige me, and when you shall be stocked with such other sorts of seed as are not usual in this country, I would gladly participate in your sparings.[17]

A further interest of Van der Kemp as a scientific farmer was the improvement of livestock, especially sheep. Livingston had given or sold a pair from his excellent flock to Van der Kemp, who was pleased when people admired his sheep. Though he thought the ewe far superior to the ram, he considered their lamb "an excellent animal with fine wool." He asked Livingston for an additional, better ram if at all possible because he wanted to try to get "more and finer wool." [18] Livingston improved an already good flock by importing merinoes from France in 1802 and, with Elkanah Watson, encouraged Americans to adopt the breed for greatly superior wool.[19]

The Van der Kemps and Livingstons exchanged occasional visits. His mother was fond of the Van der Kemps and was interested especially in Mrs. Van der Kemp because they were distantly related through the Beekmans. Early in 1790 Margaret Beekman Livingston, in reply to a request, sent the Van der Kemps information about the Beekman family genealogy. The letter included an invitation: "I beg to be affectionately presented to my cousin Mrs. Van der Kemp and to assure her that I shall expect the pleasure of seeing her and yrself here as early as is convenient—" [20]

Politics were seldom discussed in the Livingston–Van der Kemp correspondence. Their common enthusiasm for experimental agriculture and scientific theory apparently excluded other subjects aside from personal or family news. In only one letter Van der Kemp brought up a different subject by asking Livingston to provide answers to a list of queries about America for a friend who wished to emigrate to America from England.[21]

With Adams, Van der Kemp corresponded freely on politics and international affairs. Science was a lesser subject in the earlier years of their friendship. He kept Adams informed of his activities although he sometimes feared to impose on the vice president's busy life. In 1790 he asked advice on the procedure necessary to recover the residue of the considerable amount of money which had been paid on his release from prison. He explained carefully that the money had not been a fine, but a sum levied against possible damages. He thought the stadholder might consider repayment and believed an interposition by President Washington or by Congress would bring restoration of at least part of the money. He argued fluently that his changed citizenship made no difference in a matter of financial justice similar to the Dutch government's interpositions in behalf of its merchants in foreign lands. Therefore, such action by the president of the United States would not constitute meddling with the domestic affairs of the Dutch Republic. Francis asked for Adams' help.[22] It is improbable that Van der Kemp would have profited from the restitution. De Nys had paid the release money, and Van der Kemp was obligated to make an effort with or without hope of gain.

Adams was mildly optimistic. He advised writing to the president and also asking assistance through the United States minister in the Netherlands "as far as may be proper." He thought it would "probably produce an Instruction to assist you at least in a private way." [23]

The request and explanation were duly sent to President Washington and were handled by Secretary of State Thomas Jefferson. The response was negative, partly because the United States had no minister at the Hague at that time. Jefferson added that he questioned the expediency of interposing for property left behind by an immigrant although he hoped that the Dutch government would be just without an interposition.[24] Van der Kemp called it "a polite refusal" and apparently gave up the project.[25]

Another request to Adams was for assistance to Adam Mappa, former commander of the Free Corps. Late in 1789 Mappa left Europe with a letter of recommendation from Van Staphorst to Adams.[26] When his old friend and brother refugee arrived in New York with his family, Van der Kemp wrote to Adams asking for support of Mappa's plan for establishing a printing business. On the advice of Jefferson, Mappa had brought with him to America a letter foundry for various western and Oriental languages, worth some £3,500. Van der Kemp knew of no similar American type foundries in 1790 and was as hopeful of Mappa's success as was their mutual friend, Thomas Jefferson. Van der Kemp proposed encouragement of the venture by a tax on the importation of foreign letter-types. The industry would "be of an infinite profit to American literature," provided Mappa could provide a sufficient quantity of good quality type. The proposed type foundry would result in a small addition to the public revenue, increase literary production and provide for Greek and Oriental books printed in America at a reduced cost. Van der Kemp wrote a second letter dated January 9 asking Adams to introduce the

bearer, Mappa, to President Washington.[27] Adams replied
that he would be happy to make the presentation and "serve
in any other Way in my Power." [28] In spite of diligent efforts, Mappa was not successful and his equipment passed
to others to be used.[29]

Van der Kemp recommended two men to the national
service while he lived in Ulster County. In 1793 he asked
Adams to receive Major Peter van Gaasbeck, recently
elected to Congress from Van der Kemp's district. He believed Van Gaasbeck would support the administration
and praised the man generously.[30] Adams promised "to see
him and converse with him. . . ." [31] The other recommendation was for Captain Benjamin Weeks of *L'Henriette* on
which Van der Kemp crossed the Atlantic. The captain's
former passenger heard of the resolve of Congress to arm
six frigates and thought Captain Weeks would make an
excellent commander of one of the ships. Weeks was unaware of the letter,[32] a typically out-going gesture of gratitude and admiration by the amicable scholar, Van der
Kemp.

The success of various of his prominent neighbors in land
holding and development plus disappointing results in
clearing up his financial affairs in Holland seemed to
arouse a restiveness in Van der Kemp. In 1790 he made a
trip to the western branch of the Delaware River, perhaps
accompanied by some of the Livingstons. He described the
area in such glowing terms to Adam Mappa that the latter
termed it a fanciful description.[33] During this time, the
development of western lands was a popular topic of conversation. Prices were low and, if peace and prosperity were
uninterrupted, a venturesome and industrious man could
gain wealth for himself and family.

Van der Kemp had lost a considerable sum of money
through the treachery in Europe of a man who called himself his friend. Van der Kemp had depended upon having
these funds when he came to America. He now felt he could
not provide sufficiently for his family on the farm near
Kingston. He said

this would oblige me to retire further to the back-parts of America, in order to insure my own independence, and provide in time for the subsistence of my children which I should not wish to leave in a worse condition in America, than they would have enjoyed in Europe—I intend therefore—to settle on the Oneida Lake [having] made a purchase sufficient, I hope, for my intended purpose, and offered my beautiful and improved farm for sale. . . .

He advertised his farm in the *New York Journal and Patriotic Register* in July of 1793. He described it as having a large meadow, an orchard of excellent bearing apple trees, a good house, granary, poultry house, smoke house and other buildings, some of them new and all in good order. His letter to Adams said he would leave with regret but expected hardships to be replaced with pleasures in a few years. He did not expect war with Great Britain; otherwise he would not risk his family on the frontier. He was prepared to sell most of his library, which now comprised some 800 volumes, if necessary.[34]

Van der Kemp did not choose the site for a new home without careful deliberation. In the summer of 1792 he took a leisurely journey to Oneida Lake, and from there to Oswego on Lake Ontario to view the possibilities of good living in the Oneida country. He had prudently sought out information regarding fair prices for western lands, and was reasonably certain the area would be safe from Indians and war. Whether inspired by old world ambitions or new world dreams, he was impatient to see the West and judge its opportunities for himself.

Van der Kemp shared this longing with thousands of his fellow Americans in the region east of the Appalachians. Others traveled by more difficult passages and settled in more dangerous locations, but Van der Kemp made careful inquiries, considering both traveling ease and the future comfort and welfare of his family. Bartha, now forty-six years old, had come to America not by choice but by force of circumstances. Francis was determined to provide a good home—and an inheritance for their children.

Future prospects for roads and improved waterways in the Mohawk Valley were good. His enthusiasm was unbounded as he set forth on his journey of exploration. He had the western fever.

❧ VIII ❧

The Trip West

GEORGE SCRIBA must have stopped at the Van der Kemp home on the Esopus. There seems no other way that Van der Kemp could have become so interested in the Oneida Lake region and could have made such careful plans for his trip. When the time came, George Clinton encouraged the journey and provided letters of introduction to people along the route including Jonas Platt, who became one of Van der Kemp's best friends. Van der Kemp planned to travel to Fort Stanwix (now Rome); there a guide was to take him by water through Oneida Lake and the Oswego River and back, allowing time for spying out the land.

Van der Kemp kept a careful diary, later sent to Adam Mappa after his unsuccessful venture in printing, in an effort to persuade this valued friend to settle nearby.

The trip probably began in mid-June and ended in mid-July. The account is included here in greatly shortened form.[1]

I had not rode a horse, except in 1788 from Alexandria to Mount Vernon, when I visited General Washington. Now it was a journey of nearly two hundred miles. But I was resolved; my good neighbor provided me with a saddle, and other accoutrements of a cavalier—I risked to take one of my own horses—and proceeded slowly on. About noon I had passed the *Grooten Imbogt,* about twenty miles from

home, went on after dinner to Catskill, and took tea with
Mr. Bogardus at the Landing, which is indeed a very agreeable spot. The increasing population of the western country gave birth to this little hamlet on the North [Hudson]
river. Several merchants from New England and this State
had established themselves; last year their number was augmented to twenty, and this year seventeen new buildings,
houses and stores, were finished. The situation is indeed
delightful on the banks of a large creek, and not far distant
from the North river, very well adapted for trading with
the western country. The inhabitants were chiefly respectable men, while the family of Mr. Bogardus peculiarly
might have tempted you and me to fix our residence on the
spot, could we have contemplated it, on our arrival from
Europe, so it now appears.

Towards evening, I rode on to Cough Sagie [Coxsackie]
and stopped at the house of John Bronk, persuaded after
having travelled forty miles at the first onset, that I could
accomplish my purpose. My supper was but indifferent—
tea, bread and butter, with a bit of warmed mutton, but in
full compensation of it, the mistress of the house was very
civil. Next morning, I went to Albany, where I met with
a cordial reception from Dr. Marcius [Mancius?], whose
hospitality, frankness, and amiable character, leave you
scarce time to do justice to his professional merits. Every
instant the decision of the election of a new Governor was
expected, and, as the city was pretty equally divided between
the two illustrious candidates, Clinton and Jay, a painful
anxiety was legible in every countenance. At 8 o'clock it
was known with certainty that George Clinton was re-
elected for the sixth time. In the morning the sound of guns
proclaimed the Governor's election to the neighborhood.

On Friday morning, I rode on to Schenectadi, where I
spent a few hours with the Rev. Romeyn, one of the most
learned and eminent divines of the Reformed Church in
this State. He communicated to me many important observations with regard to the soil, the stupendously increasing population of the western country, with its vast in-

creasing strength. He assured me that fifteen hundred families passed by his house during the winter of '91, to various
parts of the western lands.

I proceeded after dinner about twenty miles further;
stopped a few moments at the ancient residence of Sir William [Johnson], now occupied by Mr. Jacob Cuyler, and
remained at night on Trip's Hill, at Mr. Putnam's, six miles
from Caughwaga. On Saturday morning I breakfasted at
Simon Veeder's Esq., rode on eight miles farther to Bankert's Inn and arrived about noon at the mansion of the re-
pectable widow of Col. Phil. Schuyler, in Palatine-town.
There I met with a cordial reception: Mrs. Schuyler appeared most interested in the welfare of Mrs. v.d.K. and our
John, who with us four years past had been entertained
under her hospitable roof. I was again much pleased with
her animated, intelligent conversation, and gathered more
real information from a desultory discourse than I might
have received from an elaborate discussion of a philosopher
who had never seen the country. She informed me too of
the best houses on the road.

After dinner I crossed the Mohawk three miles above
Palatine-town, and did see Canajohari. After a ride of seven
miles further, I tarried at a *ci-devant* Indian castle, now a
very recommendable inn, kept by Mr. Hudzon, to drink a
dish of superior good tea. It was my design to proceed to
Herkimer but my good horse was scarce able to lift one
foot before the other; consider further that this good beast,
by often going and returning, to examine one or other object a little more carefully [,] by always pacing even on the
roughest road, was thoroughly fatigued; that the sun was
set; that I was ignorant of the road, and, as you would say,
not much to be trusted where I knew it; and that, above this
all, Capt. Bellinger, the landlord of a homely tavern, endeavored to persuade me that I ought to stay with him.
And then reflecting that the cavalier longed for rest as
much as his beast, you cannot be surprised that your friend
yielded so soon to the urgent entreaties of that noble captain. My supper was not above mediocrity; my bed and

sleep of the first-rate. The hope of repairing my loss of the
evening by a good breakfast, made me stir early, so that
I arrived at eight at Mr. Aldritz, in former days another
Indian castle. The respectable appearance of the landlord
and his lady, soon convinced me that my conjecture would
not dwindle away in an airy vision. Good bread and butter,
excellent tea, fresh eggs, with a dish of salmon trout, a sort
of European sorrel, worthy to be presented to the best man
in the State, was more than sufficient to satisfy a craving
hunger. Now was I in Herkimer; crossed again the Mohawk; paced slowly through the German Flatts, a beautiful plain, whose rich fertility must strike even the inat-
tentive eye; from the charming fields covered with all sorts
of grain: here wheat, corn, potatoes; there oats, peas, barley; there again another variety of the same products, at
intervals surrounded or separated with clover. These flatts,
terminated from one side by the Mohawk, from the other by
the rising hills, at whose bottom the farm houses and
churches were constructed, maintain many thousand descendants of native Germans, who, searching a refuge from
infatuated despotism, in this land of liberty, have chiefly preserved the manners, language and religion of their ancestors. The same is true with regard to their neighbors in Ger-
man-town and Herkimer—all of German origin, somewhat
tempered with British, Dutch and American blood.

Col. Staringh [Henry Staring] was the man by whom I
intended to dine if it was obtainable. Although his honour
was at the same time a Judge of the Common Pleas, thus
high in civil and military grandeur, yet he kept a public
house, and my imagination was highly inflamed when I
glanced on his mansion and its appurtenances. The Colonel was gone to the meeting; his barn was the place of worship. I went thither; the assembled congregation was very
numerous; our Lord's Supper was celebrated with decency,
and as it appears to me by many with fervent devotion.
Four children were baptized by the Rev. Rosekrantz, of
the German Flatts, who made this pastoral visit to direct
these religious solemnities. After service the flock crowded

promiscuously in the Colonel's house and used sparingly some refreshments. The large majority gloried at the renewed election of George Clinton.

The presence of the Rev. Pastor; the solemnity of the sacred festival; the presence of the fathers of the baptized children, some of them related to the Colonel, procured me a good dinner.

At nine miles distance, near old Fort Schuyler, I crossed the Mohawk River for the last time; took my tea at Mr. John Post's; reached Whitesborough about evening and stopped at the house of Judge [Hugh] White, the father of this flourishing settlement, to whom and Mr. Jonas Platt, his Ex. [Excellency] Geo. Clinton had favored me with letters of introduction. I met on the road to Whitesborough a group of Oneida Indians, some of them on horseback, others walking and jumping; the one with a bottle, another with a jug or small keg with rum; for the most part merrily jolly: some deeply soaked by the beverage, distilled from the cane. Their number increased in proportion as I approached nearer Whitesborough. There I saw about two hundred, of every age and of both sexes, around their fires near the road, eating, drinking, smoking, singing, laughing, all [of] them in perfect harmony together, though many a little before had tried their strength and agility upon one another.

The occasion of this unusual concourse was that they came to receive the corn from the State, which had been stipulated in one of the articles of the late treaty. But they soon changed this corn, certainly for a large part, by the merchants for money, which they changed again for chintzes, silk, handkerchiefs, linen, &c.

Judge White was commissioned to distribute among them, the stipulated grain. He is a man between fifty and sixty years of age, of a middle stature, corpulent, and of a comely appearance. He enjoys now that exquisite gratification of being the *creator of his own fortune,* and placing all his children in an independent situation. Judge White resided in Connecticut in the year 1785. He made a journey to the western part of this State; made a purchase of the land he now lives on; moved thither in 1786 with his five sons, built a log house and barn; went the next year for his wife and remaining children, although there was not at that time one single white man in the nine miles around him. In 1788 he constructed a saw and grist mill; possessed in the fourth year all which he wanted for his convenience, ease and comfort in abundance; built in the fifth year a convenient frame house and substantial barn, and is now encircled by a number of respectable families; amongst these, two of his married sons and Mr. Jonas Platt, a son of Judge Zephaniah Platt.

The society here is already pleasing; so is the situation of this little village; more adapted for the enjoyment of rural retirement, than luring in a commercial point of view. The houses are more built for convenience than for show; the roads are daily improving, of which you may form a partial opinion from the fact that while I was here, Mr. and Mrs. Livingston [parents of Mrs. Platt] came in their own carriage, in four days from Poughkeep to Whitesborough.

That I do not exaggerate to render you enamored with this charming country, one proof shall be sufficient. By the last census the number of souls in Whitestown, was 5,788—a stupendous number indeed within the small circle of five years. In Whitesborough itself there is scarce an acre for sale. Dr. Mosely paid for three acres, for a building spot, £50 per acre.

The soil is a fertile rich loam: from thirty to forty-five bushels Indian corn per acre is an ordinary crop; often it gives fifty, sixty, and more. The article of fish is scarce; firewood has already become an object of so much importance that it is saved and sold to advantage; and salt cannot be obtained below a dollar the bushel.

I crossed about two miles from Whitesborough the Oriskany Creek, where many of the Oneida Indians resided in former days. Several farms have already been taken up, and the woods resounded when I passed there, from the strokes of the hardy axe-men: one year more, and the one farm shall be joined to the other, as here on the *Esopuskill*. I had only advanced a few steps when my attention was fixed on a number of skulls, placed in a row, on a log near the road. I was informed by the workmen that this place was the fatal spot on which the murderous encounter happened between General Herkimer and his sturdy associates, and the Indians, when this brave and gallant soldier did fall with a number of his men.

On Monday about noon, I arrived at Fort Stanwix. The Baron [Frederick Augustus] de Zeng, industriously employed in laying out a kitchen garden, had already seen me, and gave me a cordial welcome. He then introduced me to Col. [William] Colbreath, a revolutionary soldier [who lived with De Zeng].

The Baron De Zeng, a German nobleman, descends from a noble family in Saxony, and arrived in America during the revolutionary war. He was married to a respectable lady in New York, and did now intend to begin a settlement in this vicinity. He had engaged to accompany me on this tour, and I expected, as I really experienced, that he not only should be an agreeable companion, but very useful to me in many respects.

The baron was so kind, to charge himself to purchase a grand canoe [dugout], engage two servants, and procure the required provisions for our voyage. As he had before rowed through this wilderness he knew best what was wanting to lessen the hardships of a similar enterprize. A well made tent with a good carpet stood foremost on the list, and his spouse took care that a sufficient quantity of bread and biscuit was prepared. While all this was brought in readiness, I had the satisfaction to explore the country; examine the woods with the contemplated slate [site?] for the canal, to join the Mohawk with the Wood creek, and convince myself of its practicability. But this is only the dwarf, fixing his eyes upward to the gigantic canal, yet in embryo. The soils differ little from that of Whitestown, except the summit of the highland, on which the fort is erected, generally not less fertile, often too rich for wheat, as the first crop. Elm, ash, beech, heavy oak and walnut are in the upper part: on the lower ground, chiefly beech, maple and birch. As no apparent obstruction is visible, the canal may be executed nearly in a straight line.

Scarce a day passed in which not two, sometimes three, bateaux arrived, whose destination was towards the Genesee lands, Onondago, Cadaraqui [at Ft. Frontenac], or other parts of the Western District. We met daily with groups of five or six men on horseback, in search for land. During the time I tarried here, a large bateau with furs, arrived from the West; two yoke of oxen carried it over the portage. This was the second cargo within one week. It may be conjectured from this single example what riches the waters of Oneida Lake may carry on to Fort Stanwix, if every obstruction shall be removed. Now it makes a fortune to individuals; then it shall become as productive to the Nation as a gold mine.

We walked on Saturday towards Woods creek; we saw our baggage stowed: stepped in the canoe and pushed off. [In three miles they passed the site of Fort Bull.] As we indulged ourselves from time to time, in angling, we hooked a few trout and several large chubs, without reflecting that the sun was setting; our lusty boys waded continually to drag our deeply loaded canoe over rifts and shoals.

Now we proceeded quickly and discovered after a few minutes a light in a small cottage. It was that of the widow Armstrong, on the corner of the Wood and Canada creek, seven miles from Fort Stanwix, the part of land where Roseveld's [Nicholas Roosevelt] purchase begins, with which you and some of my best friends desire to become acquainted, and which, if I am not mistaken and disappointed in my wishes, may be once a goodly heritage, under God's Almighty blessing, for us and our children.

A simple statement of courses is sufficient to lay open the water communication with all the circumjacent lands; by the Wood creek to the Mohawk eastward, and so on to the North [Hudson] river, through the Seneca river, southwest of the Oneida Lake to the Genesee lands, whose settlements are daily increasing; through the Onondago and Oswego rivers, in Lake Ontario, through the St. Lawrence and the North river in the Ocean.

Both Salmon rivers emptying in Lake Ontario, to the north of this tract of land and the Fish creek in Oneida Lake, are in the spring and fall, full of salmon. One Oneida Indian took with his spear, forty-five salmon in one hour. They are equal to the best which are caught in the rivers of the Rhine and Meuse. The eel of the Oneida Lake is equal to the best of the Holland market, and far surpasses every kind which I have ever tasted here, in size, in fatness, in tenderness of the fish.

Everywhere are salt springs, and but few miles from Oneida Lake in Onondago is a copious salt lake, encircled with salt springs, the domain of the people of the State of New York. A considerable quantity is already transported to Canada, and thousand American families make never use of any other. How the copiousness must be increased when rock salt too is manufactured and carried to the South and West of our immense continent.

This country, so abundant in water and fish, is, if possible, yet more profusely endowed by our bountiful maker with wood. Every kind of timber of the northern and eastern States, is here in the greatest plenty and perfection: butternut, walnut, white oak, sugar maple, chestnut, beech, black ash, pine, hemlock, the lime tree, white wood or canoes wood, and several other species.

It is true, my dear sir, a good soil, good water, and plenty of wood for fuel and timber are strong inducements to settle in a new country—more so, when the price of all this is enhanced by the prospect of a good market in the neighbourhood; but if thou art there alone without neighbours, if from the vicinity you obtain nothing even for ready cash, if, as is the situation of the largest number who transport their families in the woods—their all consists in an axe, a plow, a wheel, a frying pan, kettle, bed and pillow, with a scanty provision of flour, potatoes, and salt pork—then

what? Then, my dear sir, something else besides is required
not to suffer during the first season. It is true a little wheat
is often saved [sowed?] in the fall, a small spot cleared to
plant in the spring corn and potatoes, while they live in
the hope, if their health is spared, to prepare the soil for
sowing flax-seed; but something more yet is required to the
maintenance of a numerous hungry family, and in this respect, too, Providence has in this district graciously provided even to satiety. Never did I see yet a country where
all kind of fish was so abundant and good.

The salmon is generally salted and sold at £4 the barrel;
cat fish at £4 and £4.10; the eel is smoked, and with the
two preceding sorts, preserved for the winter provision;
others are consumed fresh. Hundreds of gull eggs may be
gathered on the islands. Ducks and geese visit annually the
lakes and creeks in large flocks; the swan is but seldom seen
in this vicinity—while bears and deer are roving in the
neighbourhood of every cottage.

On Sunday morning we bid adieu to the good widow,
who left nothing undone which was in her power to render
her homely cottage comfortable to us. We left our canoe now
and then to look at the land; it was low and flat near the
borders of the creek, and had the appearance of being annually overflowed. At some distance the land became gradually more elevated, and was adorned with oak, beech,
maple.

The approaching night compelled us to look out for a
convenient spot for our encampment, in which we soon succeeded. Our tent was pitched, and a blazing fire prepared
by the boys. We spread our carpet, and made our beds ready,
waiting for our supper. Here thousands of muskitoes welcomed us in their abode, obtruded their company, and
exhausted our patience by their treacherous caresses, in
which they continued till we had encircled our tent with
smoke.

We covered our faces with a veil before we went to sleep.
This was the first time in my life I slept in the woods, and
yet my sleep was sound, but short and not very refreshing,

as I awoke fatigued, and was not at ease, till I drove the sleep from the eyes of all my companions, and had hurried them to the canoe to pursue our journey.

We did so, and had scarce proceeded a mile, when the Wood Creek, increasing imperceptibly in breadth, lost the appearance of a ditch, and appeared a handsome river. Now we hurried on, and encouraged our raw and unexpert hands to row on with alacrity, as we longed impatiently to see this vast expansion of water. Our wishes were ere long gratified. We stopped our course about nine o'clock, unloaded our canoe, pitched our tent, and brought firewood together, that we might have full leisure to contemplate this beautiful lake.

De Zeng left me with the canoe and one hand to take a short excursion on the Oneida creek, to the south side of the lake, to fetch some implements, left there the year before by one Peter Frey. While Major De Zeng continued his course in exploring the Canada creek, I took a walk along the eastern sandy shore of this charming lake, and examined its northern salient angles, of which the first was four, the next about nine miles distant, in this circuit from the mouth of Wood creek. Within a few moments I saw three canoes, one with Indians, among whom [was] Capt. Jacob Reed, and one bateau from the south and west, while two bateaux with four families, from the Fish creek, landed a little below our encampment. The soil is a barren sand; the trees near the shore dwarfish and of little value. At first, when I entered the woods, I met with a swampy ground, but further proceeding, a good loam, increasing in depth and richness as I went on.

The baron returned about twelve, with two most capital eels, presented him by an Oneida—Good Peter, who had been hired by him the last year to follow him on a similar expedition as that in which we now were engaged.

Having loitered here away the afternoon in examining shells and stones, and plants and shrubs, we pursued our course the next morning; then rowing, then using the setting poles along the shore, till we reached the point from which its northerly side may be calculated. From here the shore was generally covered with pebbles. A small creek, called by the Indians who were with us Little Fish creek, falls here in the lake.

We had now lost a great part of two days in fishing, without an adequate reward to our exertions, and might have suspected that the exuberant abundance of this lake in fish, of which we had heard so much boasting from white men as well as Indians, had been exaggerated, but we soon discovered the cause of our failure. The lake was now covered as with a white cloak of hundred thousands millions of insects which we call *Haft* in Holland, and which lay in some parts of the shore one and two inches deep.[2]

We were, a little after sunset, surprised at a number of fires in a semi-circular form on the lake. I numbered nine, others several more. These were made by the Oneida Indians spearing eel. They are usually two or three in a canoe, one steerman, one who spears in the bow, the third takes care of the fire, made from dry, easily flaming wood, in a hollow piece of bark, first covered with sand.

We proceeded on our course, and arrived, at no great distance, to another, but much smaller creek emptying its waters in a pretty bay [This became the site of Rotterdam, now Cleveland. Van der Kemp purchased land lying between this creek and Black Creek which flows into Bernhard's Bay.]; here was the land to some extent towards the lake low, and could only be appropriated for pasture or hay land; but it gradually ascended about 20 feet, where it was covered with a deep, black, rich, fertile soil, mixed with a small portion of black sand, and covered with majestic oak, beech, butternut, walnut, ash and maple. Here the prospect was admirable indeed. Imagine that falling plain near the lake, cleared from trees and stumps, and covered with verdure, embellished with a dozen of cows, the lake in front, a wood to the south, while behind you the noblest fields invite you to admire the rich produce of the soil, equal to the best tilled in our country.

Major De Zeng walked slowly with his gun on shore,

With head upraised and look intent,
And eye and ear attentive bent,

while we rowed on; he gave us a signal; we pushed to the shore; he told us that he saw a bear on the next point; in an instant we left the canoe and dispatched our boys, well armed, in the woods, to cut off his retreat; De Zeng and I advanced in his front from the lake side; when within a pistol shot of this surly lord of the woods, he stood still, trotted on a few steps and received a shot from the woods which broke his left hind leg, another glanced his brawny side. De Zeng missed his aim, and while I stepped forward with the cocked gun, De Zeng, throwing his gun aside, sprung impetuously forward with the tomahawk in his hand, attacked him in front and knocked him on the head twice; bruin lifted up his paw, twice he opened his mouth, at last staggring he falls, in blood and foam expires; we dragged him with difficulty towards the canoe, as he was indeed of a monstrous size, lifted him in it, and returned by land to the little creek, while our men rowed towards the same spot. Here we resolved to make our encampment for that night; in the morning it proved to be the most delightful spot which we had yet seen. If you never tasted it, you might have declined to share in our breakfast. Stewed slices of surly bruin, was the principal dish.

We entered once more our canoe; discovered two bateaux steering towards the south, and arrived about noon at the Black creek, the largest at this side of the lake, after the Fish Creek or Oneida river; here we dined on an excellent rice soup, from one of Brown's gammons [bacon ends], which we had saved. Here was a broad piece of fore-land, watered by this creek, and about a hundred rods further on another creek, sufficient to turn a wheel, joined it. The upland was excessive steep, high and barren; the soil, fine yellow sand; the trees, fir, hemlock, pine, and a few oak. At some distance the land gradually descended, the soil became richer and the timber was improving; and again the same rich black soil, not subject of being so soon exhausted or baked in intensive hot weather, as the Whitestown loam.

We continued our course after dinner along the shore, and hoped that we might reach the Fisher's bay. It was late before we reflected upon it, and a rising thunder storm urged us to take quickly hold of all our oars. I ought to have said *pagays,* as we were in a canoe. We did run, by our hurrying too fast, and through the inattention of our man at the helm, with our canoe on a hugh stone; at length we got again afloat, and arrived safe in the creek at Mr. Bruce's, in former days a Connecticut merchant, now an independent inhabitant of the Oneida Lake, maintaining himself by the chase and fishery, and what he earned from a small potatoe spot. He fetched directly upon our arrival, a fine catfish, from a *reservoir,* constructed from saplings and twigs, so well twisted that no escape was possible.

This catfish weighed ten pounds; we obtained afterwards one of twenty-four pounds. When Bruce had prepared him, he showed us a handful fat, as yellow as gold. It was indeed a delicious repast for our supper. Roasted, as this was, and no cook could have done it better, or boiled or stewed, as we did eat after a while.

In the morning we made an excursion in the country, took a straight northerly course, and returned through the west and south at the other side to our encampment. The fore-land near the lake, at the east side of the creek, appeared but indifferent to the eye, now somewhat used to contemplate first-rate soil, and the timber stood in the same relation. At the distance of about one-fourth of a mile from the lake, the ground rises gradually and continues to do so, if you proceed another quarter of a mile. Then the soil increases in fertility from step to step, and in the same proportion in depth.

We crossed the creek a little above a beaver dam, and found the same excellent soil at the west side, with the same gradation, and in the same proportion as that which we had explored on the east, till we arrived again at the plain, covered with fir and pine.

This is a barren plain, De Zeng, so it seems, but it has good water, it has good building spots, and by manuring and good husbandry, will make good gardens. It is barren indeed, De Zeng, although it may be meliorated, but you do not reflect on the advantages of that creek; art thou not convinced by what thou hast seen, that with small exertions to improve it, full laden bateaux may go in and out, may do it actually now? Did your eye not discover the mill seats on this creek?

We left Bruce's creek on Friday evening about six; the sky was serene and delightful; a soft breeze curled the waves and fringed them with white, while the sun sinking towards the west beautified the whole scenery. I did not witness such a grand or majestic sight since I crossed the Atlantic. It must be seen before it can be fully appraised, and then it must be a brute whose bosom does not glow with an ardent love towards his Creator, and adores His goodness and wisdom so majestically displayed in every part of the Universe. In proportion that we penetrated deeper in the lake, the beauty of this diversified prospect was more and more enhanced, the islands, the shores, the woods, the mountains obtruding themselves to our sight, seemed to vie with [each] other for the preference.

We landed half after seven at the largest and most westerly island, towed the canoe on shore, and walked by an Indian path in the woods.

This island might in ancient days have been the happy seat of a goddess, in the middle age that of a magician, or a fairy's residence in the times of chivalry. Proceeding on one after another through the stately trees, through which we perceived yet the last glances of the setting sun, we were at once, after a few rods, surprised with an enchanting view. We did see here a luxuriant soil in its virgin bloom; we did see industry crowned with blessing, we did see here what great things a frail man can perform if he is willing. It seemed a paradise which happiness had chosen for her residence. Our path did lead us to the circumference of a cleared circle, surrounded with lime trees; at both sides of the path was planted Indian corn, already grown from four to five feet, while a few plants towards the middle of this patch were six feet long, and this in the middle of

June. A small cottage of a few feet square stood nearly in the centre of this spot. It had a bark covering, and to the left of it a similar one, three-fourths uncovered and appropriated for a kitchen. Here was the residence of Mr. and Madame de[s] Wattines, with their three children.

They lived there without servants, without neighbours, without a cow; they lived, as it were, separated from the world. Des Wattines sallied forward and gave us a cordial welcome in his desmenes. The well-educated man was easily recognized through [in spite of!] his sloven dress. Ragged as he appeared, without a coat or hat, his manners were those of a gentleman; his address that of one who had seen the higher circles of civilized life. A female, from whose remaining beauties might be conjectured how many had been tarnished by adversity, was sitting in the entrance of this cot. She was dressed in white, in a short gown and petticoat, garnished with the same stuff; her chestnut brown hair flung back in ringlets over her shoulders, her eyes fixed on her darling Camille, a native of this isle, at her breast; while two children, standing at each side of her, play'd in her lap. Her appearance was amiable indeed. Esteem for the man filled our bosom, and when you considered how indefatigably he must have exerted himself; what sacrifices he must have made, what hardships endured, to render her situation comfortable, and rear roses for her on this island, so deep in the western wilderness then, notwithstanding all the foibles which a fastidious cool observer might discover at his fireside, he becomes an object of admiration. I, at least, gazed at him in wonder. Des Wattines introduced us to his spouse. She received us with that easy politeness which well-educated people seldom lose entirely, and urged, with so much grace, to sit down that we could not refuse it without incivility. This couple was now in the second year on this island, and all the improvements which we had seen were the work of Des Wattines' hands exclusively.

Few trunks, few chairs, an oval table, two neat beds, was the principal furniture; a double barreled gun, a pretty collection of books, chiefly modern literature, in the French language, the chief ornaments of the cottage.

At our return to our encampment [on the island], our tent was pitched, the fire blazing, our boys snoring, and we too fell soon asleep. I awoke with daylight, and made the circuit of this fortunate island. When returned to the place of our landing, I crossed the corn plantation and went on, to contemplate more carefully what might have escaped my sight the preceding evening.

Des Wattines had laid out behind the cottage a pretty garden, divided by a walk in the middle. The two foremost beds, and *rabats* [borders] against the house, were covered with a variety of flowers; sweet williams, lady slippers, with a few decaying hyacinths. At the right hand were bush beans, large kidney beans, at poles, cabbage, turnips, peas, salade, with that strong scented herbage which we call keovel; at the left, water-melons, cantelopes, cucumbers, persil [parsley], string peas, with a few of the winter provisions, all in great forwardness, with few or no weeds among them; behind the garden a small nursery of apple trees, which was closed with a patch of luxuriant potatoes, and these again were joined both sides by wheat, describing a semi-circle around it.

All this was the workmanship of Des Wattines' industry; without any assistance, not even of a plow or harrow, having no other tools but an axe and an hoe. It was true it was all in miniature, but it required, nevertheless, an indefatigable industry to be able to accomplish all this to such a degree of perfection. When I approached the cottage Des Wattines was yet employed in dragging pretty heavy wood for fuel towards it, which he chopt and split in a short time; and in less yet the fire was blazing, when he came with a catfish of sixteen pounds for our breakfast. While he was busily engaged in its preparations, Madame appeared, brought him a handful persil, and dressed the table. The tablecloth was of neat damask, a few silver spoons and forks, the plates and dishes cream coloured, remnants yet of their former affluence; while the contentment legible in her eyes, spread a fresh glow over her countenance, and made a deep impression on our hearts, and whetted our already keen appetite. De Zeng was meanwhile arrived, and complimented Madame with his usual politeness. Salade, roasted and stewed fish, well baked, warm bread of Indian corn, with good Hyzan tea, which she accepted from us with kindness, soon filled the table. I was seldom better regaled. The fish was delicious; the sprightly conversation gave a fresh relish to every mouthful we tasted; and we might have desired to be inhabitants of that enchanted spot, had it been in our power to withdraw our attention from the hardships to which they were exposed, and banish the idea that they seldom could obtain anything else but fish.

Des Wattines inquired in the boundaries of our journey, "to Lake Ontario," "and in what manner?" "Well with our canoe," was the reply. He sprung from his chair and stared us fully in the face with a *"Par Dieu!* with your canoe! to Lake Ontario! *nanny! prenez le bateaux,* take it Major, it is at your service, *Prenez le."* We did not hesitate long to accept his offer. We soon had our baggage transported in it, left our canoe behind at the island, with our frying pan, through the slothfulness of our hands. We started thus on Saturday morning about ten. There are appearances [along the shore here], and very strong indeed, of rock iron. The land had again a very promising aspect at some distance from the shore, and shall, I doubt not, be transformed, within a few years, in productive farms. We arrived at Fort Brewerton about noon, situated at the northwestern corner of the lake. Here is a location of about four hundred acres, obtained by Mr. Kaats during the late British war. It was now inhabited by two families, viz, that of one Captain Bingham, and one Mr. Simonds, the latter from Caughnawagha. They had rented it at £20 a year, and desired to make a purchase of it, but Mr. Kaats, acquainted with its value, had constantly declined their offers.

I was highly gratified with excellent bread and butter, feasted on milk for my beverage, and purchased two pints of it, which we carried to our bateau. The soil is clay, of which a large quantity of brick was made; somewhat further a sandy loam was covered with stately trees, oak, then beech, ash and maple.

We arrived in the Onondago river, which, even as the Fish creek, has generally very steep banks, more so, however, at the west side. To the west, joining Kaats' location, is an excellent tract of land, the property of Mr. L'Home Dieu; to the south the military lands, chiefly a valuable fruitful soil. A sudden shower compelled us to land about three miles below Fort Brewerton, where we encamped that night, being resolved, if the rain might abate, to take a view of the land.

I had ventured, rather imprudently, perhaps, a few miles in the woods; the beauty of the spot had lured me deeper and deeper, till at last I knew not from where I came or whither I went; the sun being set, I had lost this unerring guide; my only refuge was now my pocket compass, by which I again discovered the course which I had to steer towards the river. This, nevertheless, would have brought me two miles below my encampment, had not De Zeng, apprehensive of this issue, sent out the boys to hunt the straggler.

Next day, about three in the afternoon, we reached Three River Point, eighteen miles from Fort Brewerton; here join the Onondago and Seneca rivers, that of Oswego flowing to Lake Ontario in [from] a southwesterly direction. One Barker lived at the east side of this point, whose chief employment was to conduct the bateaux over the falls in Oswego river.

We hired Barker at five shillings a day, to bring us over the fall, and stay with us till our return. We started from the point at four. We distinguished at a considerable distance the grumbling noise of the water on the first and second rift. Near the first is a remarkable good mill seat; here were the Onondagos collected in large numbers; some fishing, some smoking in their huts, others from time to time arriving and passing us in their bark canoes, with much art constructed, so light and easily manageable, that a squaw with her little daughter gained on us, and left us soon behind her by her velocity. We concluded to encamp about ten miles from Three Rivers Point, opposite to a handsome island in the Oswego river. The pickerel often weigh here thirty pounds, pike is of a similar size; we took a catfish of four span and a half; perch too, of which we obtained a few, is here in abundance.

At a short distance from the river is a good fertile soil; further, of a rich clay; the timber pretty similar to that which we had seen before. We started again pretty early on Monday morning, and arrived at the falls, twelve miles from the point. This indeed was again a very interesting sight. At the south side is a farm of three hundred acres, of one Mr. Valekenburg, who intends to build him this year a saw and grist mill. It is a noble spot for constructions of this kind.

Here we unloaded our bateau; dragged it about a hundred rods over the carrying place, and there, below the falls committed her again to its proper element. In [a] few moments our baggage was again on board and we in the bateau. Here Barker did give us a proof of his dexterity and alertness; with a rapidity which dimmed the sight, with an incredible swiftness, we passed over stones, between rocks and islands, as an arrow on the wing and lost the falls out of our sight and hearing. At twelve we arrived at Oswego, yet secured by a British garrison, notwithstanding it ought to have been surrendered many years before to our government in conformity to the treaty of peace.

The commanding officer [of the fort], a Rhode Island man by birth, Captain Wickham, treated us with a great deal of politeness, and regretted to be unable to offer us refreshments. He enquired carelessly in the object of our expedition, and made us an offer of his aid whenever he might be of any service to us; and he did so effectually; it was through his management that the British Interpreter, thoroughly acquainted with Lake Ontario and its shores, agreed to conduct us to the Salmon creek.

This Mr. Price spent a part of his youth with Onondago Indians. He was in the beginning discreet enough and civil through the whole of this excursion, but his society otherwise, far from indifferent, lost a great part of its worth by his incessant swearing; it was, indeed, [as] if he deemed it an accomplishment.

This Mr. Price was our Palinurus [the pilot of Aeneas] as soon as we had entered our bateau, which was about four in the afternoon; our raw hands rowed; Price was at the helm. We did sit on the middle bench; ere long we reached deep water. We arrived, with a fresh breeze at Four Miles Point, hoisted now our sail, passed it and obtained then a view of a range of perpendicular rocks, which rendered a landing impossible and dangerous to approach them nearer. Bernhard, one of our hands, boasted on his seamanship and experience. He doubted not, as he might bring a vessel in safety in the harbour; he had seen the narrows between Long Island and Staten Island. Price swore that he was tired with steering, and called, with another curse our pilot to take care of the helm. Now he placed himself between us and smoked his pipe. Our new steersman pointed every time towards shore, which he as often was compelled by a general command to steer more towards the middle, as we were now between the tremendous rocks at Four and Nine Miles Point. The wind suddenly increased, our pilot turned again towards the shore, and was anew for a moment by Price's tremendous curses, overawed to steer once more to deep water. But his increasing fear—not longer within his control—a desultory animated conversation between De Zeng, Price and myself, permitting him to follow the bias of his alarming impulse and a pretty rough western wind carried us within a few moments at a distance of a few rods only, towards those horrible perpendicular rocks, of which some seemed suspended over the watery surface. At once a loud pityful cry, "hold towards shore," struck our ears. Price did tear the oar from Barker's hand, commanded to lower the sail and bring out the oars, but all in vain. The pilot wept and cry'd, "hold towards shore, Mr. Price, good Mr. Price! push on shore—I pray God Almighty—dear Mr. Price, set on shore!" Price's reply was, "God damn you rascal! down the sail, out the oar, obey or sink!" The surge rose higher and higher; our united strength and weight, viz: De Zeng's and mine, were scarce sufficient to prevent the bateau turning upside down. At last the sail was struck, the oars out, and we were only in part exposed to the first shock, while Price, who remained calm and alert, succeeded in forcing the prow into the waves, and bringing us again in safety in deep water. When the danger was past the terror of our crew abated, and I praised in my soul the Almighty, as I do at this instant, for our hair-breadth escape.

Price remained now at the helm, and we proceeded on our course with a steady breeze, very pleasantly, except that De Zeng and I were thoroughly soaked over the right side from top to toe. We entered, notwithstanding the foaming breakers, a creek of the middle size, three miles to the south of the Little Salmon creek, towed our bateau in an inlet, and chose the heights for our encampment. Before our tent was pitched, and our fire in full blaze, Price and Barker returned with a large eel and huge catfish, which were more than sufficient for our supper.

We arrived on Tuesday at the Little Salmon creek; there was fish in the greatest abundance. The salmon collects here and in the Big Salmon creek, in nearly incredible numbers, during the fall and spring. The wind was too vehement on Wednesday to proceed on our journey with such an ignorant and cowardly crew; even the daring Price advised us not to run the risk; but he could not on any account be persuaded to remain longer with us. He grasped his gun, left his great coat with us, and flew out of sight in the woods. We heard the report of a gun, another, and there was Price returned; he threw a couple of partridges at our feet, and departed finally.

The lake became more and more tempestuous; the wind

blew a gale, and our Typheus had left us. The violence of the tempest increased with the falling night, and did not abate till the morning, when we compelled our pilot and crew to enter once more in the bateau.

When we perceived that Barker brought us nearly in the same situation as before, we listened to prudent advice and considered it our duty to land in the same creek which we had entered on Monday. We took here, after we had rowed up this creek for two miles, a large quantity of trout of various sizes—to regale us at dinner.

Nothing, my dear sir, resembles nearer the small rivulets and canals in South Holland than these creeks, as far as these are navigable. You see the same water plants and flowers—in some parts the *conserva*,[3] covering a part of the surface—the same insects, the same serpentine windings. We took a walk after dinner a few miles in the country where we found a rich soil, and here and there a mill seat. We returned about six o'clock to our encampment, but our pilot and one of our hands were unwilling to embark that evening; to-morrow morning—this night they would start —the lake was yet too high; at last, however, having prevailed on one of our lads, we got them all, willing, unwilling in the boat. We placed him whose good will I had secured at the helm; the pilot with his mate in mutiny at the oars, and pushed forward deep enough in the lake, while De Zeng and I took a pagay in the hand to prosper our course.

A fresh westerly breeze with the falling evening induced us to look out for a landing spot, in which we sooner and better succeeded than we could have expected. We hauled our bateau on dry land so that we might not lose her during the night. At six o'clock [the next morning] we rowed already with all our might, and arrived about ten at the fort, to our great satisfaction and joy. We left the fort at 1 o'clock, and made our encampment that night three miles from the falls, after having walked one mile to lessen the freight of the bateau.

Our breakfast was in readiness at an early hour, neither

did we tarry long; all hands to the bateau! speed, boys! speed! and the command was promptly executed. Our boat seemed to acquire a new vigor, either that he was satisfied fully with the length of this trip, or that he actually longed for his home. We arrived at Three River Point about seven, discharged Mr. Barker, and pitched our tent in the vicinity of his house, crowded with travellers from several bateaux and canoes.

Need I tell you, my dear sir, that Fort Brewerton, which we reached at four in the afternoon was to us a delightful sight. Captain Bingham was from home on the salmon fishery, and Captain Simonds, with the women, on a visit to the Island. His eldest daughter, nevertheless, a smart young girl, prepared us a good supper, a bass of two pound, a dish with stewed eel, with fresh bread and butter. Our breakfast was congenial, having secured two capital eels, with a pot of milk and rice; we hurried to the Island and complimented Mr. and Madame des Wattines, on Monday morning between nine and ten. We were again congratulated with a hearty welcome, and a new zest was added to our gratification, when Des Wattines proposed to conduct us to the Fish creek, or Oneida river, as he was compelled to go to the Oneidas for Indian corn. His garden was yet more pleasant, its value unquestionably had increased. Head lettuce, parsley (porcelain) string peas, and kidney beans, were in full perfection.

[At the departure the next morning] Madame des Wattines, with her Camille to her bosom, her eldest boy between her, and his sister at her side, motionless, staring at us, with an expressive countenance, with features portraying what her soul so keenly seemed to feel in that distressing moment of separation, *adieu, Des Wattines!* was all which we could distinguish. There stood that lonely, deserted fair one! not deserted as Ariadne, but nevertheless left alone with three helpless children—alone! on an island on Oneida Lake.

We took our dinner by Bruce, where our milk and rice, which we purchased at Fort Brewerton, was to all a palatable dish; then we returned towards evening to the mouth of the Fish creek or Oneida river, from which we started for our expedition. Des Wattines prepared our *soupé* of eel and catfish, while we superintended the pitching of our tent and making a good fire.

Here we were gratified with a visit [from] the first Judge [John] Lansing and Col. [Morgan] Lewis, the Attorney General of the State, and Major Farley, who all went to attend the circuit. We separated after conversation; they doomed to remain there till it pleased the westerly breeze to abate; Des Wattines parting from us in his bateau to the Oneida creek, and we proceeding with our canoe to the Fish creek or Oneida river. Here we met with one of our old acquaintance, Mr. Abraham Lansing, who, with one Mr. Fonda, went to Niagara. We stopt at the mouth of Wood creek. I concluded, while De Zeng with one of our lads was preparing our dinner, to take with the other a view of the Fish creek.

We rowed up the creek about three miles, and then landed on the side between the Fish and Wood creeks; here we met first with a broad girdle of fertile flat land, nearly east by west; then a long tract of pine chiefly, then beech, maple and oak. I ordered the boy to proceed higher up, and took a similar course landward in, and examined the soil from time to time, which I found generally fertile, although of a less favorable aspect towards the lake and richer again in proportion, that I took a northwestern course. I reached my canoe near the mouth of the Wood creek, entered it and found, after an absence of three hours, the pease porridge ready. We remained that evening two miles at this side of the Oak Orchard, where we breakfasted, and met about one mile from it, Mess. [Gerrit] Boon and [John] Lincklaen, who, assisted by Mr. Morris, a land surveyor, proceeded on a similar excursion. It was 2 o'clock before we arrived at the Widow Armstrong's cottage.

Amos Fuller, who resided now with his family at the widow's till he should be successful, as he said, in purchasing a farm in this neighbourhood, informed us, that two—past three Massachusetts men, amongst whom one of his brothers, had taken an accurate view of the tract from this point between the Canada creek, then westward between the Wood and Fish creeks, and considered it upon the whole so valuable that they had offered to purchase a whole township, to pay a £1,000 by the deed of the land, and the residue within a year, obliging themselves further to settle it before April, 1794, with thirty-five families.

Fuller tacked his old horse to our canoe, and dragged it to Fort Bull; here I strode on towards Fort Stanwix, where the baron, after a little while, arrived. The canoe arrived next morning. We dined, in part, on the new potatoes of Des Wattines, the welcome cup flowed over and I sincerely thanked the baron for his hospitable reception, for his manifold services and entertaining society, during a journey which required such a good companion to smooth its roughness. His lady was by her attentions entitled to the same civilities. We took a cordial farewell; I stept on my horse, which was neat and plumb, rode to Whitesborough, visited Mr. Platt; and then made a call to the good hearted Hugh White, asked for their commands and slept that night at old Fort Schuyler, by Mr. Hansje [John] Post. I was again on horseback early in the morning on Friday, and crossed the river. My oiled silk surtout coat defended me from the rain, which continued without interruption from five till eight. I had missed the road near German Flatts, but met good people, who with kindness convinced me that I was on a bye-path. I crossed again the Mohawk, took breakfast at Mr. Aldritz's, visited the Rev. Rosekrantz, and arrived at Capt. Billinger's, where I obtained for my dinner good chicken broth. I stept at four on my horse and associated to another traveller, passed Canajohari, baited our horses by Hudson, crossed the Mohawk for the last time, tarried about an hour at the widow Schuyler's, and slept that night nine miles farther at Bankert's inn, much fatigued and thoroughly wet by a copious perspiration.

The sight of several fields, from which they were reaping

the rye, of others where the sheaves stood in array, made me double my speed. I breakfasted at Putnam's on Trip's hill, staid over noon at Mabee's, six miles from Schenectadi, without tasting a morsel, providing quietly for my beast, as the landlady declined the trouble to prepare a roasted chicken for my dinner. I might have got some pork. I enjoyed the satisfaction to find the Rev. Romeyn with his lady and family in a perfect health. A good dish of tea, with the delightful society of that respectable clergyman, revived my spirits, so that I passed two agreeable hours with them. I rode the same evening yet five miles farther, and was before eight next morning under the hospitable roof of my worthy friend, Dr. Mancius.

The Rev. de Ronde, a clergyman of four score years, who expatriated from one of the Land Provinces, and settled in this State, many years past, was to officiate in the Dutch Church. I was tempted to be one of his hearers. The good old father, I believe, did as well as he could. I retreated after dinner, in silence, from the city with the fear of the constable, ignorant that I did attend Divine worship in the morning, continually before my eyes, slept at Cosachie, and rode early on Monday morning through an incessant rain, to Mr. Sax, in the *Imbogt.** My breakfast was soon in readiness, and I could not deny him the satisfaction, to give him the outlines of my excursion. From here I continued my route to Capt. Hendrick Schoonmaker, where I took a dish of tea, till a heavy thunder shower shall have passed. My patience was exhausted at length, as the day was far gone, and submitted to ride nine miles further, through a violent rain, before I could reach my dwelling. But not one single drop made any impression, except on my hat, face and hands, thanks to my silk oiled coat.

---

* Travel on the Sabbath was forbidden unless the traveler had attended church services on Sunday morning. Van der Kemp was afraid the constable would make him return to town to verify his statement that he had indeed attended divine worship before he set forth. Therefore he says he traveled "with the fear of the constable . . . continually before my eyes."

Joy was legible in every countenance; my heart was glad and thankful when I did see me so cordially received, when I felt myself embraced with so much tenderness by all who were so dear to me.

My dear John alone suffered, under an intermittent fever, but that unwelcome visitor left us ere long, so that everything is again in its old train; the children at school, father in the field, mother unwearied, attentive to her many domestic concerns; all is bustle; ten loads of hay, eleven of rye, and fourteen of wheat are secured; the remainder mowed and reaped in the field, so that I must take hold of a few moments early in the morning and late at evening.

My companion, more sanguine in his projects and more ardent in their pursuit, had a much higher conception of this tract than your friend; to him it was superior, far exceeding all that he had seen, in situation, in luxuriant fertility, in natural riches. No doubt it was gifted with it; it might by an active industry, be transformed in an Eden! The soil, in my opinion, is even less rich than that in Whitestown and at the Oriskany creek, but its cultivation shall be easier, it shall not bake, it shall not be hardened in the same manner in a dry season.

I visited and examined this tract with the view to fix there my permanent residence, and obtain a valuable possession for my children and your family. I did not shrink at meeting in face some hardships, but visited it and endeavoured to examine it from creek to creek, not only near the water side, but often several miles in the interior, to obtain a sufficiently correct knowledge of its situation, of its real and relative value; and in this mind I do not hesitate to make you this frank and honest confession, that I have not yet encountered in this State an equal extensive tract of land on which I should prefer to end my course, if joined by a few respectable families, in the vicinity of a tolerable settlement, of which, if my wealth was equal to its acquisition, I should, in preference to all which I have yet seen, desire to secure its possession.

→≫ ≪←

Van der Kemp begged Adam Mappa to join him in the venture toward which his own mind was firmly set. Perhaps Mappa would have accepted the suggestion had he not received an offer to become assistant to Gerrit Boon with the Holland Land Company at Oldenbarneveld, a position which he filled with great success.

Van der Kemp was determined to found an estate in the Oneida wilderness, with its richer soil and more extensive lands than he now owned at Esopus Creek. His conclusion: "My determination may be modified, it cannot be shaken."

❧ IX ❧

Adviser to
Vice President Adams

NEW YORK STATE made Van der Kemp a citizen less than
a year after his arrival in America. The federal government
recognized such citizenship as binding on the nation. Van
der Kemp valued his citizenship as an opportunity for
service as well as a privilege conveying human rights.

His education was superior to that of most Americans
and his view was worldwide. He had experienced the inter-
relationships of political, economic and cultural affairs in
Europe and recognized the ties of the new United States
with the system. He could evaluate relations with the rest
of the western world better than Washington or Clinton,
perhaps better than even Adams and Jefferson who had
gained breadth through their diplomatic posts. Van der
Kemp knew Europe well through books as well as experience. He had studied political philosophy both ancient
and modern.

In late 1789 Van der Kemp decided it was time for him
to make his experience and learning useful to America.
After all, he had met and conversed with a number of its
leaders. He had become a property owner (with a mort-
gage). He was on a firm basis of friendship with the vice
president and with the governor of New York State. Adams
and Van der Kemp exchanged frequent letters in this

period. The letters indicate clearly that Adams appreciated his friend's advice.

Van der Kemp became interested in John Adams' three-volume work, *A Defence of the Constitutions of Government of the United States of America, against the Attack of M. Turgot.* The French statesman and scholar had criticized the American people for following too closely the English pattern of constitutional government and for setting up a separation of powers. He stated in a letter to Richard Price in England that the American states should have cast off the English system and established a single house of representatives with no "competing" executive or judiciary branches of government. Price published Turgot's letter appended to a small book of his own containing advice to the Americans on government. Adams in London felt that he had to defend the American system of balance of powers, particularly since the constitutional convention was meeting. Adams advocated two or three legislative bodies chosen independently of each other, and executive and judiciary branches with independent powers. He believed these powers could be balanced and checked in a way that would insure freedom, protect property and encourage progress.

In the *Defence* Adams stated his views on checks and balances and supported the balanced plans of most of the thirteen states. The work also contained analyses of the governments of Europe since the Middle Ages plus some consideration of the ancient Greek and Roman states. He thought his examples were proof that the three branches of power existed in "every society natural and artificial." [1] He looked upon the executive as "the natural friend of the people, and the only defense which they or their representatives can have against the avarice and ambition of the rich and distinguished citizens." [2] The writing was not as scholarly as Adams wished but the occasion demanded a speedy publication. The first volume was published in London in 1787 and reached the members of the Constitutional Convention in Philadelphia before they adjourned.

Reviewers were critical, particularly in Europe, some of them because Adams showed too ardent a love for democracy, or at least had too much democratic support to be acceptable to the aristocracy. Van der Kemp read the reviews and the complete *Defence* as soon as he could get it. He had approved of a strong executive in Holland but not a tyrant. The *Defence* convinced him of the wisdom in checks and balances. He intended to study thoroughly the whole doctrine of republican government.

By this time (1790) the new Constitution was in effect and working successfully. However, the French Revolution had begun and Francis was reminded anew of the difficulties and dangers of regaining lost liberties. He asked Adams to give the Americans a warning, however disagreeable, as to what courses they must follow to retain "political and civil liberty." [3] Francis felt the French could have avoided violence if they had translated and heeded the *Defence*.[4] Van der Kemp expressed his sincere wish that every sensible American would read the work and that every lover of religious and civil liberty would "devour" it. The scholar's letter then proceeded to four and a half pages of detailed criticisms and comments.[5]

If the American cause looked hopeful, the French situation looked full of trouble and sorrow. The Revolution had brought forth and firmly established the Declaration of the Rights of Man and had destroyed the Bastille, symbol of despotism. But it had also made virtual prisoners of the king and royal family, and had incurred the enmity of other nations. Van der Kemp was hopeful at first for the rights of all men in France but soon became pessimistic. He regretted the bloodshed and was convinced the French had missed a great opportunity to secure their rights and liberties by establishing a strong constitutional government with checks and balances. When the prominent editor, Jacques Pierre Brissot, and others fled to escape the French oligarchy, Van der Kemp was sure it was only the vanguard of *émigrés*.[6]

Adams was at the national capital, New York, and answered Van der Kemp's letters in late February in spite of busy schedules. He commented briefly on the criticisms of his *Defence* and boldly declared his view on the American Government.

> I will candidly confess, that an hereditary Senate, without an hereditary Executive, would diminish the Prerogatives of the President and the Liberties of the People. But I contend that hereditary descent in both, when controled by an independent Representation of the People, is better than corrupted, turbulent and bloody Elections. And the knowledge you have of the human heart will concur with your knowledge of the History of nations to convince you that Elections of Presidents and Senitors, cannot be long conducted in a populous, oppulent and commercial Nation, without corruption, Sedition and Civil War.[7]

Adams mentioned numerous letters of commendation and flattery received from Europe on the *Defence* but doubted that his books would be widely read. They were too offensive to kings and senators, to democrats and rabble. "A wish for Unlimited Power is the natural Passion of each of these orders, and no Doctrine pleases but that which flatters the ruling Passion." He ended the letter with the declaration, "I will never cease to preach my favourite Doctrine [checks and balances], untill I die." [8]

In a letter the following month, Adams again commented pessimistically on French developments, especially the single assembly. He compared a number of French leaders to various American leaders. He mentioned disorders and threats of disorder in America, telling of a political quarrel in Massachusetts in which one man was burned in effigy and another was threatened with tar and feathers. He feared that a trifle could have started killing and sedition, just as in France. He described an intrigue intended to deprive him of the vice-presidency in 1788. He contended that senatorial elections had been notoriously corrupt, and continued vehemently:

When Bribery, Corruption, Intrigue, Manoeuvre Violence, Force, shall render Elections too troublesome and too dangerous, another Convention must be called, who may prolong the Period of Senators from Six Years to twelve or twenty or thirty or forty or for Life, or if necessary propose the Establishment of hereditary Senators. . . . And if the Election of President should become terrible, I can conceive of no other method to preserve Liberty: but to have a national Convention called for the express purpose of electing an hereditary President. These appear to me to be the only Hopes of our Posterity. While Washington lives Elections may answer. . . .[9]

The bloody French Revolution alarmed Adams during this time when his own country was still in the throes of adjusting to its first major change of operation. When some of his thoughts on hereditary officials became known to his enemies, he was openly accused of being a monarchist. Van der Kemp probably discussed Adams' opinions with other people but specifically denied on one occasion quoting or showing confidential statements. Van der Kemp, himself, was not disturbed by Adams' ideas because he believed in freedom of political thought. He agreed that the French Revolution had demonstrated the irresponsibility of the rabble and Adams had pointed out signs of intrigue and violence in America. Van der Kemp did not know enough of public elections in his adopted country to condemn or defend them but he pursued the topic.

Van der Kemp wrote that he wished Adams had explained how the election of senators and president could be changed without sedition and civil war. He had doubts. It seemed to him also that the elections for members of the House of Representatives might be corrupt even though Adams saw no danger of it. Shouldn't there be fear of bribery and corruption "when but one representative can be chosen for 30 or 40,000 Citizens?" And wouldn't there be troubles in the continuation of hereditary offices in large land-holding families? How would a vacancy be filled? It might be a useful experiment to recognize Kentucky and Vermont as independent nations in alliance with the United States on the condition that they try a system of hereditary president, senators and representatives. Then it would be seen if this removed bribery, corruption and sedition and promoted civil liberty. Perhaps a division of the whole country would be preferable whenever the population multiplied sufficiently.[10] Thus Van der Kemp, living in an age when a republican form of government was often a questionable experiment, questioned but did not condemn elections.

Van der Kemp expressed further concern over the French Revolution. "Love of mankind and Liberty make me wish that Liberty may prevail in every part, althoug I fear that she is more and more declining in Europe. The French people are the last to enjoy it . . . [on the continent]." He feared that the bulk of the French, after the delirium passed, would join some foreign power in restoring a monarchy with the old despotism unless they were awakened to the dangers of their present course. He still thought the French should read the *Defence* and had recommended it to Baron Jean Dauerhoult (of Dutch origin) in Champagne. He was impatient for an answer, yet how could he expect the French to appreciate it when "American scriblers" were abusing the work so roundly? [11]

When Adams won the very close vice-presidential contest with George Clinton in 1792, Van der Kemp congratulated the winner but stated clearly his respect for his good friend, the loser: "I am not angry that men of principles and character honour Governour Clinton with their suffrage— He is it worth in my opinion. . . ." He believed Clinton had been unfairly treated in the campaign by some of his enemies. Adams replied that he, too, was a friend of Clinton but regretted that Clinton lent his name and influence to the opponents of the Constitution and the administration, inviting anarchy by their notions.[12]

In the winter of 1792–93 Van der Kemp read from the works of Machiavelli, including *The Prince*. He thought

the work was instructive and that "modern politicians could
learn a great deal of sound reasoning by this so universally
damn'd Italian—" He agreed with Adams that the writer
actually favored democracy. Adams remarked that the
French had adopted one of the alternatives suggested by a
Machiavellian maxim, to either destroy or be very generous
to defeated enemies, when they got rid of their nobility.
He still doubted the success of the French unicameral system and thought France would be a "shambles of Carnage"
until she changed it.[13]

When Adams became vice president in 1789, he recognized a need for a sequel to his *Defence.* The new Constitution had been formed only by much compromising. Even
at this time Rhode Island had not ratified the document
and New York State had voted for ratification very reluctantly. Many important leaders still believed in a dominant national legislature and a weak executive. Adams was
obligated to defend the balanced system again, to defend
his ideas against attacks of Condorcet and to make obvious
the weaknesses of the French system which was influencing
Americans. He published a series of papers in the *Gazette
of the United States* at Philadelphia. These were in the
form of commentaries on the French history written by the
Italian historian Enrico Caterino Davila. The *Discourses
on Davila* were rejected by Adams' political opponents,
who selected isolated statements to use against him. Van
der Kemp was anxious to get not only the *Discourses on
Davila* but also Davila's history. References in letters and
newspapers were not enough.

Adams wrote in further support of his thesis, "The French
Revolution is every day furnishing the World with fresh
Proofs of the Necessity of Checks and Ballances. Unlimited
Power is as dangerous in many as in one. . . . I have no
Idea of any greater Wickedness, than an attempt to govern
Societies by single Assemblies." [14] Van der Kemp agreed in
principle. He thought Louis XVI deserved some punish-
ment but he doubted the wisdom of destroying the king
and the nobility. Nor was he yet "an adept at their levelling

system," a total lack of respect for property as well as lack of respect for position. Van der Kemp wanted the French people to be free but also secure under a sound constitution, enabling France to serve as an example for the rest of Europe.[15] Later in the year Louis was beheaded. Van der Kemp heard the news with regret, as he thought Louis, with his power controlled and limited, could have been a competent constitutional monarch: "France would have been in Europe what America is in the New World independent and free—a scourge to despotism, and asylum for the oppressed." [16]

But not all was perfect in America. Van der Kemp warned Adams that, if he "had not such a high opinion of the good Sense and Political ability" of the government of the United States, he "should be fearfull indeed that the Americans should be seduced to some rash steps by the cunning intrigues of a French Minister [Genêt]." [17] A few months later he advised Adams more directly about Genêt. "I hope that Congress will not leave unnoticed the daring attacks with which a foreign Minister insulted our Constitution, by libelling the Executive Power with desultory adpellations, for whose excuse no shadow shall be adduced." He strongly opposed having a French emissary give orders to the United States; [18] the hatred of foreign domination learned in his military school days had been reinforced when he had seen his native Holland submit to the French and the British.

Genêt continued his agitation until it appeared that he would push America into war with Great Britain. When Van der Kemp heard that a declaration of war had been defeated by only two votes in Congress, he had mixed emotions. He knew a war would be sure to hinder the progress of the new country, even threaten its existence. However, the *threat* of such a war might cause Britain to give up its western posts, including Oswego, near the site for his new home, and restrain British cruisers and privateers from attacking American commerce. He felt France was not to be trusted because it was headed for an oligarchy backed by the army. Van der Kemp offered an idea that probably deserved more consideration than Adams gave it.

He suggested that our government offer to mediate between the French and the combined powers for the practical purpose of gaining time, depending on the emotionalism of some of the partisans in the United States to insure public support of the idea. If we could avoid war for a year, affairs in Europe might be considerably changed and the pressures on Congress considerably lessened.[19] Adams rejected the proposal on the basis that he dreaded contagion by contact. He said the United States ought "if possible, keep wholly out of the Vortex. Enthusiasm is as contagious as Mesmerism alias Animal Magnetism [a fad at the time]." [20]

When Van der Kemp moved to Oneida Lake in 1794, he immediately became more conscious of threats of war with Great Britain. His land was only 25 or 30 miles through the woods from Lake Ontario, a few more to Fort Oswego. The British had closed the Oswego River in 1793 and, in case of war, this river and Oneida Lake might be a path of invasion for both British and Indians. Saint Leger's attack on Fort Stanwix and the Battle of Oriskany were fresh in the minds of frontier families. Van der Kemp hoped for peace, and tried to be confident that peace would continue, but admitted that "in case of war the neighbourhood of Oswego would not be desirable." [21]

Van der Kemp was in favor of John Jay's mission to England in May, 1794, to draw up a treaty. He probably did not know that Jay planned to use the threat of war as a weight against English demands, much as Van der Kemp had suggested. Jay had little with which to bargain when Hamilton got word to the British that the United States would not declare war.

One of Van der Kemp's business friends on the frontier was Leonard Gansevoort of Albany. In October, 1794, Van der Kemp included in a letter to Ganesvoort, "I congratulate you, with the joyful tidings from our ambassador at the British Court—I hope in that part, our most sanguine expectations may be fulfilled, and Jay—may—at his return, receive the thankful applauses of America—once more." [22] This was premature. In August, 1795, Van der Kemp wrote to Gansevoort again, saying: "The prospects of peace seem not to be so near at hand, . . . but how ardently I wished it universally established. I shall consider America happy if ours is not disturbed or infected by European influence." [23] At last the treaty was official and Van der Kemp wrote: "I wish you joy with the ratified British Treaty, here [at Oneida Lake] every one considers it as an eminent blessing." [24]

Not everyone in the state of New York or elsewhere shared the view that the treaty was a blessing. Van der Kemp himself considered it a mixed blessing in his correspondence with Adams. "I rejoice with the ratification of the treaty, though I could have wished it more favourable. . . . Washington and the Senate have merited our confidence. [T]hey would have been unworthy of it, if the clamorous vociferations of a considerable Party could have intimidated them. . . ." [25]

The clamors of Jay's vilifiers, the hangings in effigy, the heckling and stoning of those who spoke in favor of the treaty, all reminded Van der Kemp of the violent French mobs in the Revolution and the swift changes of public sentiment. Jay had been elected governor of New York before the treaty was made public. Was there danger to Jay, to Washington and the Senate? Every time that Van der Kemp commented on the troubles of France, he must have said a silent prayer that the same thing was not beginning in America. Throughout the country there was violent debate. In France, the Directory was forbidding the expression of opposition to its policies. Despotic leaders were displaced by other despotic leaders. In 1796 Van der Kemp predicted that the despotism of the French oligarchy would lead ultimately to a crown for a "Disinterested Patriot." [26] He deduced from his study of ancient and modern history that from such unstable conditions a new Julius Caesar would arise.

The puzzling political situation in the Netherlands interested Van der Kemp as much as the French turmoil. The French had assisted in the ousting of the stadholder, but had made a severe treaty with the Dutch. Heavy payments were required in return for the assistance and for further French protection. The little country was reorganized by Patriots on a French pattern, with "liberty, equality and fraternity," a constitution, and a single national assembly. Peter Paulus, an old friend of Van der Kemp, led the reorganization and was chosen president of the Assembly. The nobility was abolished, public gallows and whipping posts were removed, coats of arms were taken from the churches, tolls were abolished and taxation exemptions were eliminated.[27] The constitution of the new Batavian Republic was much like the old Articles of Confederation of the United States. Van der Kemp approved of these democratic actions but doubted that his native country could prosper under the direction of a violent, treacherous France. He thought the Dutch would feel the expense of the settlement with the French for a long time if they were forced to join in "Proclamations of liberty, equality or *death.*" He was not sure the reorganized government held promise.

> If the Dutch people had preserved more of a National character and Patriotism than I believed in the years 81–87—If they can become superior to party prejudices, . . . If the majority as wel[l] as the pars potior are united without any controul from abroad—if they are sure that France never will . . . betray the Dutch to England and Prussia—just as she betrayed them in 87—and if the Dutch then can agree to adopt a good constitution and return to the good faith—industry—and frugal life of their ancestors . . . [they will again be prosperous].

In spite of his concern and hope for the future of his fatherland, Van der Kemp told Adams that he never wished to return "though the most scanty circumstances may be my share—through the rest of my days—in the lonely woods—"

But he said he would rejoice if the Dutch became a "free independent People" with a good constitution.[28] Not until 1814 was he able to rejoice for Dutch freedom.

When George Washington delivered his Farewell Address, Van der Kemp immediately thought of Adams as the probable successor to Washington, and wrote to him:

> Washington's resignation, which crowns that Excellent man with glory, opens the career for my worthy and much respected friend, to bestow new obligations upon his countrymen, if they are wise enough to take hold of this favourable opportunity. Can your Excell[ency]—without compromitting yourself procure your old friend a place among the Electors in this State—you know upon whom he shall pay the tribute, which every American owes to your meritorious character.[29]

Realizing that Adams had relatively little control of the choice of electors, Van der Kemp wrote a month later that though he had wanted to contribute in this way to Adams' election, he could understand that it was necessary to choose someone else to be elector in order to keep his support. He said he would be satisfied if it worked out successfully.[30] The election was very close, Adams receiving 71 votes while Jefferson had 68. The "someone else" chosen from Western New York was Van der Kemp's friend, Peter Smith,[31] an important land speculator. Smith voted for Adams and Pinckney as did all twelve of the New York electors. Van der Kemp was satisfied.

When Adams became president, Van der Kemp corresponded less with him. The life in the wilderness was hard and it was difficult to get the information that was needed to keep himself informed. Van der Kemp was too proud to waste the time of Adams as president even though he had offered advice and guidance to Adams as vice president.

On March 4, he sent his congratulations to Adams:

Permit me to address you with [a] few words upon your election to the Presidency of the United States. My wishes in this part are certainly accomplished— May America remain happy in peace and prosper under your administration— So that the name of Washington and Adams may be combined at every new election—as those of August and Trajan . . . Sensible of my obligations towards you in so many respects, and of my duty with regard to your exalted station in not abusing your precious time.

    I am with sentiments of the highest esteem and regard
        Sir!
              Your Most obed. and oblgd st
              Fr. Adr. Van der Kemp [32]

❦ X ❧

An Estate
on Oneida Lake

EARLY in June, 1794, Francis Van der Kemp stood for the first time as owner on his own estate, a thousand acres of virgin land. His family was staying with the Adam Mappas in Oldenbarneveld, a good day's journey to the east. Seven years before, the number of houses in this whole area west of the ford at Old Fort Schuyler was twenty-one, some of them mere huts. Now the movement to the Genesee country had begun and villages dotted the area. In 1794 more than six thousand people lived on farms and in villages, with Whitesboro, Fort Stanwix, Clinton, New Hartford and Old Fort Schuyler as the centers of population. A little to the west of Van der Kemp's land was the Indian town of Oneida with 500 or more inhabitants. Few of the white settlements had more than 200. Also to the west, but north of Lake Oneida, was the beginning town of Rotterdam. General stores and taverns had been established in the villages, but the closest grist mill to the Oneida Lake lands was at Fort Stanwix. Roads were chiefly the cleared paths from village to village.

Van der Kemp had purchased his land from George Scriba, owner of a large tract lying between Oneida Lake and Lake Ontario. Originally the state had sold this land to John and Nicholas I. Roosevelt in 1791, but when the Roosevelts failed to fulfill the contract, Scriba was allowed to buy a large part. Scriba was from Germany and had become a successful merchant in New York City. He decided to speculate in Central New York lands and obtained the patent in 1792 and 1794. In these first years Benjamin Wright, an early surveyor, had laid out the tract into twenty-four townships with "great lots." The section of the north shore of Oneida Lake purchased by Van der Kemp was called Scriba's Location. George Scriba moved to nearby Rotterdam where he opened a store, and promised land and road improvements to prospective settlers. Thus, he convinced Van der Kemp to buy the choicest great lot bordering the lake, No. 130, and in 1795 sold him three adjoining lots, farther back from the lake on high ground, in the names of the three Van der Kemp children.

Van der Kemp's land was covered with hardwood trees and in one section had a gentle rise to a pond. The soil was sandy and well drained. Near the lake shore was a flat area, some twenty feet higher than lake level, where he would begin his buildings. As he viewed his land and planned the locations of his buildings, he thought of Hugh White's success at Whitesboro and of the way in which Des Wattines had made his island bloom. Perhaps he thought also of Robert Livingston and George Washington with their fine houses and noble estates. Here he began the building of his family estate and named it Kempwick.

The first task was to clear a patch of land and put up buildings sufficient for modest living. He engaged local woodsmen to fell trees but they failed to do more than a small part. Folk stories have it that the wealthy Van der Kemp brought a large number of Negro slaves with him. But the scholar was not wealthy and owned few slaves, perhaps one family. There is brief mention of a Negro child dying in 1796 and the sale of a Negro "wench." He hired carpenters and other choppers. After modest shelter was completed, Van der Kemp moved from the Esopus farm. He transported household furnishings, stock, and farm supplies to Kempwick, and brought his family to stay with the Mappas until he could fashion a home good enough to share with Bartha, John, Betsy, and little Peter.

No existing records explain which route the Van der Kemps traveled from the Esopus Creek to Oneida Lake with their possessions. They could have gone by sloop to Albany, from there by bateau to Fort Stanwix and then overland to his lands. It is more probable that the hardy pioneer-scholar went by road the entire distance of about 175 miles, a difficult trip taking from three to four weeks. Two or three oxcarts were carefully loaded with Mrs. Van der Kemp's prized furniture and other household goods along with seeds and farming equipment. Chickens were in cages, and cows were tied to the backs of the carts. Francis rode on one horse with five-year-old Peter in front of him, while Bartha rode double on another horse with Betsy, now nine years old. Young John Van der Kemp helped herd sheep along the road or took turns riding on one of the carts. He was eleven.

Francis had planned the trip carefully. He knew where to stop for rest, for the best food, and for the night. However, no amount of planning could make pioneer traveling easy or comfortable. Rain increased the depth of the mud and raised the level of the river at the several fords along the route. The well-packed cargo sometimes shifted, requiring a half hour to adjust it. An axle, wheel, cart tongue, or perhaps only a piece of harness could break, causing frustrating and tiring delays. More than once friends, old or new, stopped the family to talk. When the party reached Old Fort Schuyler, Bartha and the children, with one of the hired hands, turned to the north to stay at Oldenbarneveld. Francis continued west, superintending the moving of his goods over the last part of the journey. Here the road was worse, scarcely more than a wide trail with churned mire, frequent boulders, and overhanging tree limbs switching the faces of the cart drivers. Fish Creek was forded on the initial journey, as the bridge across it was not finished until early July.

At last the creaking oxcarts arrived at the clearing.

Francis had little time to savor his satisfaction at the completion of the long journey, as it was necessary to care for the animals and carefully put the furniture under roof.

His mind had been busy with plans during the difficult trip. After an inspection of his clearing, he was ready for the next stages of pioneering.

He did not expect perfection in one season. He had written in May,

> . . . Mrs. Van der Kemp is great-minded enough to dare encounter this new and difficult struggle and sacrifice, with out reluctance, the comfort of society and the allurements of an applauding circle, to the calm pleasure of domestic happiness and a retir'd life. A beautiful situation, a fertile soil—three beloved children and a selected library shall be our amusements and our ambition, to reap all the possible advantages from these united sources and spread so much happiness around us, as our narrow circle shall allow— [1]

His buildings were planned as intelligently as his most arduous research project. He constructed the small house of logs, probably with a loft overhead. The scholar-turned-carpenter built his barn of solid Dutch construction, 60 by 26 feet, 6 feet high at the eaves and 18 feet high at the main posts. The chicken house was 16 feet square, with a peak for pigeons.[2]

Construction difficulties on the frontier were many, and took strange twists. At one time, he ran out of nails and instructed Leonard Gansevoort & Company at Albany: "[S]end me with all possible speed . . . [since] the carpenters shall be waiting on them in a week *forty thousand 9^d nails of the first quality for putting on shingles.*" [3] The carpenters could not use the local nails because they were too short to fasten securely Van der Kemp's better than ordinary shingles.

A month of hard physical labor passed and the house was not yet ready to receive his family. He wrote in a spare moment, perhaps when it was raining, to John Adams:

The situation here is delightful—the soil rich enough
—and my seat in particular would admit every improvement of taste if my finances were adequate to it. . . .
All will be surmounted in time if once I may be happy
enough to see my family on the spot. Mrs. Van der Kemp
is still . . . with the family of Mr. Mappa where she
shall stay till I have prepared the outhouses and a convenient log house, as was intended for a temporary residence. She is resolved to make few sacrifices more, and
more yet, if by necessity it is required. . . . To avoid this
however and to make our retirement more comfortable
to my worthy consort as accustomed to another manner
of living, I am resolved to repair for a small part of our
losses to offer my Library for sale in the hope that the
amount shall be sufficient to build a conventional house.
. . . I value it between 400 and 500 £ and shall prepare the Catalogue this winter.[4]

Only store records of fall purchases signify the completion of Van der Kemp's buildings and the arrival of his
family at Kempwick toward the end of the summer. During this period of the writer's life his pen was laid aside for
much of the time. The daylight hours were too short for the
tasks to be done, and the night too short to rest his tired
body. Supplies for the family were obtained from Scriba's
store at Rotterdam and George Huntington at Fort Stanwix. In one of Scriba's account books are listed for Van der
Kemp one barrel of pork and two of beef, two barrels of
country rum, one barrel of gin, groceries, seeds and trees,
and a "washing machine" purchased from Domine Gross.

When Bartha came, she directed the arrangement of furniture for more comfortable living. A small stream nearby
furnished water until some later time when a well was dug.
Probably the chinking of the house had to be redone to be
sure the cabin would be warm for Bartha and the children
during the long winter.

In another of Scriba's account books, for September and
October, are listed three pairs of hinges, 1992 feet of boards,

50 common boards, nails, sugar, rice, molasses, tea, a de-
canter, a dozen cups and saucers, yellow flannel, three
blankets, brandy, mustard, vinegar, flour and thread.[5] Some
hunting and fishing was necessary to supplement the supplies. Firewood had to be cut. The fences for the animals
had to be kept in repair, and hay cut or bought for their
winter feed. Always there was clearing to be done for the
spring planting. But Van der Kemp embraced all of these
activities as part of the developing frontier with his usual
vigor and enthusiasm. His beloved books would have to
wait until winter.

Rotterdam, a few miles to the west, was the main village
established by Scriba. Solomon Waring settled there in
1793 and opened a tavern within a year or two. In 1794
Scriba had a road cut from Rotterdam to Vera Cruz on
Lake Ontario at the mouth of Little Salmon Creek. Scriba
built a sawmill and gristmill in 1794–95 and set up a store
soon after.[6]

In 1795 John Bernhard brought his family and tried to
live on what is now Bernhard's Bay in a poorly built and
abandoned log hut. The Van der Kemps compassionately
invited the Bernhards to live with them during the winter.
With two families closely confined by bitter weather in a
small house, perhaps it was inevitable that trouble should
arise. During the course of the winter, Van der Kemp and
Bernhard had a sharp political disagreement, and the Bernhards went back to the hut in anger. But they chose a poor
time. A heavy snow with wind came that night drifting
snow through the holes in the roof and walls. Van der Kemp
welcomed the family back under his roof. In the spring the
Bernhards built a good house on the bay and the two families were friendly ever after.[7]

In June, 1795, the French Duke La Rochefoucauld-Lian-
court visited this area but remembered it adversely.

> Rotterdam is a new establishment begun . . . by Mr.
> Scriba, a wealthy Hollander, and a merchant, . . . At
> present his establishments amount to but little. A dozen

poor log houses, built almost entirely at Mr. Scriba's expense, constitute all there is of the city of Rotterdam, so named in honor of the native place of its founder. The dams for the use of the mills that he has built have cost much money, and being always poorly built he has been obliged to recommence them several times. The grist mill is not yet built, and the dam appears too feeble for the pressure it will have to sustain. Some work and considerable money has been expended at the mouth of the creek to make a landing, but the accommodation is very poor. They estimate that Mr. Scriba has expended over eight thousand dollars here, and if the work had been well applied it would be a profitable investment. Mr. Scriba is now building a fine frame house in which he intends to place a store. In this he will share the profits with two associates whom he has as his agents for all these works. . . .[8]

In 1796 Rotterdam's building program progressed, but the town suffered from lack of business as a lake port. The agent wrote to Scriba that the boats had passed by in the middle of the lake all summer. "There seems to be a combination at Ft. Stanwix against Rotterdam." [9]

Management of his estate kept Van der Kemp busy during the first year at Kempwick. He paid for materials purchased in Albany chiefly through the payments for his Esopus farm by Abraham Van Gaasbeck. Transportation for articles from Holland had to be arranged, one lot containing 52 pairs of wooden shoes and some optical instruments.[10] The latter were lenses for magnification or use in telescopes, while a ten years' supply of wooden shoes for the Van der Kemps, hired hands and tenants resulted in a rather large order.

Van der Kemp also arranged for a box containing farm tools and ordered a beehive.[11] With other citizens of the region he signed a petition to the state assembly asking for the improvement of the roads in the "Western district." [12] In

January of 1795 he became Scriba's agent for land sales in the vicinity of Kempwick.[13]

The dispensation of justice also demanded some of the energy of the champion of liberty. Van der Kemp's Oneida Lake property was in Herkimer County. By 1794 the people were sufficient in number to require a term of the court of common pleas and general session. In January the first court session was held in the meeting house at Whitestown with Henry Staring as judge, Jedediah Sanger and Amos Wetmore as justices and twelve others having the position of assistant justice and justice of the peace (a combined office).[14] In September, 1794, Van der Kemp was added to this list by the council of appointment at Albany. In addition to handling minor cases of local justice and attending sessions of common pleas, justices presided over town, district, and precinct meetings. When Van der Kemp accepted the post, he proudly informed Adams that his "particular situation, in an infant settlement in the Western parts with other considerations" had overcome his resolutions to stick to the development of his estate. He recognized these duties would take time and even some little expense but declared he would try to do a good job.[15] On October 21 he purchased for three pounds, six pence a copy of the *Law of the State of New York* and two weeks later paid two pounds for his commission.[16] A month before the appointment was made, he wrote, "Though I place so much confidence in the principal rulers that I am less anxious to trouble myself with the subalterns [,] I love to make me thoroughly acquainted with the principles on which good government must be conducted—" He had been studying local justice and deserved the title of judge that the new position gave him.[17]

The majority of court cases at this time were assault and battery or eviction from lands. This was the West in the 1790's, and the first inhabitants were mostly men of self-reliance who sometimes exercised justice with their fists or with clubs and who insisted on "natural" rather than

legal rights to land. In these adolescent years there were
at least two murder trials, one an Indian defendant, and
one case of the theft of a yoke of oxen.[18] The lawyers, the
constables, the sheriff and the justices, particularly those
who held the general respect of the community, no doubt
settled a great many disputes on the frontier. Van der Kemp
said he was giving considerable attention and effort to establish "some order and decency in the court where ignorance and stupidity prevails." [19]

A description of a session in Judge Sanger's court in New
Hartford reveals the rather startling informality of some of
the frontier courts and explains Judge Van der Kemp's
resolution to establish "order and decency":

> A gentleman who attended the court as a spectator in-
> formed me that the day was one of those cold "January
> days frequent in our climate," and that in the afternoon,
> and when it was nearly night, in order to comfort them-
> selves in their by no means very well appointed court
> room, and to keep the blood at a temperature at which
> it would continue to circulate, some of the gentlemen of
> the bar had induced the Sheriff to procure, from a neigh-
> boring inn, a jug of spirits. This, it must be remembered,
> was before the invention of temperance societies. Upon
> the jug's appearing in court, it was passed around the bar
> table, and each of the learned counsellors in his turn up-
> raised the elegant vessel, and descanted into his mouth,
> by the simplest process imaginable so much as he deemed
> a sufficient dose of the delicious fluid. While the opera-
> tion was going on, the dignitaries of the bench, who were
> no doubt suffering quite as much as their brethren of
> the bar, had a little consultation, when the first Judge
> announced to the audience that the court saw no reason
> why they should continue to hold open any longer, and
> freeze to death, and desired the crier forthwith to ad-
> journ the court. Before, however, this functionary could
> commence with a single "Hear ye," Colonel Colbrath
> jumped up, catching, as he rose, the jug from the lawyer

who was complimenting its contents, and holding it up towards the bench, hastily ejaculated: "Oh, no, no, no, Judge,—don't adjourn yet; take a little gin, Judge; that will keep you warm; tant time to adjourn yet;" and suiting the action to the word, he handed his honor the jug. It appeared there was force in the Sheriff's advice, for the order to adjourn was revoked, and the business went on.[20]

Although exploitation of the soil and other frontier resources was prevalent, Van der Kemp continued his interest in scientific farming while at Kempwick. He took his fine sheep with him, his numerous experimental seeds, and a good stock of chickens and cows. He apparently made converts in the area, resulting in a meeting in Hugh White's tavern at Whitesboro for the formation of an agricultural society. On April 7, 1795, the interested citizens met with Van der Kemp. In June they had an organizational meeting at which Van der Kemp delivered an address which led to the formation of the Agricultural Society of the Western District of New York. The state society had not been organized yet but a group had been formed in Albany in 1791.

At the Whitesboro meeting Van der Kemp expressed his objective to be "no less than the erection of a *Society of Agriculture and Natural History,* in these western parts." He spoke with feeling about how country living invigorated one's health and strengthened "the faculties of our soul," eliminating the petty passions of long-settled regions and accenting in the country the rigorous and bold. The eminent statesmen, lawyers and heroes, including the foremost—Washington—were from the country. Van der Kemp mirrored his own life in the statement:

What pleasure! what raptures we enjoy in the contemplation of a cleared, fenced acre of the first crop of corn, wheat or grass, that ever covered that spot, since the creation!

He continued a bit later:

> In the evening he [the farmer] endeavors, if possible, to keep his family employed to advantage, or instructs his children in the duties of rural and domestic life, acquaints them with the history of his country, with our laws and government, with the precepts and excellence of virtue and christian religion; or studies a Sidney—a Locke—a Montesquiou—an Adams, and cryes out, by comparing their doctrine with human nature and experience of past ages and modern times, in extasy—*I too am a free American.*

It is unlikely that more than one or two of his hearers had read or heard of Sidney, Locke and Montesquieu. Perhaps Jonas Platt was so educated, if he was there. Van der Kemp pointed out that the greatest handicaps to success were indolence, ignorance and "prejudices against all improvements unknown to their fathers." An agricultural society would combat all three, but especially the ignorance and prejudices. He outlined a constitution and suggested a number of projects including correspondence with other agriculturists in Europe and America. Then he said that he could not be active in the society because "the subsistance of my family requires my continued presence and uninterrupted labour, in order to preserve our contentment and independence." [21]

Perhaps the society did not prosper because the energy and guidance of Van der Kemp were not available. However, the address was published and the society gave encouragement to better farming for a few years. The historian, Hedrick, says this effort paved the way for the New York State Agricultural Society founded a few years later.[22] Van der Kemp said of his efforts:

> The Society is established—not in every part as I could desire—but a trial to controul other inclinations would have destroyed the whole. There may be in time raised a

more permanent and lofty edifice upon the foundation I laid.[23]

During this first busy year, Van der Kemp found time to read and to write letters, in spite of protestations to the contrary. He wrote to New York, Philadelphia and to John Adams in an effort to obtain a copy of Adams' *Discourses on Davila*. At this time they had been published only in the *United States Gazette* at Philadelphia and Adams had no copy. Van der Kemp also tried to get a copy of Danema's *Revolutions of Greece and Italy*. He read the *Works* of King Frederick the Great and from the writings of Condorcet. And he eagerly read newspapers and materials on law and agriculture whenever they were available.

In the summer of 1796 Jeremy Belknap and Jedediah Morse made a journey to western New York. Adams gave them a letter of introduction to Van der Kemp, who was delighted with the prospect of receiving them at Kempwick. However, the two men got only as far as Old Fort Schuyler and decided to turn back. Philip Schuyler of Albany wrote to Van der Kemp that he could not persuade the two men to go any further.[24]

Van der Kemp made a trip to Cazenovia in February, 1797, to preside at the wedding of his friend, John Lincklaen. This appears to be the only marriage ceremony performed by Van der Kemp after coming to America.

As agent for the Holland Land Company, Lincklaen had done much to develop the Cazenovia area. The beautiful falls of Chittenango Creek first attracted Lincklaen and he made the first settlement there in 1793. The following year Lincklaen persuaded the Holland Land Company to build a saw and grist mill at the site.[25] The fine house, still standing, which Lincklaen built for himself at Cazenovia a few years later, overlooked Cazenovia Lake across a spacious lawn and rivaled the house that Mappa built. Lincklaen never failed to stop for a visit with Van der Kemp on trips from Cazenovia to the east, and the Van der Kemp and Lincklaen women became close friends.

On another occasion Van der Kemp left Kempwick for a trip to Oldenbarneveld to join Adam Mappa and Harm Jan Huidekoper, both employed by the Holland Land Company, on a business trip to Kortenaer (Boonville), eighteen miles to the north. Van der Kemp persuaded young Huidekoper to visit Kempwick and the young man reported his observations. He went by road through Fort Stanwix, which had recently been renamed Rome. He was impressed with the increase in number of houses, some of them of three stories. He viewed the canal works along Wood Creek as an outstanding and pleasant sight in this rough, undeveloped country. The land to the north of Oneida Lake appeared to be less fertile than elsewhere and even unhealthy in the Rotterdam region. "The exhalations from the marshes and the stagnant water cause[d] a fever among the inhabitants" which seemed to him very much like the Zeeland fever. Poor soil, the fevers, and bad management were cited as the reasons why Rotterdam was growing so slowly.[26] Probably another reason was the superior attraction of available lands farther to the west, especially the Genesee country, and the improvement of the road south of Oneida Lake.

Van der Kemp had some difficulties getting special orders delivered to him from Albany or farther away. Usually arrangements were made for small boxes to be sent with some large shipment for a local merchant, or to be left with a merchant or friend in Whitesboro, Old Fort Schuyler or Rome. Van der Kemp relied upon Jonas Platt, John Post, or George Huntington. Huntington and his brother had set up a store in the tavern at Fort Stanwix in 1793. By the time Van der Kemp was settled at Kempwick, the Huntingtons had built a store and a house and thereafter carried on the business for a long time.[27] Since George Huntington became a judge of the Common Pleas in 1798, he probably was associated with Van der Kemp on problems of justice as well as business. Van der Kemp had stayed overnight with Post in 1792.

Van der Kemp had written in 1794, "Rather a laborious

life of a forgotten farmer in the Western Parts than the brilliant greatness of those Parisian leaders, who today are Patriots and tomorrow traitors—and rather the approbation of few honest neighbours than the noisy applause of an infatuated mob—" [28] In spite of this sincere sentiment, the physical labor and hardships of frontier farming often dismayed the scholar. Although he complained very little, he admitted in 1796 that his strength of mind and body were much impaired.[29] A later letter concerning his neighbor Des Wattines also discloses the loss of animals of considerable value to the frontier farmer.

George Scriba had given the Frenchman, Des Wattines, a small farm in the vicinity of Kempwick, where he first prospered, then deteriorated in "manners and worth." Van der Kemp wrote:

> Through the carelessness of one of my men a yoke of my oxen was drowned in the Lake—after a fortnight—Des Vattines on a morning before breakfast came to ask what I intended to do with my drowned oxen "leave them in the ice" Parbleu they are worthy to be taken care of "at your service" if I was in earnest "yes" would I permit him to take hold of this advantage—"yes" and away he went—with a stout Canadian Frenchman—skinned the oxen, and returned with the skins and about 40 weight of meat, which you could smell at a distance—all was carried to his Seat—and he told me a few days after—it made *une soupe excellente*. His dogs had destroy'd [at a later time] two of my ewes, on which I placed a high value, as an extraordinary breed—and a present of Ch. Livingston. I wrote him a line requesting him to be more watchful—as the damage could neither be paid nor repaired by him.[30]

Van der Kemp mentioned the illness of his wife and children late in 1795, and it seems that Engelbartha never did become accustomed to the frontier hardships and simple society. It grieved her to see her husband and children without common comforts. It must have humiliated her when

Francis had to send for four yards of cloth saying his drawers were "actually and entirely worn out" and that she would be "greatly obliged" if the store sent the cloth soon.[31]

On one occasion a large moose came to the Van der Kemp clearing, and Tom, apparently an Indian of the vicinity, frightened Mrs. Van der Kemp. When sickness occurred, it was sometimes impossible to persuade the doctor to come from Rotterdam. Although the family had less sickness in 1796 than in the previous year, Van der Kemp wrote to Scriba that the situation was alarming and promised nothing but sadness.[32]

Although Bartha knew Francis' dreams for the development of the estate, she could not bear to see the formidable hardships of frontier life sapping his strength and energy. He had little time for books, and few contacts with well-educated friends for the intellectual conversations he enjoyed so much. But worst of all was seeing him work in spite of ailments. Life in this isolated area was a struggle for a man with a family.

At last she must have broken down. Francis agreed to move. He loved her dearly and he wanted the best for their children.

The brief paragraph in the autobiography eloquently expresses the mental struggle and the sacrifice:

> There once more duty compelled me to make my greatest sacrifice of all my prospects—of which I sometimes yet feel the sting—to the peace and comfort of your excellent mother, and conducted her, who had given up country and ease, and relatives and friends, to follow her consort to the Western hemisphere, to Oldenbarneveld, to enjoy there the society of our few friends, Gerrit Boon, and Mr. and Mrs. Mappa, and there, I expect the end of our course.

Leaving a tenant in charge of Kempwick, the Van der Kemps made their way during the early winter of 1797 across the hills to Oldenbarneveld.

❧ XI ❧

The Move to
Oldenbarneveld

In 1797, the settlement with the impressive name of Oldenbarneveld had little more than its name. This had been taken from a town in the Netherlands named for a spirited liberal, John of Oldenbarneveld, who had been executed for his political nonconformity.

The village in the Oneida woods was off the most logical route north from Fort Stanwix to the Black River Valley and Lake Ontario. The West Canada Creek route from the German Flatts region toward the lake was only a vague possibility. The location of the village at the junction of Cincinnati and Steuben Creeks had the advantages of countless other mill sites. The land in the vicinity was well drained and much of it lay in gentle slopes suited for agriculture. The soil was somewhat rocky but rich enough to support general farming. Most budding settlements in the Adirondack foothills had the similar disadvantage of being off the main trade routes.

The location of the Holland Land Company office in Oldenbarneveld was a major advantage in the competition to attract good settlers. Gerrit Boon, the company agent in this part of New York, took a special interest in the growth of the village. With the assistance of LeRoy, Bayard, Mc-Evers and Busti, he purchased in trust for the Holland Land Company 46,057 acres of Outhoud's Patent, 6,026 acres of Steuben's Patent, 1,200 acres of Machin's Patent and 23,609 acres of the Servis Patent, the latter tract including the site of Oldenbarneveld.[1] In 1793 Boon blazed a trail north from Old Fort Schuyler to Cincinnati Creek. Who accompanied him is uncertain but either shortly before or shortly after this time, John Garret and his sons, Cheney and Peter, bought land near Nine Mile Creek on the trail that Boon blazed.

Three Garret boys, Cheney, Peter and Samuel, had come from Connecticut to Old Fort Schuyler, perhaps as early as 1791.[2] The following story of their arrival, passed down by Cheney's grandson, is true in spirit, if not in detail:

> In the spring of 1792, a man standing on the bridge over the Mohawk River at Fort Schuyler . . . was looking at a boat down the stream, which was being propelled or polled up the stream against the current and as it came nearer, he discovered four young men and some boxes or chests on the boat. He hailed the party with . . . , "Have you any *carpenters* in your party?" The reply came, "Yes, we have four." The man again hailed, "I want to talk with you, do not engage until I have a talk. I want to hire you." On reaching the shore, the man on the bridge was on hand, and said, "My name is Thomas Hicks, I'm looking for carpenters to work some 14 miles from here, at a place called "Olden Barneveldt" for Mr. Boon, and you will be well paid in yellow coin if you suit him." [3]

The three Garrets and William Palmer agreed to work with Hicks, but apparently first built some houses in Old Fort Schuyler and went to Boon's holdings the following year.

Boon pitched a tent on the site for his village. As soon as the Garrets and Hicks arrived work was begun on his house, on the location where Adam Mappa later completed the beautiful Mappa Hall. Other settlers built houses on the site and the community soon longed for a grist mill. The nearest mill was at Whitesboro, a walk of some eighteen miles, never an easy journey over a crude trail, but particularly hard when the traveler carried a sack of corn or flour on his back. Boon built a dam and mill on Cincinnati Creek below the village and placed in the gable of the building a stone bearing the date 1798 and the word "Valonia," the acorn cup for the hopes of the village.[4] Soon muskrats tunneled the earthen dam, making the mill short of water. Shortly afterward a flood severely damaged the mill. It was abandoned, apparently without ever operating. Some time later, the Holland Land Company built both a grist mill and saw mill at a better point on the creek. Shortly after their construction, the mills were sold to Peter Schuyler for operation.

In 1795 Adam Mappa came from New York to be Boon's assistant. In order to get him started Boon advanced Mappa $6,500 from company funds for his buildings. Boon was determined to attract and assist industrious settlers, as a few good people attracted more, and company land prices could be raised. The village had to have a mill and a store, a business leader and a doctor. Boon got them. He tried, though without success, to establish the cooperative production of maple syrup as an industry for the area. Boon probably welcomed Van der Kemp to his growing community as a respected judge, industrious farmer, and renowned scholar.

Van der Kemp acquired a cottage near Mappa's big house, borrowing $800 from the Holland Land Company to finance the purchase. Since Van der Kemp did not sell his Oneida Lake lands immediately, the loan was secure. Though the practice of loaning company funds to settlers was common, Boon was later required to make good several of these loans. The Van der Kemps paid.[5]

The Van der Kemps moved their fine furniture and simpler possessions into the one and one-half story cottage. They brought some of their domestic animals but probably left more with the tenant at Kempwick. Francis placed his beloved books, almost like family gods, in the new home, placed the sword and pistols of his revolutionary days in the bedroom and hung up the sword acquired by one of his ancestors from Baron de Haersolte, a factional leader of Overyssel.[6]

Engelbartha was more contented in town. Margaret Beekman Livingston wrote, "It gave me great pleasure to hear that my cousin had again a good and pleasant home . . ." [7]

Dutch friends and neighbors in Oldenbarneveld soon learned that Van der Kemp's wit matched his learning. Knowing that the people of his native Kampen were accused of droll stupidity, his townsmen now took advantage of the absent-minded scholar, and Francis became a good-natured target for their humor. In good fun the people who loved and respected him told how he planted beans upside down, transported a wooden barn frame hundreds of miles into a region of fine trees, and, forgetting where he had hired a horse and buggy, drove around the streets of Philadelphia asking people if they recognized the horse.[8]

The Van der Kemps were hardly settled before public service called Francis. On March 24 the state legislature passed an enabling act for the organization of a new town of Trenton, the first meeting to be held in the home of Thomas Hicks.[9] Van der Kemp as justice of the peace, presided at the meeting on April 4, 1797. Adam Mappa was elected first supervisor and all other town offices were filled, including Thomas Hicks and Cheney Garret as assessors, Peter Garret as commissioner of the poor and Gerrit Boon as a fence viewer. Van der Kemp himself was chosen to be overseer of the most important highway, the road to Old Fort Schuyler.

Records of the town of Trenton in succeeding years reveal the efforts of a frontier community in trying to become civilized. Roads were a great concern, particularly those leading to Old Fort Schuyler, the Black River and the Military Road to Johnstown. The town financed several bridges for the Utica Turnpike Road Company in 1808 by selling stock. The fencing in of hogs, sheep and rams was required. Cattle, though not restricted, had to have a brand or ear mark. The state bounty on wolves ($10) was supplemented in the town by $5, later raised to $10 and $15 extra, but rescinded altogether in 1820. Van der Kemp may have presided at town meetings in the first years. He received the ballots for election of officers through 1803.[10]

Van der Kemp was appointed federal surveyor of revenue for the year starting October 15, 1799. His duties were the collection of tariffs on imports from Canada. In the next decade and a half Van der Kemp served from time to time as assistant justice and justice of the peace, as master in chancery, and as fence viewer. The records show his notarization of deeds and other legal papers and there is a copy of the oath of office which he took.

> I, Francis Adraen van der Kemp appointed to the Office of a Master in Chancery do solemnly Sincerely and Truely affirm ["promise and swear" were marked through, with the "affirm" phrase substituted], that I will in all things to the best of my knowledge and ability faithfully perform the trust reposed in me.

Two other affirmations follow, all signed by Van der Kemp:

> I, Francis Adraen van der Kemp appointed to the office of a Master in Chancery do solemnly, sincerely and truely affirm that I renounce and abjure all allegiance and subjection to all and every foreign King, Prince, Potentate and State in all matters Ecclesiastical and civil and that I will bear faith and true allegiance to the State of New York as a free and Independent State.

> I, Francis Adraen Vanderkemp Solemnly Sincerely and truely declare and affirm, that I will support the Constitution of the United States—[11]

In a new community fence viewers were important. The law required a certain type of fence if the land was in use. Fence viewers settled disputes about construction, upkeep, and effectiveness of fences and other questions not requiring court action.

The master in chancery drew up legal papers both during and between sessions of the court of chancery. He made initial reports on cases of lunacy and guardianship, certified testimony in cases of adultery, and performed a number of other legal duties, all with fees ranging from twenty-five cents to five dollars. The most common activity was probably the examination of deeds and ordering them to be recorded at the court house. It was convenient for the Holland Land Company to have Van der Kemp nearby when deeds were drawn for property sales.

In 1804 and 1806, brief records show that Van der Kemp did jury duty for his county. In the "Court of Oyer and Terminer and General Gaol Delivery holden at the School House near the Gaol in the Town of Rome in and for the County of Oneida," he sat on the jury for three different cases. The circuit court was in session at Whitestown on the same day and Van der Kemp served on the jury for seven cases. It must have been a busy day for him. In 1806 he served on the grand jury for this court at the Whitestown session and in another case appeared as a witness.[12] He was appointed assistant justice and justice of the peace five times for three-year terms, the last in 1804. One of these, 1801, he declined.

In national politics Van der Kemp was, of course, a Federalist, as were the majority of Oldenbarneveld residents. In state politics he was torn between the party of Clinton, and the party which supported Adams. In 1808 he attended a political meeting in Utica and served with Mappa on a committee to support the Federalist nominees.[13] Long afterward the story was told that Dr. Luther Guiteau, who settled here in 1802, was a Democrat in the Federalist village. When party spirits rose two new doctors (presumably Federalists) were brought in. "But alas! when sickness came the people would call in Dr. Guiteau, and the last of the political doctors quit the place in disgust, declaring that he would not stay here and shake the bush for Dr. Guiteau to catch the bird." [14]

When George Washington died in 1799 the people of Oldenbarneveld planned a memorial service. At the request of his townspeople, Van der Kemp delivered a eulogy to the assembled community on February 22, 1800. It touched on international and national affairs. It related national political affairs to the local community. Van der Kemp waxed sentimental; once again he saw Washington "under his hospitable roof," "in his unassumed original grandeur" and with his "dignified character." He outlined the great man's personal sacrifices and services to the nation in improving agriculture, establishing national credit, increasing commerce, securing liberties and rights and putting national felicity and independence on a firm basis. Van der Kemp implored his audience to emulate Washington, to be "temperate, frugal, industrious, tender loving husbands," to be "obedient, active, good citizens." So then would felicity, peace and plenty keep a constant abode, "even in the western woods." [15]

Van der Kemp's oratorical advice to his neighbors followed his own philosophy as well as that of Washington. Francis was an affectionate husband, took a hand in the educational and religious training of his beloved children, and served his community and nation according to his abilities.

In 1799, or possibly the year before, John Van der Kemp, now sixteen years old, became a clerk for the Holland Land Company under the supervision of Adam Mappa, who had succeeded Gerrit Boon as agent. John was a good penman and his sentences were clear. The boy made steady progress with the company and later became agent in the Philadelphia office. In 1800 Van der Kemp wrote in regard to the three children, "Thus far they are growing up to their advantage and the two oldest principally are deserving the love and esteem of all who surround them—which is something . . . [as] it will be their chief inheritance." [16] Peter was the slow child.

Along with his legal services, his correspondence, his reading, his writing, and his religious activities, Van der Kemp continued his interest in scientific farming. In 1800 he renewed his correspondence with Chancellor Livingston and reopened their old discussion of agriculture. He said that he had not seen any of the *Proceedings* of the Agriculture Society since he left Esopus, could not afford to buy them, and hoped to borrow them. He continued:

> My endeavors in these Western parts to promote the study of Agriculture—have been greatly in vain—in part by want of my inability to afford sufficient encourage-ments—We have made some experiments on the wild Buckwheat—on the canary-bird seed—the last comes here to perfection— We tried it only in small quantities in our gardens— It would be worth a new trial in the neigh-bourhood of a market— The ars veteranaria is much neg-lected.[17]

Van der Kemp told Livingston that he and Mappa planned to investigate a deposit of gypsum a half mile from the village, also a slate stratum to see if it overlay a coal seam as in Europe. The Chancellor thought the gypsum might be good but said that the western lands were too fertile to need it yet. In later years it would "prove an in-estimatable treasure." In return for a list of Dutch articles on agriculture, he promised to send the *Proceedings* when he went to the meeting of the state legislature in Albany.[18] Van der Kemp also asked for himself and Mappa a bushel or so of Sicilian wheat, of American growth preferred, and some cantaloupe and cauliflower seeds. He had grown cauli-flowers the previous summer "as big as the largest plate" and had brought one, not fully developed, from the garden for Engelbartha on the sixteenth of December. He said he had been reading the first four parts of the *Proceedings* and would send for the next one at Albany. He said a "Mr. Laurentius" had brought to Oldenbarneveld from Albany small samples of both the Sicilian winter and summer wheat, both of which were growing. An additional request for this wheat was made to Livingston. However, the mem-bership to the New York Society for the Promotion of Ag-riculture, Arts, and Manufactures which Livingston secured for him was regretfully declined by Van der Kemp. He said it was "beyond his power to become an useful member" due to his financial situation and that he would not be a useless one.[19]

Adams and Van der Kemp said little in their letters about farming although it was necessary for both of them to grow their food. Upon his retirement in March of 1801 Adams began the regular tasks of plowing and planting and Abigail that of milking the cows and feeding the chickens. Only occasional comments indicated regular farm chores during the growing seasons. Van der Kemp wrote a fragment in November, 1802, stating he had been busy gathering seeds and preparing his fields and gardens for spring. The following March when the late snows lay deep around his cottage and garden, he said he longed for spring. He added that for two years he had grown excellent cauliflowers, equal to Holland's best, for his own and Mappa's family.[20] He boasted some years later that although his garden spot was small he often was able to make a distribution of surplus among the neighbors, sometimes being more successful than Mappa's gardener.[21] Yet the inclinations of the writer were always stronger than those of the farmer. A letter to Adams in 1808 reported he was compelled to write "tho a beautiful fair day and work enough in the garden to perform—but Adams! the garden shall remain, when either of us—when both shall be no more—" [22]

Chancellor Livingston received more details, especially about Van der Kemp's experimental planting:

I succeeded here with greens, which I tried in vain at Esopus—I was compelled to content myself there with the Snasfagan[?]—here I cultivate the broad Windsor bean in the highest perfection—and doubt not or the horse and pigeon bean would succeed here, which I tried there in vain. Among the culinary herbs we have two sort of white beans—of a superior quality, prepared in various manner for the table—*green*—*pickled dry*—The *Scorsonera*—the Sellery—The *Red cabbage* and *cauliflower*—These two sorts I had in as high perfection as I ever did see them in Europe, and never equalled at N.Y.

Here I again must make an application to your politeness with a request for a few seeds of *cauliflower sellery*
—*Endivy* with broad leaves and uncurled—cantaloup
melon—and *watermelons*—which you may—if to spare—
join to the M.S.—when they are returned. I intend next
summer—if I remain alive—to send some seeds to Batavia [Dutch East Indies] —to my old friends the Mars-
chalk and Governor Daendels and Gristier Blok [who
had visited in Oldenbarneveld] —and by you, my Dear
Sir! I may be enabled to render this boon more valuable—[23]

Dutch materials on agriculture came to Van der Kemp's
hands from time to time, and these he perused carefully.
Then he attempted to make any new ideas useful to America by sending notes to Livingston and by submitting excerpts and comments to the Agricultural Society. When
Livingston returned from France, Van der Kemp hoped
that new life would come to the society. The scholar from
his "wilderness" sent to the society "Observations Concerning the Lea-Bug," "The Cultivation of the Poppy," "The
Cure of a Particular Disease in Cattle," and a wooden model
of a maltboard (a special platform for drying germinated
barley) used in Zeeland. In return, he had only curt messages saying they had been received.[24] He wrote to the chancellor to tell about the Dutch May harrow. It was simple to
make and to use, and could be drawn by either horses,
oxen or even one stout horse. If the soil was clear of stumps,
a great deal of soil could be prepared in one day. He explained that his friend Cau had described it in a letter.[25]
Van der Kemp was welcome as a member of the state
agricultural society but had too much competition from
Livingston, Samuel L. Mitchill, David Hosack, John Jay,
James Duane, Simeon De Witt and Elkanah Watson for his
contributions to be noted. His agricultural efforts were appreciated chiefly by his neighbors in Oldenbarneveld, while
he shared them by correspondence with Livingston, Adams,
Washington, and other far-away friends.

⚘ XII ⚘

Establishing
a Free Church

WHEN the Van der Kemps lived on Esopus Creek, they were near the Dutch Reformed Church at Kingston. Francis had long outgrown his youthful antagonism to that church, but he remembered Adams' warning to stay out of religious controversy when he settled in New York. Knowing he could not avoid expressing his opinions if he took an active part, he probably attended church only occasionally, but more often held religious services in his home for his family and the hired hands. On Oneida Lake no church was near and the family services were continued. Oldenbarneveld also had no church when the Van der Kemps settled there. Houses and cleared fields, mills, roads and schools came first on the frontier.

In 1802 the Reverend John Taylor recorded observations made during a missionary journey to the Mohawk and Black River region. Whitesboro and Clinton were the most prosperous settlements, with Clinton having the most prosperous church. The report for Floyd, some six miles southwest of Oldenbarneveld, was unpromising, even to a missionary:

> I know not what remarks to make upon the inhabitants of this town—a half a dozen excepted, they seem to be the fag-end of man in disorder, and confusion of all

147

kinds. The baptists have some regularity; but the methodists are producing the scenes which are transpiring in Kentucky. Women here methodists, pray in their families instead of ye men—and with such strength of lungs as to be distinctly heard by their neighbors. . . . In fact, this is a most miserable place,—as to inhabitants. The land is good—too good for such inhabitants.[1]

The missionary was looking for Calvinists. He regarded those of other sects with various degrees of disfavor. He was much interested in the "falling down" of several of the fervent religionists at Floyd in a two-day outdoor meeting. He preached to the people, visited the school and left books and tracts to save the inhabitants. At Remsen, just a few miles north of Oldenbarneveld, Taylor described the people as a "broken society," "very ignorant and very wicked." He found what he believed to be a "notorious villain" preaching in the schoolhouse. No church organizations existed in any of the villages. In Norway he found a mixture of Presbyterians, Methodists, Baptists, Universalists and Deists.[2]

When Taylor went to Oldenbarneveld he stayed with "the Revd. Mr. [Peter] Fish, a gent. who was once settled in Connecticut Farms in N. Jersey, and is now employed part of the time by the people of this town." The Reverend Mr. Fish was a "sensible, judicious man" and appeared to be doing "great good" but with a "poor reward." Taylor reported that a majority of the people were Presbyterians with some Baptists, Methodists and "persons of no religion." [3] Perhaps Taylor placed the Van der Kemps in this latter classification.

Taylor visited the school, a hundred yards from the Van der Kemp cottage, and found fifty students with a good instructor. However, many of the children had no catechism and some had no school books. Taylor left for distribution "4 bibles, 10 catechisms, 4 of Janeway's Tokens, and 10 of Dodridge's Addresses." [4] Janeway's Tokens were religious tracts written by a non-conforming English clergyman over a century before, and frequently reprinted: "Token for Children . . . Account of the Conversion, holy and exemplary Lives and joyful Deaths of Several young Children, &c."

The missionary represented the Presbyterians and Congregationalists of Hampshire County, Massachusetts. He respected the Reverend Fish and tried to help him rather than taking away his followers. Both of these men may have inspired and assisted in the society started by Van der Kemp, Mappa and Guiteau. The society that was organized had the imprint of Van der Kemp indelibly upon it and was different from all the new congregations within the immediate area except that which developed at Whitestown in 1805 as a Universalist society.

In the late summer of 1803 a meeting was held of those interested in a religious society. No record exists of the action except a list of twenty-three men in attendance, with the name of Francis Van der Kemp first. Also listed were Adam and John Mappa, Thomas Hicks, and John Van der Kemp. They subscribed to a resolution that they would unite in the promotion and support of a religious society.[5]

At a second meeting on September 19, 1803, sixteen additional persons were listed, with a few more in succeeding months. On October 22, these earnest people met at the school house and agreed to incorporate themselves into the United Protestant Religious Society of Trenton, for the purpose of providing religious instruction. Van der Kemp and Jacob Hochstrasser were chosen to receive the ballots and three trustees were elected. A charter of incorporation drawn up by Van der Kemp and Hochstrasser was registered at the court house the following June. Van der Kemp had successfully averted denominationalism. The probability is that the Bible was read, commentaries were made occasionally by Van der Kemp himself, and itinerant preachers such as the Reverend Taylor addressed them.

In the summer of 1805 the Reverend John Sherman came to Oldenbarneveld to visit his brother-in-law, Joshua Storrs.

Sherman, pastor of the First Church in Mansfield, Connecticut, had displeased some members of his congregation. Although he had been an orthodox Calvinist in 1797, he had been swayed from the Trinitarian concept by the writings of Joseph Priestley and others. A series of meetings and letters in the Mansfield area about his preaching made Sherman's situation uncomfortable. He came to Oldenbarneveld for a vacation.

He was asked to preach, and the village people were impressed and pleased. "He was quick in his perceptions, ready in his utterance, and had the power not only of commanding his thoughts and feelings on any sudden emergency, but of rising under the pressure of an occasion." [6] Shortly after Sherman returned to Mansfield, the society made its decision, duly publicized:

> NOTICE—At a meeting of the Inhabitants of the town of Trenton, holden at the Schoolhouse in the village of Oldenbarneveld on the 11th Aug. 1805, the REV. JOHN SHERMAN of Mansfield, (Con.) was unanimously elected Pastor of the *United Protestant* Religious Society in said place.
>
> By Order of the Society,
> LUTHER GUITEAU, CL'K.[7]

A letter was sent to Sherman written by Van der Kemp and signed by a committee of Guiteau, Hicks and Storrs. It said that the Christian Revelation had greatly influenced the lives of the inhabitants of the "new settlements." But they needed regular public worship to "purify our hearts and to enlighten our understandings." While members of the society differed in religious convictions, they agreed heartily on calling Sherman as pastor because they believed he would allow differing views.

The letter than stated basic beliefs. As Protestant Christians they believed in Christ and in a life to come. They believed the Sacred Scriptures to be the only true guide of faith and conduct, "without intervention of any human authority whatsoever." They observed the Reverend Sherman to have great zeal, piety, talent and prudence. They expected him to teach the children, hear the doubts of the adults with patience, "explain our difficulties with meekness, comfort us in our afflictions, and reprove firmly and sincerely our follies, transgressions and weaknesses." They hoped he would come as soon as possible because they were "a flock without a shepherd, newly brought together, wandering at random in the wilderness." Citizens of Holland Patent, a nearby village, agreed to help support the Reverend Sherman in return for his preaching to them once a month.

Sherman accepted this call after he was released from his Mansfield church. His recommendation by a committee of pastors noted his anti-Trinitarian views. On February 18, 1806, he accepted the new appointment for three years at $600 per year, with four weeks' vacation. The society immediately took steps to form a church. A committee of four drew up the plan—Van der Kemp, Mappa, Storrs and Ithamar Morgan. Eight articles were submitted and accepted on March 8, and the pastor was installed the following day.

The articles mirrored Van der Kemp's experiences and beliefs in a remarkable manner. The first declared the Old and New Testaments to contain the revelation of God's will to mankind, to be used as the only standards of doctrines and rules. Article two accented this idea by applying to baptism only the Scriptural demands, which were cited. Article three was surely written by Van der Kemp:

Liberty of conscience shall be preserved inviolate. Every member shall be maintained in his right of free inquiry into the doctrines of Scripture; in publishing what he believes the Scriptures to contain, and in practising according to his understanding of his duty. This liberty shall not be abridged as to his understanding and practice respecting the ceremonies, ordinances, or positive institutions of Christianity.

Article four established the church's executive authority

in the minister, elders and trustees but provided for a referral by request to the congregation at large, while article five stated that the church officers were to be chosen by ballot. Number six made membership a matter of character rather than creed, remindful of the days at Leyden when Pastor Van der Kemp successfully resisted establishment of a creed requirement:

> The mode of admission to the Church, shall be, that any person wishing to become a member, shall make known his desires to the Consistory, the Minister, Elders and Deacons, who shall, if the applicant be a person of good moral character, refer his case for decision to the Church at large.

Article seven provided for the celebration of the Lord's Supper twice a year at each village. The last article gave the name as the Reformed Christian Church (meaning "formed again" in the likeness of the original church). Van der Kemp would probably have joined a church such as this at any time after his withdrawal from the Dutch Reformed Church at Groningen. His friend John Adams would also have fit easily into this company. Though this church adopted Universalist-Unitarian practices in later years, in the beginning it was designed only to be free and Christian.

Nothing could have been more fitting than the arrangements for the installation on March 9 when Francis A. Van der Kemp gave "a suitable lecture" in the morning and the Reverend John Sherman delivered his introductory sermon in the afternoon. The free church was under way.

The controversy over Sherman's beliefs in Mansfield did not end with his move to Oldenbarneveld—and Van der Kemp became involved as a staunch supporter of his minister. Sherman had written and published a book in 1805 with the title, *One God in One Person Only: and Jesus Christ a Being Distinct from God, Dependent upon Him for his Existence, and his Various Powers; maintained and*

Defended. William B. Sprague in *Annals of the American Pulpit* called Sherman's work "the first formal and elaborate defence of Unitarianism that ever appeared in New England." [8] In the summer the work was noted and reviewed in a respectful, though somewhat non-committal, manner in the *Monthly Anthology.* Van der Kemp wrote a letter of praise to the editors about the May and June issues in general and commented on the Sherman review in particular. He admired the candor of the reviewer and thought the criticisms just. He felt publications of material such as this would encourage deserving authors and promote learning while discouraging the "stupid block-head" who wrote only to be agreeable to editors. A few further comments were made including an exception to the use of the word "childish" in reference to Sherman's work. [9]

The Reverend Daniel Dow of Thompson, Connecticut, soon published a pamphlet of criticism of Sherman, *Familiar Letters to the Rev. John Sherman, Once Pastor of a Church in Mansfield, in Particular Reference to his Late Antitrinitarian Treatise.* The sixteen letters attacked Sherman's character as well as his doctrine. Van der Kemp answered this attack with as severe a castigation as a religious man could write. He had not lost the spirit that long ago led him to attack the stadholder and the aristocrats in the Estates General. The pamphlet was entitled *A Wreath for the Rev. Daniel Dow, Pastor of a Church in Thompson, Connecticut; on the Publication of his Familiar Letters in Answer to the Rev. John Sherman's Treatise of One God in One Person Only &c.* and was published in Utica in 1806, anonymously. His authorship is revealed in a later letter to John Adams.

The introduction describes the immediate affection and respect for Sherman felt by the congregation of the Oldenbarneveld church:

> When the Rev. John Sherman visited our neighborhood in the course of last summer, and preached to us for several weeks, the gospel of salvation, numbers of

us were struck, at seeing various important doctrines of
our holy religion placed before us in a new point of view.
His unassuming modesty and candor—his uncommon,
plain and nervous diction—his pure scriptural language
—. . . his devout prayers breathing and [an] ardent love
towards his God and fellow creatures; his amiable manners and instructive behavior in the ordinary walks of
life, occasioned a wish in the bosom of every one of us,
to hear more of this worthy young man.

Van der Kemp explained that Sherman had held nothing
back. He had told his new friends about his change of
views in Mansfield and about the activities against him.
When he had accepted the unanimous call to be pastor at
Oldenbarneveld, he had presented his treatise in favor of
the Unitarian doctrine. It was accepted by some members
of his congregation, rejected by others—but all were pleased
to have him preach from the Scriptures. After this introduction Van der Kemp berated Dow for fifteen pages and
ended by giving the articles of the new church.[10]

Van der Kemp joined in another phase of religious activity in 1806. A society for "promoting the knowledge of the
Sacred Scriptures, and the practice of the Gospel Doctrine"
was formed in the town of Trenton. One of its first activities was to cooperate with the General Synod of the Reformed Dutch Church in a religious study project. Records
indicate that the organization was formed by members of
the new church. One newspaper notice was signed by the
Reverend John Sherman, secretary, and included the name
of Colonel A. G. Mappa as treasurer. Perhaps Van der
Kemp was president. The following year the society proposed three questions as subjects for an essay contest. The
writer of the winning essay would receive fifty dollars and
have his essay published. The questions are similar to some
of the statements in Van der Kemp's *Wreath:*

1. What are the principle causes of the increasing
fanaticism, enthusiasm and infidelity, within the limits
of the Middle and Eastern States?

2. What are the most potent remedies for these moral diseases?

3. In what manner may these remedies be the most successfully applied?

The question for 1808 was, "What degree of knowledge in Oriental and Greek literature, Jewish antiquities and Ecclesiastical History is requisite to qualify a minister of the Gospel to silence the cavils and successfully to refute the objections of ancient and modern infidels against the Jewish and Christian revelations?" [11]

The society also proposed to collect money, books, tracts, and Bibles to promote the knowledge of the Christian doctrine. It was planned that similar groups could be formed to join in the work of the Trenton society.[12] Van der Kemp persuaded Jedidiah Morse to publish the question for 1808 in the *Panoplist,* an orthodox religious periodical. Van der Kemp asked Morse if they could unite "against the common enemy of infidelity" represented by the writings of Paine and Volney (Count Constantin Chasseboeuf) which were being spread through the distribution of tracts by peddlers in wilderness regions. How could this be stopped? [13]

Neither the Reformed Christian Church nor the community of Trenton prospered during the next few years when trade was disrupted by the Embargo. It was difficult to pay Sherman, but at the end of his three-year appointment, he accepted reappointment upon the request of the committee of Van der Kemp, Ephraim Perkins and Benjamin Brayton. Church pledges were allowed to include produce and Sherman was encouraged to preach at a third place, probably Newport. Financial conditions became worse and Sherman submitted his resignation February 6, 1810, to the trustees, Van der Kemp, Hicks and Brayton. The liberal clergyman established a successful private school and in later years set up a hotel at Trenton Falls with continued success. He remained a faithful member and firm financial supporter of the church.

The church was determined to continue, even without a pastor. The congregation held meetings every Sunday and had Communion service whenever a visiting pastor was available. Luther Storrs and Jacob Hovey continued to lead the singing, while Francis Van der Kemp, John Mappa (son of Adam), Canfield Coe and others agreed to read sermons. Van der Kemp wrote to a friend in England, "Some of us have engaged to read in turns so we are edified sometimes by Clarke, and Tillotson, and Blair, sometimes Lindsey, Priestly, Price, Toulmin." These informal programs held the church together but only with difficulty. In November, 1810, Van der Kemp was the only person to appear at a scheduled meeting to elect a new trustee. In the succeeding months a growing sentiment to dissolve the organization led to arguments. At a meeting in October, 1811, words were spoken against the leadership of Van der Kemp and on the next day he resigned in a letter to his fellow trustee, Ephraim Perkins. He declared that the opposition was "lawless" but that Perkins still had influence with them. Van der Kemp said he would resign as the "only obnoxious person" in the hope that Perkins would succeed in keeping the organization together. On November 8, 1812, Van der Kemp wrote that he had resumed worship in his home since the meeting house (school) had been taken from the society, apparently through the efforts of the discontented members of the church.[14] For two and a half years the church and society were both rather unsettled. There was not enough wealth in the little community to allow liberal contributions to the church. The whole nation was suffering because of the dislocation of trade caused by the struggle between Napoleon and the British. In most of central New York prices for products were high but prices for the things the residents had to purchase were even higher.

After the war, church members once more regained the old feelings of fellowship and cooperation. In October, 1814, Isaac B. Peirce, a licensed reader who was visiting Sherman, was asked to preach. He met Van der Kemp and others and shortly was asked to serve the church on behalf of the "liberal minded Christians" in the vicinity. Peirce was installed the following March. Van der Kemp took part in the planning and rejoiced at the revival of Oldenbarneveld's free church.

The time was right for the important step of erecting a church building. Economic conditions were better, the Reverend Peirce was vigorous, and his congregation happy. Money was raised, a building lot contributed by the Holland Land Company, and the building erected—a near copy of King's Chapel in Boston. When the pews were auctioned, the Van der Kemps took the fifth on the left for $46.50. Only thirteen families paid more; Francis was generous with his limited funds. He could not know that one day the church was to receive from his daughter his own cottage to be used as a parsonage.

As for now, Van der Kemp was content. He had helped to establish a free church in America.

⚜ XIII ⚜

Writing
in the Wilderness

FENCE viewing, agriculture, and religion were not enough
to submerge the scholar's desire to write. In the long win-
ters and during the rainy weather of the growing season
Van der Kemp spent much time with his own books and
those he could borrow. And of course he read eagerly the
newspapers and periodicals which passed from friend to
friend. It was meager intellectual fare but Van der Kemp
was living on the edge of civilization, isolated from other
scholars except by letter-writing. In spite of the handicaps
of the wilderness and that of writing in an adopted language, Van der Kemp essayed to be a productive scholar.

The enlightened people of the late 1700's took an avid
interest in natural history and natural law. Van der Kemp's
education and personal philosophy attracted him to this
study, of which scientific agriculture was a facet. His reading of Jefferson's *Notes on Virginia* inspired him, and
Chancellor Robert Livingston's letters encouraged him.
The finding of a huge animal skeleton in Ulster County
in August, 1801, greatly aroused his curiosity.

The *Notes on Virginia* contained several pages dealing
with mammoths and other prehistoric animals. Jefferson
disagreed with the popular French naturalist, Count George
Louis Le Clerq de Buffon, especially in regard to the
Frenchman's conclusions that animals were smaller in

America than in Europe because America was wetter and colder than the Old World. Van der Kemp was intrigued with the differing opinions and soon acquired or borrowed the major work of Buffon, printed in 1764.

He wrote of his interest to Chancellor Livingston in late 1800, saying that for "some time" he had been "ruminating" on the theories of Buffon and Jefferson. He intended to put his own ideas in a letter to Livingston with the hope that it would "find its way to our illustrious Philosopher [Jefferson]." [1] Livingston replied that Van der Kemp's contributions could be valuable. European naturalists were prejudiced against America, but American naturalists had defended their country with warmth. "You who are at once an American & a European will see the points in dispute with more coolness & probably detect errors in both." He was certain Jefferson would be interested.[2]

Upon reading a "masterly" report on natural science by Dr. Samuel L. Mitchill of Columbia University, Van der Kemp hoped that scholar would be interested in opposing Buffon. He then looked up some animal descriptions by Livingston in the agricultural society proceedings, but found only sketches of the moose, elk and reindeer. Van der Kemp expected "exact descriptions of every one of them with their comparative anatomy and characterising differences with accurate drawings of them!" He wanted all the data necessary to understand and explain the theories of Buffon and Jefferson.[3]

The following June he told Adams that he had "amused" himself during the winter "gluing together [a] few cursory remarks on Buffon's and Jefferson's theories." He wanted to submit the work to Adams but his present "hard working life" permitted writing or copying only in off seasons. He then opened up the subject of a study of the northwest coast, with numerous questions to Adams. Believing that Captain James Cook never reached the American mainland, Van der Kemp thought the government should support research to refute the British claim. He wanted to know more about the voyage of Captain Robert Gray, who discovered the mouth of the Columbia River. Would it be possible to see Gray's journals from 1787 to 1789? How far eastward did Gray's first voyage take him; did he make astronomical observations (if not, why not); did he sight land and what was its appearance? What was the view north of 55°, and why did Gray not make sure of the location of the continent?[4] Van der Kemp's search for knowledge never ceased. He believed the whole world was knowable and could be made useful to mankind.

Adams laughed at Van der Kemp's interest in the natural history of Jefferson and Buffon, particularly the mammoth. He expressed credibility in such large animals but saw less value in such research than in comparable work on agriculture. Buffon's writing style pleased Adams, and he was interested in his facts "when he is correct"—but not in his theories. He asked Van der Kemp if Buffon's molecules were any different from Epicure's atoms. In regard to the northwest coast, Adams promised assistance in Van der Kemp's research and suggested a look at the journal of Captain Joseph Ingraham who made a voyage in that area. He concluded his letter by saying he had been too busy with schemes for the public good over the past forty years to enjoy curious inquiries and, therefore, he was the least qualified man Van der Kemp could have chosen to assist.[5]

Livingston offered some of his ideas on mammoths and natural law and received Van der Kemp's first essay in the summer of 1801. It began:

> I was and am yet enamoured with Buffon's theory, and most cheerfully submit to your judgment in crowning him with laurel above all his competitors—but even this splendid sun of our Philosophical world—has in your opinion his spots. His proofs, it is true, are so numerous, his facts so indisputable, the appearance of mathematical exactness so artfully display'd and so much analogy preserved in his most excentric whim, that he often compels our assent by his bewitching eloquence, when cool reason

discovers, that this immense fabric of solid materials is
raised in quicksand—

Van der Kemp doubted some of the reports on the
Shawagunk bones which had been taken to Charles Willson
Peale's museum in Philadelphia. Peale had made quite an
expedition to Ulster County and reconstructed two skeletons in his museum. Van der Kemp contested Livingston's
idea that an early race of men had killed off the mammoths; surely sufficient carniverous animals inhabited
North America to have reduced the number of huge beasts.
He accepted Livingston's offer to send a fuller description
of the Shawagunk bones and asked, "Was the head entire?
Did the Judge [George Graham] examine the jaw-bones?
. . . Have you explored their enamel? Are the teeth bone
or of ivory?" Van der Kemp presented six or seven pages
of ideas, queries and opposing opinions about the mammoth.[6] From this grew a manuscript of 270 pages.

Van der Kemp organized this work in the form of letters
—a common practice at this time. These were supposedly
to Chancellor Livingston and Gerrit Boon and were twelve
in number. A short introductory letter contained the
reasons for writing the material, praised Jefferson as
writer-president and praised Buffon for his perception in
his *Natural History*. In the first numbered letter the subject of the creation of the earth is treated, followed by discussion of the possibility of the deluge as an explanation
of fossils and shells of sea animals on high lands. Van der
Kemp could not believe God would allow creation of the
earth through an errant comet knocking a chunk out of the
sun, but the theory that the earth was originally a molten
mass which cooled interested him. He explored writings
and presented ideas of his own concerning the theory. This
chapter was concerned more with Buffon than Jefferson,
although the latter was criticized for his unsupported rejection of the deluge. Gottfried Wilhelm Leibnitz and
other great scientists were cited frequently, with quotations
in French and Latin. The second letter continued the ex-

amination of evidence for a deluge which deposited shell-fish and other sea animals on the mountains of Europe and America. He included comments on fossils collected by John Lincklaen, probably near Chittenango Falls, and some found by Peter Smith at Peterboro. Van der Kemp himself had observed fossils at various places, and collected many at Esopus and Trenton Falls.

Prompted by his curiosity about fossils and the deluge, Van der Kemp had made some further geological studies. He had followed the West Canada Creek and its branches from the falls toward Rome and found "unquestionable proofs of disappeared lakes and rivers." He felt that if the land at Cohoes Falls and Little Falls were compared with that around Canada Creek and the vicinity of Rome, it would be found that

> The Mohawk shall be transformed in an immense River—our vicinity shall be proved to have been a lake —whose circuit *yet* may be ascertained—and the Oneyda —Ontario and other adjacent lakes were a vast expanse of water within its lofty barriers.

Van der Kemp used this example and many others to show that numerous convulsions had changed the pattern of the earth's lands and seas.

His next consideration was the origin of the American Indians and the extent of their civilizations. He saw similarities between the Indian artifacts and habits and those of the Mongolians. He thought the Indians must have come across Bering Strait but that more investigation was needed, especially of the Mississippi and Ohio Valley mounds. The mammoth bones that were being discovered in America and Siberia probably belonged to animals that used the same connection of Asia and North America. However, he believed the mammoth was not carnivorous, as some thought, and that it was, perhaps, not extinct. Maybe the unexplored parts of our Northwest or the interior of Siberia contained living mammoths.

In the last letters Van der Kemp jumped from one minor

scientific problem to another, apparently with the aim of showing how many areas of research were inviting educated men. Then he concluded with a strong theme that the Almighty Creator made every thing and every part for a purpose or a service and these purposes could be discovered by man.

Many sources were cited and explanations and quotations were placed in extensive footnotes. Sometimes additional materials or citations were put in the margin. At the end of the manuscript were some addenda, a table of contents and an index. The complete manuscript includes research done as late as 1812.[7]

The earliest manuscript was sent to Livingston, with a second copy laboriously copied and sent to John Adams in the late summer of 1801. Adams wrote soon that he had read the paper "with great pleasure" but that there were "too many subjects of curious speculation" for him to comment further.[8] This reception encouraged Van der Kemp to ask Adams to mark the weak places in the manuscript. He reported that Livingston proposed to write a criticism from France. Livingston had sent the paper to Jefferson and received the president's polite approval of the author's exertions, of his wide reading and observations and his proper estimation of Buffon's unphilosophical but eloquent dissertations.[9]

Professor Sereno [?] Dwight of Yale offered to read and comment on Van der Kemp's research but there was no copy to send him. As soon as the Adams copy was returned it was promised to John Mifflin in Philadelphia.[10] Adams made his first comments in January, 1802.

I can afford you no ideas on the subject of the mammoth because I have none. The Spirit of Political Party has seized upon the Bones of this huge Animal, because the head of a Party has written something about them, and has made them a subject of more conversation and Investigation than they merit. The Species may yet exist in America and in other quarters of the globe. They may be carnivorous, or they may subsist on the Branches of the trunks of Trees: but as I see no means of determining these questions, I feel little interest in them, till a living Individual of the kind shall be found. Mr. Peeles Skeleton may determine whether he is graminivorous or carnivorous or both, but our knowledge of the globe and even of this Continent is not sufficiently advanced to determine that the Species is extinct. We have so little of final causes as well as of physical causes of the phenomena of nature that no certain conclusion can be drawn from the Wisdom of the Creator against the Extinction of a Species. There may have been reasons for their existence at one time, which may not remain at another.[11]

He added in a second letter that every word of panegyric on Jefferson and Buffon must be erased since Buffon was an atheist and Jefferson was president of the United States. He thought the Academy might publish it.[12] Van der Kemp was pleased with the prospect of publication and agreed to alter the manuscript as suggested by Adams. He also said he would "soften" the panegyrics and "mollify" the censures.[13]

During his perusals of the early manuscript Adams raised the question of the generation of shellfish. He suspected generation on the surface of the ocean and further suspected that the Portuguese man-of-war was a shellfish in embryo.[14] The New Yorker knew only one author on shellfish who wrote in English and a few in Dutch and French. He could not yet agree with Adams' ideas but was intrigued by their novelty. "Iterated experiments more than doubtful observations would be required" before he was persuaded. However, Adam Mappa was less doubtful, as he had observed in the eastern Asiatic seas various species of foam that might be the beginnings of shellfish.[15]

Perhaps Adams was stung by the reference to his "doubtful observations." He elaborated with a long description of his careful observations of the externals and internals of the Portuguese man-of-war while on a voyage across the

Atlantic. With this clarification of his "conjectures," he asked Van der Kemp to procure Mappa's observations.[16]

Mappa was busy with the annual reports of the Holland Land Company and Van der Kemp was doubtful if he could be prompt with his observations. Mappa had been pulled into a number of agricultural and other scientific investigations and had complained good naturedly that Van der Kemp was making him "a Naturaliste par force a la Moliere." However, Mappa did write to Adams promptly.[17]

Van der Kemp busily searched for information on shellfish and included five pages of observations and data which he found. He also included notes on his own observations in Oneida Lake and the Oswego River of a fresh water fish which heaped stones over its egg deposits.[18] Some of the ideas on shellfish were ultimately included in the *Researches* manuscript.

During the winter of 1802–03 Van der Kemp worked further on his manuscript, chopping off some "useless branches" and taking away the "meretricious tinsel." He thought it was vastly improved in its "more simple guise." Then he sent it back to Adams for submission to the American Academy of Arts and Sciences.[19] Adams liked the revised work and placed it before the Academy at the May, 1803, meeting. It was referred to the regular committee and Adams declined to predict what action would be taken. His own opinion was that the work was a "learned and ingenious performance." The compliments to Buffon and Jefferson made no difference to Adams but he was apprehensive that the committee and the Academy membership would object since "Neither of these illustrious Personages is held in much veneration among our New England Philosophers." "In plain English" the Academy had classed Buffon's theories and purported discoveries as "the most Stupid things that were ever committed to the Press." He also thought the extraordinary length, the complementary episodes and the handwriting might be against Van der Kemp's manuscript while the style was probably "not to the Taste of American Readers." However, his own vote would certainly be for acceptance and publication.[20]

Van der Kemp was honored by the submission but certainly not encouraged by the comments. He asked if it would be publishable if Jonas Platt were to polish it.[21] After eight months of waiting for the committee's decision, Van der Kemp asked Adams if his "doom" had been "fixed." He proposed to devote another winter to it inasmuch as he had additional materials. He said he would be willing to have the Academy publish part of it, as it would probably add to the value of a later publication.[22] In March, 1804, Adams inquired of the committee what was happening to Van der Kemp's manuscript and found it had been referred to a sub-committee.[23] The following November, the decision came. "All who had looked into it, express themselves handsomely of it, as ingenious and learned, but all agree that it can not be inserted in the Transactions." [24] Van der Kemp had hoped for the publication to be included in the "Records of New England's Worthies" but said he was not humiliated. In fact, he decided to spend the latter part of the winter of 1804–05 in retouching the work.[25]

The *Researches* was not Van der Kemp's only scholarly effort in these years. The field of political science received his attention as an extremely important facet of the natural world. His work in this area is recorded in the following chapter. He also gave some time to a literary pursuit with minor scientific significance. This was his *Use of Copper by the Greeks,* an essay of sixty-nine pages. It depended largely on materials sent by friends from Europe and was concerned with the period of the Trojan War. He wrote the first draft in the winter of 1802–03 and sent it to John Adams with a request to send it on to John Mifflin or J. B. Boardley of Philadelphia. Van der Kemp thought maybe the Philosophical Society would be interested.[26] Adams read it with pleasure and sent it to Boardley but it did not attract the Society.

In February, 1804, he wrote that he had collected "considerable ingredients" to improve the *Use of Copper among the Greeks* and a "vast heap of undigested materials" on the northwest coast. Would Adams be reminded to send some of Ingraham's *Journal?* Van der Kemp asked for more information on shellfish to strengthen his "firm belief that no genus is annihilated." What did Adams think about Clavigero's history? "I am now in an European correspondence to investigate Particularities about the Arabian incursions from the 7–11 Cent. in the N.E. parts of Asia," an attempt to add to his understanding of the American Indians.

> A correspondence with a German Mineralogist induced me this winter to take a course of chemistry, and how deeper I dive in this and other branches of Nat. Philosophy, how more glorious appears to me—the goodness—the wisdom—and our thought surpassing greatness of our glorious maker.

He had also renewed his study of canon law and wished to borrow Adams' old study. How many volumes of transactions had the American Academy published and at what price? He expected to induce a friendly neighbor to buy them and "allow me the perusal." [27]

The northwest continued to be discussed between the two men during 1804 and for some time after. Van der Kemp collected materials, particularly extracts from journals, and in 1804 sent queries to Joseph Barrell of Boston, one of the six capitalists who financed the voyages of both Ingraham and Gray. Van der Kemp thought the government ought to provide for the exploration of the northwest coast rather than trust discoveries and settlement to smugglers and to kidnappers of island natives. He doubted if the Jefferson administration would do it. Yet he said he would write to Secretary of State Madison if he thought Madison would pay any attention to the idea.[28] He had already written to Aaron Burr in 1802 and the vice president had sent information from Secretary Madison.[29] On April 10, 1804, Van der Kemp wrote to Burr again (just a few months before the Burr-Hamilton duel) and included twenty-five detailed questions, most of which he had asked of Barrell regarding the voyages of Gray and Ingraham. The questions were pointed at the determination of what land in the Nootka Sound area (later Oregon territory) belonged to the United States and its commercial possibilities. The last question particularly inquired about the cost of a more discerning voyage. Individuals might contribute or a president might arrange it. The hints were there for Burr to support the national interest as well as the scholar's pursuit. He also told the vice president about his political treatise, his *Researches* and the essay on the *Use of Copper by the Greeks*. Would Burr criticize the *Researches?* Perhaps even give it a recommendation and help to get it published? Did Burr know where Van der Kemp could get cited sources unavailable at Oldenbarneveld? [30]

Burr was unable to assist Van der Kemp but John Adams sent extracts from Ingraham's *Journal.* The scholar was delighted. Still more knowledge was needed on the northwest, however. Why did not the merchants of Boston and New York finance a study? The seal fishery and fur trade were to be gained and the China trade would pass through this spot. Of course, Van der Kemp was still concerned primarily with disproving the British claim of Captain Cook.[31]

Van der Kemp soon gave up on this project of helping his country. Perhaps he decided that the Lewis and Clark expedition would make his efforts unnecessary. The expedition, as it progressed, actually carried out some of Van der Kemp's ideas.

Raphael Peale, son of the curator, visited John Adams in 1804 and said he believed the bones from Shawagunk in the museum at Philadelphia were those of a sea monster or at least an amphibian. Since such skeletons were always found in or near salt licks, he further believed that the bodies had been thrown up by convulsions of nature through caverns which connected the salt holes with the sea.[32] Van der Kemp replied to this report from Adams that "Mr. Peale's whim—with regard to the Mammoth—

is in my humble opinion, not much better supported than Buffon's reverie." [33] With this dismissal he reported corrections and additions to his paper during the winter and, sometime during the summer of 1805, sent it back to John Mifflin in Philadelphia. The Philosophical Society through Mifflin had made Van der Kemp a member during the spring.[34]

When Robert Livingston returned from Europe in 1805, correspondence with Van der Kemp was renewed and an interest in Van der Kemp's writing was expressed. *The Use of Copper by the Greeks* was promised if Livingston could pick it up in Albany. The *Researches on Buffon's and Jefferson's Theories* would be available for Livingston the following winter of 1806–7. Van der Kemp said that over the past few years the treatise had "increased more in value than in bulk." [35]

To a considerable extent Van der Kemp turned his research and his writing to religious topics in the next few years. These are treated in another chapter. Yet, he kept a strong interest in his works on natural history and political science.

In 1809 one of Van der Kemp's "honoured correspondents" offered to extract and polish parts of the *Researches* for insertion in the Philosophical Society *Transactions*. The author unaccountably declined the offer even though it was flattering and would have kept him from being "entirely an useless member" of the Society.[36] Livingston said he should have allowed the extraction as "an insertion in the philosophical transactions would have given publicity to the useful work & the subject is sufficiently interesting to make it a duty in you not to withhold it from the world." [37]

In 1811 Livingston read "with very great pleasure" *The Use of Copper by the Greeks* and the revised *Researches*. He regretted that Van der Kemp did not make them available "to the world by their publication." Francis sent the copies of *The Use of Copper by the Greeks* to various friends, including John Quincy Adams. John Luzac offered to edit the essay in Holland for publication, but that prospect was ended abruptly by Luzac's death.

Livingston was feeling his years and preferred to work in agricultural problems. However, he did write a long letter of comments on the origin of the earth and the great changes wrought through the ages by natural forces.[38] His death occurred only fifteen months afterwards, a great grief to Van der Kemp in the loss of his "valuable friend."

From time to time Van der Kemp worked on his *Researches* until it reached the length of the existing manuscript, 270 pages, in January, 1813. He apparently added more marginal notations when he was able to borrow the later volumes of Buffon's *Natural History* dealing with minerals. In 1811, he sent it to Josiah Quincy, son of the Josiah Quincy whom Francis had so greatly admired when he and Adams had defended Preston ten years before. He sent it to Charles Eliot in 1813, but Eliot died before he could fulfill his agreement to edit it for publication. In 1815 the *Researches* manuscript was sent to De Witt Clinton, who was especially drawn to Van der Kemp's remarks on the natural history of New York State. He asked if the petrified bees found by Peter Smith could be acquired for a cabinet of natural history. He had no suggestions for publication, and Van der Kemp gave up; the *Researches* was never published. However, it was perhaps as a result of his reading of this fine manuscript that Clinton proposed the scholar as a member of the Literary and Philosophical Society of New York. He was accepted.[39]

❧ XIV ❧

The Achaian Republic

THE letters which passed between Van der Kemp and Adams during the presidential years were few but very cordial. The chief executive of the republic should not be distracted from his serious duties. The nation faced the crises of the XYZ Affairs, an undeclared naval war with France, and the Alien and Sedition Acts controversy followed by the Virginia and Kentucky Resolutions. Van der Kemp was frequently puzzled by the intricacies of party conflict but the principles of free republican government were clear and strong. Some of the political developments reminded him of the history and principles of the Greek republics with which he was so familiar. The two friends generally agreed on the principles.

In the first year of Adams' presidency, Van der Kemp wrote that his message to Congress was well received "in the western parts," though a few thought it "too dry." Van der Kemp thought Adams had cleverly suggested alternatives to Congress in such a way that his own leadership would prevail.[1] In the middle of the Adams administration Van der Kemp introduced a letter with the following apology:

Was it not to satisfy the ardent wishes of a learned deceased friend I should consider it approaching to sacrilege to intrude upon you, and bereave you of the use of a single one of those precious moments, which you in this critical period, with unrelenting ardor consecrate to the securing and promoting the happiness of millions who entrusted themselves to your care and guardianship.

The friend, Louw Van Santen, had met Adams in one of the gatherings at the Golden Lyon during the American Revolution. As an editor and poet he sent his respects to the president through Van der Kemp. The latter now sent several of the books of Santen to Adams and said he would translate the poet's works if he were "better acquainted with the progress of the Americans in Grecian and Latin critic" and if he could be assured of purchasers.[2]

Later in the year Van der Kemp read or heard that the political enemies of Adams were going to publish a refutation of the *Defence*. Since Van der Kemp had studied the work carefully, he offered to answer the "refutation" in place of Adams if the president wished it and indicated his "elucidations."[3] It seemed like a good idea but Adams thought otherwise. He recognized that, due to haste, the *Defence* contained inaccuracies but not errors. For twelve years the work had withstood "Violence and Virulence of Party Spirit." He had never written a line in its vindication. "The more it is attacked the better." Adams had heard that Thomas Paine was to write the refutation. He asked Van der Kemp what language he proposed to answer in and where he expected to find a printer.[4]

Van der Kemp suggested that an answer might well be "protected" [supported?] by the government since such an essay would instill principles of good government in the youth of the nation; it could be followed by similar works on the criminal and civil code. By these publications, "political prejudices and animosities would insensibly subside, local interest and ambition be bereaved of its principal spur, foreign influence effectually curbed and the whole mass of Americans consolidated into one undivided People." He declared, "If Tom Paine is not better acquainted with the Classics and the times of the Middle Ages, than he was with the Oriental languages and Ec-

clesiastical history, his opposition will be very despicable."
He proposed to reply in English if a friend would correct
it but could do better in Dutch or French. He hoped for a
printer in New York or Albany.[5]

Adams assured him that he wrote "very well in English"
but that he could hope for nothing from the government.
He said he wrote the *Defence* in a hurry because of the
disturbance of Shay's Rebellion on one side and the French
Assembly on the other. He doubted the effects of his work
and remarked very cynically:

> Mankind has found more amusement in shedding
> blood than in reading. If the time which has been spent
> in gazing at the blood streaming from the guillotine in
> the Place de Louis 15 had been spent in reading my dry
> volumes and spreading the doctrine of them, Mankind
> might have understood something of the subject. I have
> come off hitherto with mere abuse. Men write not upon
> government with impunity. Sydney was beheaded. Har-
> rington died in prison distracted, and Montesquieu was
> banished ten years from his country. I have no reason
> to complain.[6]

The latter part of the comment was in response to a Van
der Kemp remark that the Americans had not paid Adams
well.

Nevertheless, Van der Kemp wrote a paper sometime in
1800 defending Adams' writings and ideas. Two publishers
turned it down, though one offered to print it if the author
would buy 250 copies. He could not afford it. The main
reason for the rejections were due to his inadequate style
in the English language. He told Adams that he had also
translated Luzac's *Socrates* and sent it to the Massachusetts
Historical Society without any response.[7]

The failure of Paine or anyone else to produce the criticism led Van der Kemp to say, caustically: "I am persuaded
at present that the boasted answer to your Defense proposed by subscription by Barber [James Barber, Virginia]
had been a low cunning electioneering trick." He indicated

further that the backers of Jefferson would do well to defend their own leaders and measures rather than attacking Adams.[8] This was not a condemnation of Jefferson inasmuch as Van der Kemp respected the Virginian. It was the remark of a political scientist—a blunt one.

A lesser friend than Adams would have felt the rough edge of another political remark dealing with elected officials. Van der Kemp said that our safety up to 1800 was due "more to the mediocrity of Talents of our rulers than to our intrinsic virtue." He meant that America had been fortunate that its leaders had no inclination to be autocrats. In George Washington he saw a man who was popular enough to enslave the Americans, and regarded Americans as weak enough to accept it.[9] He was concerned about the election of 1800 as the month of September came and the tide was running against Adams. Van der Kemp asked, "Can your Excell. who is convinced of my disinterested attachment to his person with any propriety dissipate the excruciating pangs about the future election? Is it so doubtful?" [10] As late as December 12, Van der Kemp expressed a hope that Adams would continue in office. By this time Adams had lost not only the election but also one of his sons. Van der Kemp attempted to console him by speaking of the success of John Quincy Adams and told him to think about his religion and look at his blessings.[11] Adams agreed that his sorrow required the consolation of both religion and philosophy. However, he had no sorrow about the election—only solid pride.

> Before this reaches you, the news will be familiar to you that after the 3rd of March I am to be a private citizen and your brother farmer. I shall leave the State with its coffers full, and the fair prospects of a peace with all the world smiling in its face; its commerce flourishing, its navy glorious, its agriculture uncommonly productive and lucrative.[12]

Van der Kemp complimented his friend as "the Father and Benefactor" of the country, agreed as to the fair state of the nation and said that Adams' retirement would be honorable and notable. Lest Adams misunderstand his view on the new president, he added: "May your successor's administration be as wise, firm and happy—equally respected at both sides of the Atlantic—then your utmost wishes will be accomplished." He asked Adams to continue the correspondence, to write about the history and government of the United States, and of the political weaknesses and how to strengthen them.[13] A few months later he wanted to know about the conference with Lord Howe, the Preston case, and several other incidents in Adams' political life. Was there any truth in the report during the Revolution that General Nathanael Greene said Alexander Hamilton "never would be highly serviceable to this country either in the field or in the cabinet?" Did Adams apprehend immediate danger under Jefferson, or "after having silenced a few hungry office-seekers" would the goal of the administration be the *salus populi?* [14]

Adams responded to most of the questions with interest. He refused to comment on the new president.

> You call upon me for a History of my ancient dreams. Prestons Tryal—and Howe's Conferences are like long forgotten Reveries to me. There is a printed Tryal of the Soldiers—and I wrote a letter giving an account of the Conferences on Staten Island, but I know not how long time it would take me to find it. I never had a home till now and my papers are not arranged.

He did not know of a remark by Greene but recalled one by General Charles Lee that Hamilton was very brave but he doubted whether it was a kind of bravery that would do the country any good.[15]

The two men reminisced about their friendship in the Netherlands and of their meetings at the Golden Lyon and in homes, meetings with Baron Van der Capellen de Pol and John Luzac in particular.

From time to time, Van der Kemp lashed out at an injustice or an evil in government. Late in 1801 when Jefferson sent a squadron to Tripoli, Van der Kemp criticized severely the papers Jefferson passed to Congress on December 8 and December 22. The papers dealt with our affairs with the Barbary or North African piratical states, and covered sixty-two pages in the *State Papers and Public Documents of the United States.* America's commerce with the Mediterranean countries was growing, and Jefferson wanted to persuade the African rulers through soft diplomacy and gifts not to seize American ships. A small squadron of four war vessels was dispatched in midsummer of 1801 to the Mediterranean to protect our trade. The public papers spoke of the squadron as though it were on a sight-seeing tour, and Jefferson's letter to the Pasha of Tripoli appeared shamefully weak to Van der Kemp. The fiery patriot exploded in wrath. Why should our government apologize for sending a squadron to protect our ships? Why should we embarrass our ministers and consuls with the conciliatory letter to the ruler of Tripoli? Was the squadron sent to learn the pirate trade? Van der Kemp was certain Europeans would condemn the action. Then he asked Adams to correct him if he were wrong.[16] When Adams defended some aspects of the procedures, Van der Kemp replied he had not intended to question the patriotism of the administration, but as an "independent citizen" he felt free to do so.[17]

Spurred by dissatisfaction with Jeffersonian handling of foreign affairs, Van der Kemp began early in 1802 to write an essay on the ancient Achaian republic. "The mad pranks of our ruling characters" prompted the project, but the greater consideration was Van der Kemp's feeling of obligation to do whatever he could to preserve liberty and independence. By late March he was half through the work and asked Adams to criticize and smooth the writing.[18] Adams praised the essay as "a valuable Addition to American Literature" and said it was richly deserving of publication. He hoped it would do some good for America, yet feared politicians would not be frightened out of their power "by a few paper shot." [19]

In a letter which followed shortly, Adams reconsidered his opinion on the value of "paper shot." While he agreed with his more optimistic friend that "the deadly infection" of party politics had not yet spread through "every limb" of the nation, how could sensible citizens overlook the popular journalist, James Thomas Callender, who had unfairly criticized Washington's administration, supported Jefferson enthusiastically, then shifted to bitter condemnation of Jefferson for no good reason?

The Editors of Newspapers have no Check, and yet have Power to make and unmake Characters, at their Will, to create and uncreate Constitutions; to erect and demolish Administrations. When a few Scribblers, all foreigners, whose origin history and Characters nobody knows, have more Influence than President Senate, the Peoples own Representatives, and all the judges of the Land, [what shall we say]?

In hot anger, he said that some intelligent and educated writers who had failed to succeed, perhaps because of low morals, were writing only to keep from starving. For a guinea they would write for or against anything or anybody.[20] Engrossed in the subject of the power of the press, Adams sent a second letter to Van der Kemp the next day. He had remembered a quotation of the French author, J. F. La Harpe, about the influence of writers in France during the Revolution.[21] He quoted an entire paragraph.

Van der Kemp indicated that some of these observations would be reflected in the *Achaian Republic*. He thought there were too many writers who were poorly educated "philosophatters," and regretted their ability to attract the "gaping crowds."

He recalled that the Netherlands, too, had had its share of irresponsible and vacillating journalists. But Van der Kemp's faith in democratic processes persisted; he was sure America presented more opportunities for correcting weaknesses of the state. He hoped to read more of La Harpe sometime.[22]

Van der Kemp recurrently pursued Adams for historical reminiscences, though with little success. At this time he sent Adams a number of inquiries concerning national affairs, but Adams replied to but one. Van der Kemp asked if Jefferson really believed in following the party but found himself forced to follow a clique.[23]

Adams replied that the doctrine that a president ought not think or act for himself was completely against the intent of the Constitution. It was true that he was not elected to rule by his own fancy, but he ought to have judgment and conscience enough to resist opposition "by his own Ministers in concert with a Party in the Senate aided by influential characters out of Doors." [24]

Van der Kemp was never content with the Jefferson and Madison administrations, partly because of his Federalist leanings in national politics and partly because of the open admiration for the French exhibited by prominent Jeffersonians. He himself did not depend on France as a bulwark nor consider it a worthy model for the American republic. In the revolutionary movements of the Netherlands, he saw dangers of the same fate which had befallen the French. Indeed, he saw dangers to both his native and adopted countries which his story of the Achaian Republic would make evident.

From time to time corrections and additions were made to the manuscript. In its final form in 1809 it carried the title, *A Sketch of the Achaian Republic in Letters to Colonel John Lincklaen*. It was dedicated to the memory of George Washington and had a short but solemn foreword to the "American Reader" that if he spurned the warning and continued "to dream of peace without danger" and to trample on the American blessings, "then you shall accelerate your Doom." An introductory letter of twenty-four pages spelled out the dangers of excessive political power, but ended with hopefulness:

Do not conclude from this disgusting scenery, that Liberty is a vain name—a palatable soporific, artfully administered by them, who aspire to reduce their coun-

trymen in slavery. Altho this abuse cannot be contro-
verted, it is however worth a bloody struggle to obtain
its valuable possession. Indeed, it is worth this struggle,
to secure an inestimable treasure to our Posterity, but
by what means? When some wise and virtuous individual,
when a George Washington knows and dares, after he has
broken the fetters of his countrymen to model a government or persuades his fellow citizens to adopt one, in
which the law is fixed on a firm and unmoveable basis,
and its impartial execution entrusted to an independent
body,—in which the power and inclinations of the few
and many are so controuled and balanced, that all are
compelled to do good, and cannot do any wrong. Such
a government administered by an energetic—permanent
Executive must secure the civil and Political liberty of
this true Republic—preserve a dignified equality among
its members, compell foreign applause and homage to a
rising virtuous People, raise the Public credit to its
highest summit and keep it there, till the increasing
wealth and luxury have vitiated its morals, and Heaven's
decree marked its decay and death—25

Van der Kemp assured his readers that he continued to
favor a republican form of government—if wisely administered. His hatred of tyranny had not subsided. He said that
he would still lead an insurrection against oppression and
sacrifice his life to save the Constitution and the country's
liberty.26

Van der Kemp told of the rise of the Achaian league of
cities, their development into a republic, and the reasons
for their subsequent troubles. "The history of ancient Republics is the history of those of our own times with altered
names. What an instructif, awful warning is included in
this truth." 27

From time to time Van der Kemp drew the parallels
to modern times very strongly.

When the Constitution is violated—the morals are
corrupted—venality is seated in the tribunals of justice

and party rage becomes Patriotism—when factions engage in a bloody strife for the choice of a master, and
foreigners are lurking to grasp at the throat with an iron
hand—when all shall be too much exhausted, to avert the
meditated blow—even if united in dispair—then the
nation [is] lost—and lost forever. The Achaian Republick was in this period not in a more favorable situation.[28]

Van der Kemp concluded the work with the hope that he
had shown that the "Liberty and independence of a Nation—that all the sacred rights of Individuals" could be
longest preserved under a well-balanced government.

Achaia, alas! was lost—so were the Republicks after
the Middle Age in Italy—So was Venice—Geneve—
Genua—Lucca—Holland! Hamburg! and is there a solid
hope that America shall learn from all these examples? [29]

Van der Kemp prepared it for publication and sent it to
Philadelphia. Two printers rejected it as not having enough
sales appeal. Van der Kemp could not assume any of the
financial risk and hoped there might be a "more enter-
prising bookseller" in Boston. He had no trouble getting
things published when in Europe but now his essay was
rejected while Paine's "more than Billingsgate slander"
was published with profit and greedily devoured.[30] Adams
was pessimistic; he thought studies of this kind were "not
to the Taste" of the people. He suggested sending the essay
to Joseph Dennie, Editor of *Portfolio,* asking him to edit
it and print it by instalments in his periodical. He added
that his son, Thomas Boyleston Adams, a lawyer in Philadelphia, would help with the editing.[31] Dennie said he
did not have time to condense the material and could not
use it piecemeal. Adams (of Philadelphia) praised the work.
Van der Kemp immediately sent the manuscript to his
friend, the Reverend Theophilus Lindsey, in England,
with a request for him to forward it to John Luzac after
perusal.[32]

The *Achaian Republic* was read by Lindsey in England

Francis Adrian Van der Kemp at age 24. From a miniature reproduced in *Francis Adrian Van der Kemp, 1752-1829: An Autobiography,* edited by Helen Lincklaen Fairchild (New York: G. P. Putnam's Sons 1903).

Unitarian Church, Barneveld, New York, which was established in 1803 with Van der Kemp's help. The present church appears essentially as it did when constructed in 1816.

Van der Kemp's residence in Barneveld from 1797 until his death in 1829. The original dwelling was one and one half stories high and the entrance was on the left side of the present structure. The wing on the right was added by Van der Kemp in 1820. The cottage became the Unitarian parsonage shortly after his daughter's death in 1868.

Van der Kemp at age 35, painted while he was a political prisoner in Holland. Reproduced, with permission, from a copy in the Unitarian parsonage in Barneveld, New York.

and went on to John Luzac in the Netherlands. This copy was promised to Robert Livingston for criticism. Rather than wait, Van der Kemp made another copy for Jonas Platt in the winter of 1806–7 and "in some parts materially improved it." [33]

The copying of manuscripts was a chore to be reckoned with for the scholars of Van der Kemp's day. In addition to copying excerpts from the works of others which had to be passed on or returned, Francis was obliged to spend countless hours in copying his own writings. He preferred to copy his own manuscripts, probably because of the scholar's constant desire to revise and improve. Most of the surviving Van der Kemp manuscripts are in his own handwriting; the neat, rather decorative and finely legible script of a well-educated gentleman. A very few written in his declining years appear to have been copied by Betsy.

While perplexed with the problem of getting the principles of good, safe government before the American people, Van der Kemp decided that publication of the Adams memoirs would help. He insisted that Adams begin writing, but was laughed at. Adams said it would take almost a hundred volumes, and he would be dead before he could finish even one.[34] When Van der Kemp repeated the request, Adams replied with more seriousness: "My life is already written in my Letter books as particularly as I wish it. There I shall appear as I wish with all my imperfections on my head." [35]

In 1806 Van der Kemp penned a remark intended as praise but having the reverse effect on his friend. "What less can I return to the man, of whom a Washington declared that none could more cordially than himself approve the wise and prudent measures of his administration— which ought to have inspired universal and lasting confidence?" [36]

Adams lost his temper.

For the future I pray you to Spare yourself the trouble of quoting that great authority in my favour. Although no Man has a more Settled opinion of his Integrity and Virtues than myself, I nevertheless desire that my Life Actions and Administration may be condemned to everlasting oblivion, and I will add infamy, if they cannot be defended by their own intrinsic merit and without the aid of Mr. Washingtons Judgment.[37]

Van der Kemp accepted the rebuke by saying that he appreciated their correspondence because he could speak his mind. He did not intend to flatter Adams but merely to praise him. He continued:

As Washington is no more and left no progeny—I cannot yet agree that he can be extolled too high, provided it is not done at the expense of other meritorious characters—and how little I esteem Franklin as a statesman —I join willingly in his praises as an experimental Philosopher.[38]

In April, 1807, Adams sent word of a tremendous explosion which had occurred in the university section of Leyden, when a canal boat loaded with powder was ignited. Letters were enclosed which Adams had received. When Van der Kemp learned the extent of the destruction, he was appalled and overcome:

You shall not expect an excuse, for my delaying a few days to return the inclosed [letters]. My heart was too much oppressed with grief. I took refuge to labour to assuage its pain. My young friend Mappa [John] brought me your Lett. in my garden. . . . Since the account of Webster's Gazette [Albany] of this horrible catastrophe, we have remained in that excruciating uncertainty, which is more tormenting than even the fatal dreaded events. You can form yourself an idea of Mrs. v. d. Kemp's situation, when I have told you, that in the neighbourhood of that spot, where the explosion happened, several of our relations—a Sister in Law—a Niece a cousin—our best and oldest friends—Two families of Luzac and among them John—two families of Le Pole—perhaps three—that of Gyzelaer—that of Vreede, the friend of my bosom—resided.

In the evening I communicated the event to Mrs. v. d. Kemp—Luzac had been her friend—long before she was acquainted with me—a friend of more than forty years —a friend and more than a brother to her—when I was in confinement. . . .

Coming out of the church I find a voluminous letter of Mrs. Busti of Philadelphia—informing us of more particulars—tho many uncertainties remain yet with regard to many dear to us—

About four hundred houses were destroyed and already nearly a million guilders had been collected for relief.[39] It was learned later that John Luzac and many of the others had been killed but De Gyzelaer survived and had become the guardian of John Luzac's children.[40] The copy of the *Achaian Republic* which Luzac intended to edit was undoubtedly destroyed along with the editor.

The comparisons and resulting suggestions in the *Achaian Republic* became less and less relevant as conditions changed in America and the threat of Napoleon increased. The last possibility for its publication seems to have been in the latter part of 1808 when Jonas Platt asked Chief Justice James Kent to read it. Nothing resulted from this examination and Van der Kemp reluctantly laid the manuscript aside, believing it was good, believing it could be useful, but realizing it was unacceptable.

Van der Kemp's grief upon hearing of the Leyden explosion was only one of a number of times when the friends shared their sorrows. However, they shared their personal joys also. Van der Kemp was always glad to hear about John's son, John Quincy, who had served the country as ambassador to Russia and had just returned in 1801. Van der Kemp wrote: "I congratulate you Sir! with the safe arrival of your Hon. Son and family— . . . I hope your glorious days may be so long protracted—that He—pressing the footsteps of his father—may fill the highest office of our country—without longing for or fearing to accept it." [41] The next year John Quincy ran for Congress but was defeated. The father wrote to Van der Kemp that he had been persuaded to run against both his own and the son's inclinations. He said he rejoiced in the loss of the election.[42] Some months later Van der Kemp wished to ask the son some questions. Therefore, he asked Adams to remind his son who Van der Kemp was.[43] John Quincy Adams was always very respectful to his father's friend and in later years exchanged a number of letters with Van der Kemp.

In 1806 Van der Kemp congratulated John on the "accepted station" of his son and predicted great things for him.[44] The father added that he expected his son to promote the "Taste and Litterature" of the country and that he had already done so with a fine course of lectures.[45]

When John Van der Kemp received a fine promotion from the employ of Mappa at Oldenbarneveld to the main office of the Holland Land Company at Philadelphia, his father told Adams of the great opportunity:

> My Eldest son has accepted the offer of our Mr. Busti at Philadelphia—to be employed in his ofice at a salary of 1200 £ [?] with the prospect of 400 £ [?] more, if Mr. Busti, who is a Director of the Population Society can obtain for him this combination.[46]

Once Van der Kemp asked for Adams' portrait. He said he had a small one of Washington and wanted one of Adams that he might bequeath to his children.[47] Adams made a half promise to give him a portrait that Stuart started but he did not know whether it was ever finished. Apparently the portrait never got to Van der Kemp.

During the years of Napoleon when national and international affairs were critical, Van der Kemp reread his Cicero and Pliny and avidly consumed such other works as John Marshall's *Life of Washington*.[48] Then he began to read carefully the sixteenth century writers and later authors who wrote about that century.

That era was unquestionably all-important—and contained the seeds of all the following events during two centuries and a half—while a new one—no less prolific has been opened about the time of the American Revolution. An introduction to any modern history, similar in many respects to that of Robertson's Charles the Vth but upon a larger scale, would be as useful as entertaining, but requires the hand of no less accomplished master, as it ought to comprehend history, Philosophy, Literature and commerce.[49]

He said he had spent the winter of 1808–09 "vox silentis in deserto" but certainly his mind was active. In addition to the considered scheme of the great history, he studied metaphysics and Protestant church law. When he was tired he read Chaulieu, La Tarre, Rabelais and Sterne.[50]

Perhaps in 1811, maybe a year later, he wrote his informal essay, "Dutch Conviviality." Van der Kemp described a gathering of friends in Oneida County and their heated discussions. Bantering between Dutch and Yankees and between Germans and Yankees added a touch of humor, and social customs of the day were vividly described. The Dutch nation was defended and praised for its aid to America. American leaders were discussed, including John Adams. The nineteen page essay was later given the name, "Symposium Uticense." [51] Although it was never published, it was read with a great deal of pleasure by Van der Kemp's friends. To the present-day reader, it offers a lively and fascinating view of an evening of solid enjoyment in Oldenbarneveld.

❧ XV ❧

The Threat of Napoleon

NAPOLEON Bonaparte made a good beginning on his ascent to power in Europe before Americans such as Van der Kemp were aware of danger. In December, 1793, during the Reign of Terror, Napoleon freed the port of Toulon from the British and was raised to the rank of brigadier general. At a tense moment in 1795 he broke up a mob and received further governmental favor. From 1796 to 1799 he led victorious armies in Italy and Egypt and on November 9, 1799, overthrew the French Directory, thereby opening the way for his long dictatorial regime. After the events of 1799 Americans began to take notice.

As early as 1796 Van der Kemp had predicted that the French government would disrupt into chaos, bringing a crown to a "disinterested patriot." Van der Kemp would never credit Napoleon with patriotism, but his prediction of the fall of the republic came true. While Adams was still president, Van der Kemp's desire for peace with France shaped his thoughts. In December, after Napoleon seized power but probably before it was known in central New York, Van der Kemp wrote to President Adams,

> Will you condescend to accept my thanks with those of the best of this neighbourhood for the grand sacrifice which you made again to your country in sending Ambassadors of peace to the French nation—notwithstanding the disapprobation of some of your real admirers and the

murmurs of yet a greater number pretended friends? I knowed that Adams was not to be sway'd by frowns or smiles.[1]

This referred to the commission which negotiated the Convention of 1800 ending our alliance with France.

Van der Kemp was also concerned lest Francophiles sway the government and, of course, he was concerned about his native land. He had been disturbed when John Luzac lost his position at a Dutch university, but was proud to relate that Luzac rejected a pension because "he wished not to feed on the spoils of his country when he could not deserve well of it in the office with which he was entrusted." [2]

A year and a half after Napoleon overthrew the Directory, Van der Kemp made an interesting comparison starting from the question, "Will King Buonaparte's consulat be as durable as Cromwell's Protectorship?" [3] Adams replied, "I have long ceased to conjecture, and never pretended to prophecy. The Duration of Bonaparte's Consulate is the most uncertain of things." [4] Of course, Adams had more knowledge of Napoleon than Van der Kemp since he had many reports from ministers and consuls when he was president. Perhaps he was exercising the use of discretion which he had been asked about. He said he had lots of it since he had used little in the past. He added, "I read the Newspapers and apply what I learn'd from Juvenal, half a century ago, an excellent Precept of Circumspection Digito compresse labellum, which is well translated by our vulgar monosyllable *Mum!!!* [5]

Van der Kemp had less enthusiasm for the Jefferson administration than its predecessor and thoroughly disapproved certain actions of the government. Not only did he condemn the weak action against the Barbary states but also felt that the Senate intended to give up too much in the French treaty. Van der Kemp remembered the results of French treachery in the Netherlands and was afraid of the same thing in America, saying, "Buonaparte has jaggled America fairly—and our government says—Lett it be so—

as says Buonaparte." He told Adams he had "taken up my arms again—tho an old veteran" by writing about the Achaian and the Dutch republics in order to warn the citizens of America.[6]

After finishing the *Achaian Republic,* Van der Kemp took up a defense of the Constitution again. It seemed to him that the numerous attacks on the government and the "various illusory essays" of a utopian nature called for a refutation of the criticisms and a clear portrayal of the advantages of the Constitution. He sent a rough outline to Adams, the most salient point of which was that a well regulated and balanced government "is *not exposed* to the danger of falling into a Despotism" unless its constitution is openly violated, neither can it "degenerate into Tyranny under the garb of Liberty." He asked for Adams' ideas on such a project. Then he declared that it made his blood boil to see Holland trampled upon by the "insolent Corsican at the head of his perfidious Gallic slaves." Would the Americans learn? Would they rise, banish the foreign influence and eliminate the Jacobinical stain? [7]

By this time one threat from France to the United States had been removed through the purchase of Louisiana, signed April 30, 1803. Napoleon made the sale in preparation for a renewal of war with Great Britain which came at about the same time. Britain had no allies when Napoleon made preparations for an invasion. Van der Kemp was gravely disturbed and asked how Europe could survive if its people did not oppose the Corsican usurper. He had been dismayed to hear his old friend, Rutger Jan Schimmelpennick, cringed before Napoleon. Was America in danger too? [8]

Van der Kemp read the local newspapers and sometimes papers from Albany, New York City and Washington. The local papers, the *Columbia Gazette* and the *Utica Patriot,* carried many national and international reports, sometimes taken from other papers. The reports on Napoleon were frequently inaccurate because of prejudiced sources, but mistakes were later corrected when possible, and vague reports were often verified and amplified. However, there was no question as to the sentiment of the two papers. Van der Kemp could be righteously stirred by statements like the following:

> It is evident that Bonaparte still feels himself insecure on his usurped and bloody throne. In blood he waded to it:—Like Damocles, he tastes not the dainties of his table, he enjoys not the magnificence which surrounds him; he sees suspended over his head a sword, which soon or late must, and will fall, for it is the sword of retributive justice.[9]

This statement was made in regard to Napoleon's actions toward a conspiracy involving one of his generals. Van der Kemp was an indignant wishful thinker like the writer of the statement and he received comfort from such readings, if not assurance. In a few months he again expressed to Adams his fears about the dangers of French influence on America:

> I lament with you most sincerely Sir! that our dear country is so deep tainted with Gallic principles, that it will require a very deep cut [as in bleeding for an ailment] before it shall be freed from this infection. . . . But do you not believe, that calamities will awaken the Nation from its lethargy? I do—[10]

Napoleon did not invade England but he did bring Spain into alliance with France. Austria, Russia and Sweden joined Great Britain in the Third Coalition and Napoleon moved by land to break it up. French arms were successful on land, but Nelson defeated the French and Spanish fleets in the Battle of Trafalgar. Although France had given up her interests in the Americas, Spanish lands still stretched from California and Florida to Cape Horn. The Spanish had been unpredictable at New Orleans before the purchase. Since then, there had been numerous incidents along the Florida border.

Van der Kemp expressed fear in late December, 1805,

that Europe would be ruined if the Russians did not arrive in time to defend Austria against France. The Russians arrived but Napoleon defeated both Russians and Austrians in the great battle of Austerlitz. Van der Kemp did not know of this battle yet, but had heard of Trafalgar. In spite of the destruction of French naval power, he feared the United States might be drawn into the war through trouble with Spain.[11] On the other hand, difficulties were piling up between the United States and Great Britain. Van der Kemp wrote: "I hope not that war with England shall be our doom . . ." He disapproved British acts on the seas but thought American merchants were courting trouble.[12] Various hopeful reports from Europe arrived just before the news of Austerlitz, leading Van der Kemp to say as late as February 18, 1806, "God be praised! if the latest European accounts are verified—then the vain presumptuous Corse shall yet be humbled in the dust!" [13]

Adams was anything but optimistic.

[T]he mad Spirit of Democracy in France and in Bohemia and Austria has ended in Empire a[nd] Despotism. It may do the same in all Europe. A few Dynasties of Emperors may succeed, by frequent convulsions and wars till Arts Sciences Liberty Religion Government and all may perish and Europe grow up a howling Wilderness such as our Ancestors found this country in the days of Massasoit and Pokahunta.[14]

Later he wrote: "Our government moves with moderation, and I hope will not fly out in a passion with Spain or England. But our honor, and a Sense of their own Power, in the Minds of the People must be preserved." [15]

When Van der Kemp heard of Napoleon's successes in Austria, he was as pessimistic as Adams.

Alas poor tottering Europe—Austria annihilated, Italy under the Despot's yoke—Mushroom Kings plundering their subjects to still the all devouring rapacity of a Corse—I am not indeed without apprehension for old

England— . . . I have not the remotest doubt, or [that] Napoleon's gigantic empire must crumble in pieces— even if he does not fall a victim to insulted human- ity. . . .

He believed the American nation had become corrupt and that New York was a sad example of it. The virulent Dem- ocrats had won in Oneida County and elsewhere were gen- erally successful. Now they threatened to destroy politically the Livingstons and the Lansings.[16] The following July he explained further: "The Livingstons pay now dearly in this State, for having bowed their knees to the thou- sand headed monster, and are writhing under the goad, which they permitted and assisted in cutting in their own manor." [17] He believed that the Federalists were the makers of their own ruin and that Hamilton had given his party the heaviest blow.[18]

The English Orders in Council and the French Decrees began to irritate Americans. After the Battle of Trafalgar, British interference with American shipping became far greater than that of France. John Adams had favored a strong American navy but Jefferson allowed the navy to decline for the sake of economy. To give protection to American shores a number of very small ships were built for a coast guard, but were found to be completely worth- less for sea travel and offense. One of them was reported washed up into a cornfield in a heavy sea.

Van der Kemp was scornful of these ships even before their misfortunes:

Might I not give a hint—that in case of a new broil— a few of these amphibions—I suppose with triffling ad- ditional expenses, they might be enabled to act as well on land as in open sea—stationed on Oneida Lake—near my farm is a small snug harbour—black creek—to con- ceal them—might unexpectedly descend in Lake Ontario and lay Canada under contributions. It might be a good proviso in our Legislatures address—to pray the Presi-

dent—to manage our national affairs—after his own way
—for another term—provided we may get our share in
the cursed gunboats—[19]

Napoleon defeated Prussia and the Russian forces in
the latter part of 1806, and Prussia was forced to make an
unhappy peace. Would the conqueror invade Russia? Van
der Kemp hoped the "modern Sennacherib" would fall on
the way.

I ardently pray—that the gigantic power of that daring insolent Corse may be crushed. You can not doubt
of my sincerity. What would save us from his grasp—
in our distracted situation—if he succeeded in conquer-
ing Great Britain—That and the Almighty's protection
are our only bulwarks—[20]

When Congress requested in late 1806 that the president make overtures to Britain to settle their differences,
Van der Kemp approved although he overestimated the
British willingness to compromise at this time. The Mon-
roe-Pinckney Treaty, which resulted from the negotiations,
was so unfavorable to the United States that Jefferson
did not even present it to the Senate. Without knowing
all the facts Van der Kemp was hopeful that continued
negotiations would be successful and would insure peace
between the United States and Britain.

Adams told Van der Kemp that the United States should
not despair in regard to the "Angel of Perdition" who was
desolating Europe. Napoleon would need to transport fifty
thousand men to America for a conquest and he could not
raise the ships to do it. What this country needed for defense was only ships.[21] Van der Kemp replied:

Ships! Ships! Yes Sir! with them—with a squadron of
16 men of war and an adequate number of frigates,
America should have now dictated to the Belligerent
powers, in the place of being the scorn and derision of

Europe. No Navy can endanger our liberty—a standing army must sooner or later become its bane—and its increase beyond what imperious necessity commands must be viewed with a jealous eye by every lover of his country.[22]

And Adams responded, "I neither dread old England nor old France: of the two the former have it in their Power to do us most Mischief." [23]

After the defeat of the Prussians and Russians, the Treaty of Tilsit was made by the three rulers on a raft in the Nieman River. The treaty made France supreme in the Germanies and established the French satellite, the Duchy of Warsaw, on the border of Russia. By a secret agreement Russia promised to join France in war against England. Napoleon was now free to extend his continental sway southwestward. In November, 1807, a French army invaded Portugal and in March, 1808, a larger French army began the occupation of Spain. However, opposition by the Spanish with the assistance of the British made the Peninsular War drag on to November, 1809, before Spain was subdued. Portugal continued to resist.

In the middle of this war Van der Kemp expressed the opinion that if Austria and Russia did not take advantage of Napoleon's involvement elsewhere to push the French out of north Germany, the two nations deserved to be conquered. He also thought Napoleon could be driven out if the Spaniards really tried. Van der Kemp was sincere in his desire to oppose Napoleon with arms, and favored fighting on the frontier in Europe rather than waiting for an attack in America. He wrote to Adams, "Was I young—without family—I would cross the Atlantic and enlisten in Spain—if previously I had some solid prospect that the majority of Spain would struggle to obtain the palm of victory." [24] He had faced armed conflict long ago at Wyk on Duurstede; now at fifty-six he declared he longed to take up arms again to defend his new country and help save Europe. He thought that if England fell to the continental conqueror, America would become the center of civilization and Europe would revert to wilderness.

An interesting view on the European situation was brought to Oldenbarneveld in 1808 by Bernardus Blok. With his daughter and secretary he stopped off in America, staying six weeks in Oldenbarneveld on his way to a judicial post at Batavia in the Dutch East Indies. Blok had lived at Enkhuizen and probably became acquainted with Van der Kemp at Leyden. When the Mappas fled from the Netherlands they had lived for almost two years with Blok in Belguim. His appearance was an "unexpected agreeable visit." Blok had kept abreast of movements in Europe and could "unfold a tale, which fills with horror." Van der Kemp and Mappa plied him with questions about the exercise of controls by France in Holland, the movements of armies and economic dislocations. With a goodly amount of prejudice against Napoleon before the arrival of Blok, Van der Kemp was now confirmed in his opinion: "Never was similar Despotism established—never continued by similar means." Blok told how the burgomasters not only wore large periwigs but also had donned togas and occupied pews of honor in the churches. Such worldly displays in the churches displeased Van der Kemp. He also disliked the fact that the herring fleet had not been sent into the North and Baltic seas during the past years. The Dutch economy suffered, fishermen were "reduced to beggary" and the public credit had fallen.[25] Blok apparently tried to give his friends a true picture even though he officially represented the Netherlands as it now was—a satellite of Napoleon. When Blok left, Van der Kemp wrote, "I ardently wish he may with his family arrive in safety [in Batavia]. He is an amiable man—of an excellent character with moderate talents." [26]

The coming of a treacherous Frenchman to the community later in the year increased Van der Kemp's mistrust of Napoleon's "horde of Gallic slaves." Adam Mappa called the newcomer a "respectable, thin little Frenchman," a "man of the world, once clever, agreeable in company, knowing human nature, a *philosophe* of the first rank" who married an "old lame widow," bought a farm without seeing it and went away without paying for it.[27] Van der Kemp described the Frenchman with a bitterness increased perhaps by a chronic headache which started early in 1809.

> I presume that the disease originated chiefly from the mind, which had been cruelly delacerated by the discovered baseness of a foreigner, who, recommended to me, covered the heart of a villain with the cloak of an high-accomplished Gentleman and whom I had considered it a duty, to introduce to many of my respected friends to record his views and retrieve his broken fortune. I traced him out on his own steps, and found myself in the disagreeable necessity to warn and disabuse all my friends. This is over—and he is covered with infamy.

Added to Van der Kemp's wounds, word came that the old "friend of his bosom," Peter Vreede, had become a bankrupt and a fugitive. With him Van der Kemp had worked for the Patriot cause. When the French came in 1895, Vreede became a member of the Dutch Directory. He had become a millionaire through careful investments in commerce but now at the age of sixty was disgraced. His partner, a man of "deep profligacy," had caused his failure. Van der Kemp was despondent but recovered, in part by his own prescription of light reading—Sterne or Scott, perhaps Shakespeare.[28]

Actually Van der Kemp had frequent headaches and other ailments from 1809 on. Whether it was his eyes, sinus infections or something else, it would be difficult to determine. The worries about Napoleon's despotism and his threat to a weak United States were enervating. Frustration in seeing his research and writing generally rejected added to his ailments.

In 1805 Van der Kemp had been admitted to the American Philosophical Society at Philadelphia but returned the diploma because of the ten-dollar fee. John Mifflin withheld the rejection and persuaded the society to waive fees for non-residents. Van der Kemp then accepted the diploma —but sent the fee. In the same year, through Chancellor Livingston, membership in the Society for Promotion of the Useful Arts (formerly agriculture) at New York was offered to Van der Kemp. This too he was obliged to decline because he could not afford the dues. In 1808 Van der Kemp was elected to membership in the Academy of Arts and Sciences at Boston.

Beset by fears stemming from Napoleon's continued successes, and growing dissension in the United States, Van der Kemp constantly tried to induce Adams to make known his political theories and ideas. He also urged Livingston to be active in the field of politics as well as agriculture. When Livingston returned from his embassy in France, Van der Kemp wrote, "You will preside once more at the Society of Agriculture spread a new life thro all its members and make their operations prosper." [29] Some of the letters are missing but five years later when the international affairs were much more dangerous and internal politics were troubled, Van der Kemp encouraged Livingston to take a hand.

Your indolence is enviable indeed—when you perform so much—and spread knowledge—and ease all around you, in the instant of your pretended idleness. A man of your cast places himself usually in the most favourable light—in a dignified retirement—I acknowledge Sir! the justness of your remarks with regard to Politicks—but it is no less true that the situation of a country becomes duely alarming, when the Pelhams retreat. Men of noble mind and unsullied integrity and glowing Patriotism may widely differ in opinion and choice of means, but eagerly join hearts and hands—when their country must be saved —What must become of our poor hulk in a boisterous sea, amongst shores and quicksand, with a mutinous crew— without pilots to steer it in a safe harbour—Shall the rocks to which they fled—to repose in safety—ease their mind when all is lost? Men of your station—influence and

talents—may well deserve of their country in their cabinet
—and I know an example when a single letter turned the
scales in favour of measures by a deliberating body, when
without it, often contrary measures should have been
adopted.[30]

By this time Livingston, at sixty-four, was tired of political
warring, tired of the struggle to keep the steamboat rights
on the Hudson, and interested chiefly in the further adoption of merino sheep. Some of his earlier political activity
may have been encouraged and influenced by Van der
Kemp, but not after 1810.

In order to stir up the thinkers of the Academy of Arts
and Sciences, Van der Kemp proposed that the members
discuss the problem, "Thro what means the military and
commercial spirit can be most effectually entertained and
rendered permanently advantageous to a Free Nation under
a Republican form of government." [31] Adams did not like
the proposal and said the Academy was not prepared to
discuss both sides of a political question since nearly all
members were Federalists. Adams said "such questions
would only make of our academies so many political cau-
cuses." [32]

Napoleon had failed to conquer Portugal but held Spain
in 1809. Austria had risen and had been disastrously defeated in the Battle of Wagram and other revolts of lesser
importance were promptly quelled. In 1810 Louis Bonaparte fled from his Dutch throne rather than block Dutch
commerce by enforcing Napoleon's order for the continental
boycott against England. Napoleon married Maria Louise
in the summer. Sweden and Russia went to war, Russia
won, and a revolt in Sweden overthrew the king. Van der
Kemp said he enjoyed being so far from the convulsions
of Europe but feared they would be extended to our
coasts.[33]

Shortly after Thanksgiving in 1810 Adams wrote to Van
der Kemp about a timely sermon he had recently heard.
He agreed with the preacher in many points "and in none

more cordially than in Thanksgiving to God for creating the Atlantic Ocean between America and Europe." The minister represented Napoleon "as the great oppressor, the Destroyer of Nations, the Universal Despot; and the English as a Nation to be pitied as fighting for their own Existence." With this picture of Britain, Adams could not agree. He saw no moral difference between England and France. His philosophy was to "trust neither" and "prepare to defend ourselves and assert our Might against both." He acknowledged that Van der Kemp undoubtedly agreed with the preacher.[34]

Van der Kemp was ill again during the winter and took medicine called "Bark and Steel." Not until February did he start to mend, and spoke of doing light reading. He re-read Rousseau's *Héloïse* and Scott's *Lady of the Lake* three times without interruption as part of the "course of Physic." However, he had thought about Adams' letter and commented:

> Britain is yet a more powerful Nation—can not conquer France—grasps at every object she can reach and may nevertheless sit upon a tottering throne—be ripe for destruction. The all conquering Corse is safe at home —compelled to arms by necessity—moral and physical, and can not rest till Gr. B. is ruined by him—or herself —and if we had followed the system of preparing to defend ourselves and assert our rights against Both—we were safe—We might defy both—would be cajoled by both and supply the whole world with what they wanted.[35]

In 1811 Napoleon hurt the commerce of neutrals in trying to make his continental system more effective. However, the Americans had their attention directed to the commercial interference of England as well as France. The Macon Bill was proposed as a substitute for the Embargo prohibiting trade with the two belligerents. The new arrangement provided that if one of the two nations withdrew its decrees of interference and the other did not, trade would be banned with the latter. The Federalists opposed the Macon Bill but it passed. Napoleon pretended to accede and on November 2, 1810, President Madison opened trade with France and ordered trade cut off with Great Britain. France continued to seize United States ships, while Britain continued to blockade New York City and to impress seamen all through 1811. Anger at Great Britain mounted and Napoleon seemed far away as he began his disastrous invasion of Russia. Van der Kemp and Adams, and thousands of other patriotic citizens, criticized or praised the Madison administration and sometimes wondered what was going to happen to civilization.

Early in 1811 Van der Kemp congratulated John Adams for the appointment of John Quincy Adams to the Supreme Court and added that this act made up for "many political sins" in President Madison.[36] The Supreme Court appointment was not accepted but John the father picked up Van der Kemp's phrase about Madison's sins.

You speak of Political Sins in the P. Pray what are those Sins? "In Adams Fall We Sinned All," but I really know of no more Sins committed by Madison than by Washington Adams or Jefferson.

The Government of the United States from 1789 to 1811 has been but a Company of Engine Men. Their constant Employment has been to Spout cold Water upon their own Habitation, built, if not of Hay and Stubble, with Wooden Timbers, boards Clapboards and Shingles, to prevent its being Scorched by the F[l]ames from Europe.

Europe is desolated: Millions have perished in Arms glorious or inglorious: Every Nation has been Scourged by War. The United States of America have been at peace these eight and twenty years. In Foreign Relations Washington Adams Jefferson and Madison have pursued the same system, Neutrality: but I certainly knew that Washington and Adams, and believe the same of Jefferson and Madison, in case of equal Injury from France and England, and in case of an absolute Necessity of war with one or the other, would have preferred a War with Great Britain rather than France.[37]

To prefer war with the British seemed a paradox to Van der Kemp. We were prepared for war with neither nation but Napoleon's great continental power was the more dangerous to humanity. He commented further on his lack of confidence in Madison.

I am no enemy of the President—as long as he was a Private Individual—or even a head of department. I should have courted his more intimate acquaintance— could it have been performed without appearent intrusions—or servil cringing—Indirectly I have received from him marks of civility and regard. But I do not approve His political conduct—indiscriminately—It may be that here in the Woods—my prospect is too much clouded by fogs—my eyes too grown so dim, that I can not allways see the fitness of the measures pursued.

Among the Political Sins I am this instant struck by Wolcott's appointment [Bank Board]—the President's Proclamation upon Cadore's Letters [resuming trade with France]—the Proclamation with regard to the Florida's—their invasion and retrogressive motion of the army —the appointment of Joel Barlow [minister to France]—[38]

Van der Kemp was not alone in his lack of confidence in Madison's administration and in his opposition to a war with Great Britain. The Federalists won election victories in both New York and Massachusetts early in 1812. When Congress received Madison's war message on June 1, the Congressmen from New York and New England constituted the bulk of the opposition.

Van der Kemp was greatly involved in his writing in 1811 and 1812 and made few comments on national and international events in his letters of the latter year. Patriot that he was, he could not keep still among his many friends in Oneida County. His later activities indicate this. Perhaps a comment late in 1811 shows resignation to evils which he could not prevent.

Yes Sir! No Nation on earth has so long enjoy'd uninterrupted so many eminent blessings—but I scarce know any Nation, except perhaps the Dutch—so ignorant, so insensible of these blessings—so insolently trampling under their feet, so that I am highly apprehensive that without seven stripes [of a lash]—they shall not learn wisdom—neither eventually be saved—as [except] thro fire.[39]

Would the fire be war with Britain followed by the domination of Napoleon?

❧ XVI ❧

The War of 1812

WHEN President Madison sent his war message to Congress on June 1, 1812, there was no precedent to follow. The measure was recognized as of high importance, but other measures had seemed equally important to the young republic. The congressmen regarded the message as one to be debated in the usual manner. American citizens watched with interest, registering their views as best they could. Since the end of the Revolutionary War, the United States had met many international problems irresolutely, with the actions of the Barbary pirates and the crippling of the *Chesapeake* by the British as outstanding examples. Avoiding outright war despite provocations was regarded as an expedient to allow us to develop our strength. In 1812 the young nation had neither naval nor military strength. War was certainly a fit subject for debate.

The Republicans were expected to follow the recommendation of their president although the party was not well enough organized to command a party vote. The decision in Congress was made chiefly by southern and western members, urged on by the War Hawks led by Clay and Calhoun. The Federalists opposed, although not as obstructionists to Madison. They preferred peace with Great Britain so that their commerce could continue, at least in some fashion. Proponents of war, with designs on Canada, countered by pointing to prospects of making the seas completely open to our commerce.

New York State had far more at stake than the western and southern states. War would interfere with commerce out of New York City. In addition, Canada touched New York State borders both at Niagara and in the north country. The waters of Lakes Ontario and Champlain would undoubtedly be paths of British invasion. The war question meant much to Van der Kemp as a citizen of central New York and as a Federalist. He also had a son eligible for military duty.

The *Utica Patriot* carried fervent editorials in opposition to the war and expressed its approval of peace meetings by lengthy and favorable reports. "A large and respectable meeting of the Friends of Peace, Liberty, and Commerce, in the County of Oneida" occurred at Whitesboro on October 13. Resolutions against the administration were passed.[1] If Van der Kemp was not at this meeting, some of his neighbors surely were. Sentiment against the war resulted in a "peace Ticket" in the fall election. Morris Miller, a friend of Van der Kemp, carried the town of Trenton for the Peace party by a vote of 152 to 69 and other towns by similar majorities. He was elected to Congress. Editorials called Madison's war "ruinous." [2]

In the meantime soldiers, sailors and marines were passing through Oneida County on their way to Sackett's Harbor or to Fort Niagara. Some of those going to Sackett's Harbor passed through Oldenbarneveld. Newspapers reported a few contingents to be unruly and others were accused of theft where they camped. The build-up of land and sea forces on the border continued and ultimately led to action. Oneida County was not so far away but that its invasion by the British was considered possible if Niagara, Sackett's Harbor and Plattsburg did not hold.

Volunteers from Oneida County marched away north or west. Colonel Andrew W. Bellinger led a whole detachment of locals to the north and in the fall Colonel John Westcott led the Oneida militia to Sackett's Harbor. Captain John Billings of Oldenbarneveld took one company north. At home a guard was formed of the older men and

Adam Mappa became captain of the Silver Greys. He drilled the company rigidly, "put them through the manual, marched and wheeled with the boys—left—right," and tired himself "finely." [3] The state government allowed this home guard 75 muskets and one box of cartridges on loan.[4] Van der Kemp was not one of the marchers although he would have taken a musket if an invasion had threatened central New York. At the age of sixty he could do more good as a civilian by oral and written word.

Only part of what Van der Kemp wrote and spoke was recorded. Public statements doubting the fitness of Stephen Van Rensselaer for command at Niagara because he was a Federalist and an early opponent of the war surely roused Van der Kemp to his defense. The argument between the regular army and the militia found Van der Kemp favoring the state militia. When Van Rensselaer ran for governor against Tompkins, and De Witt Clinton ran against President Madison, Van der Kemp was for Van Rensselaer and Clinton. One document indicating his activity is a letter from Mappa to Morris S. Miller, newly elected congressman, written on January 6, 1813.

> . . . I take the liberty of enclosing these two little fragments of our friend Van der Kemp; if you think they are worth a little corner in the [Utica] Patriot or Albany Gazette, the printer is welcome to them, provided that no name of the author is asked, for my friend, I believe, would not wish to be dragged before the bar of the majesties.[5]

If the "fragments" were published, they were probably signed Manlius, Pro Bono Publico, Cato, or a similar classical pseudonym. This was according to the custom of the day, and allowed "letters to the editor" to be identified in series if the same writer continued his contributions. In Holland Van der Kemp had used the name Junius and in religious contributions to the *Panoplist* in 1806 he used the name Candidus. The referral of the items to Miller gave them more weight and also allowed for secrecy. It is doubtful, however, that Van der Kemp feared any reprisals from the Republican officials for his writings.

In the winter of 1812–13 an epidemic illness spread through central New York and the north country. Physicians were uncertain or in disagreement as to how to treat it, although when in doubt bleeding seemed to be the logical procedure. The disease, perhaps a virus, spread to civilians and soldiers alike. Doctor Luther Guiteau described the spread of the epidemic as follows:

> Amidst this general gloom and alarm which overspread the country, our soldiers daily falling victims—our legislature then in session at Albany witnessing the decrease of its numbers, and our citizens in every town bending beneath its force, the inhabitants of the northern towns of this [Oneida] and Herkimer county as well as the counties of Lewis and Jefferson had their full share of calamity and were thoroughly tried in the crucible of affliction.[6]

Both Mrs. Van der Kemp and Peter came down with the disease. Peter, with the stronger constitution of a young man of twenty-three, threw off the disease after some varied treatments including bleeding. His mother was not so fortunate. At the age of sixty-four she suffered a long illness "under a rigidly antiphlogistic regimen." Doctor Guiteau regretted that he did not bleed her.[7] On May 5, 1813, Van der Kemp wrote to Adams, "The severe sickness of my Son was scarce over before Mrs. VanderKemp was indisposed. She is now—after four weeks illness reconvalescent, and will —ere long recover her strenght [sic]." Mrs. Mappa and her daughter, Sophia, also had the disease but both were on the way to recovery at this time. To add to Van der Kemp's troubles, his close friend, Chancellor Robert Livingston, died and John Mifflin, his friend at Philadelphia, was very weak with the gout. The celebration of Van der Kemp's sixty-first birthday and the twenty-fifth anniversary of his landing in New York was less than joyful in 1813.[8]

The war on the northern front was disastrous to the

Americans in the campaigning of 1812. Hull had surrendered Detroit, Smyth and Van Rensselaer failed at Niagara and Dearborn did practically nothing against Montreal from his base at Plattsburg. The War Department continued to send troops to Niagara and to Sackett's Harbor and the new secretary, John Armstrong, urged General Henry Dearborn to action. The plan was to strike at the Canadian villages of Kingston and York from the Sackett's Harbor base. The attack on Kingston was not made, partly due to an erroneous report that reinforcements of European veterans had arrived. The attack on York awaited a proper buildup of forces, the arrival of spring, or the inclination of Dearborn. One small raid was made on Elizabethtown across the St. Lawrence River from Ogdensburg and a retaliatory raid by the British and Canadians on Ogdensburg.

Van der Kemp did not like what he heard about the military confusion at Sackett's Harbor. He decided to see for himself, perhaps aided and encouraged by his political friends. Sometime near the first of March he started north on the military road, either by horseback or in a sleigh, "to take a view of the boasted powerful defence of our frontiers, after the surprise of Ogdensburg, courted so long by the iterated incursions on the defenceless and peaceable Canadians." He reported the raid to have been severe with much loss of property both public and private. When he arrived at the harbor all was confusion because of an impending attack by a superior force of British veterans. The place "had more the appearance of a crowded, noisy, European fair than that of a well regulated fortified camp." No sentinels challenged those coming and going. Morale of the troops was low because of the military situation and the increasing amount of sickness. Yet Van der Kemp thought a few crack companies would "fight the Devil" if well led. The raw militia were hardly fit to fight a human foe. However, the infant navy was "in an excellent condition, full of activity, and obeying orders at a wink." Commanders James T. Leonard and Melancthon T. Woolsey had the sailors well in hand and the marines were ready too. If

Sackett's Harbor was to be saved, the naval forces would do it.[9]

No attack came until much later in the year when conditions were vastly changed. In the meantime, General Dearborn took the best of the troops on an expedition to burn the half-built frigates and the government buildings at York. From there the expedition went to Niagara where skirmishing took place but ended with no great advantages to either side. Back at Sackett's Harbor the British made an attack, having heard of the weakened condition of the base. Van der Kemp would have been even more discouraged if he had been there then. On May 28, the British appeared, were frightened off briefly by American gunboats, but landed on the following day. At the first shots the militia fled. General Jacob Brown held a position with his regulars and rallied some of the militia. The British withdrew and returned to Canada.

Van der Kemp and Mappa were both very busy men by this time. Mappa was involved in the organization of a woolen factory and Van der Kemp was finishing his major book and planning a trip to Boston. A story has been handed down that only Federalists were allowed to buy stock in the woolen mill. Prices were high and profits were good until after the war. Then the Federalists lost money.[10] The organization borrowed money from the state school fund in 1812 and later the state took action to recover this money. Van der Kemp was concerned with Mappa's overwork and possible financial losses as a friend as well as a political brother.

Van der Kemp continued to have headaches and Adams told him not to work so hard and worry so much. His visit to Boston in August of 1813, his book on natural science, his reading, and his garden took his mind away from the war. But he was never able to escape it for long.

Harrison was successful around Detroit but Wilkinson's attempt on Montreal failed. In mid-December the American forces burned Newark on the Canadian side and the British, Canadians and their Indian allies retaliated by capturing Fort Niagara and slaughtering the garrison. Then they destroyed the villages of Lewiston, Manchester, Schlosser and Tuscarora, going thence to destroy the ships at Black Rock and to burn that village along with Buffalo. The whole Niagara country was laid waste. News of the tragedy reached Oneida County and aroused the sympathy of the inhabitants. Mappa and Van der Kemp conscientiously did what they could to help. In the *Utica Patriot* appeared the following notice:

> The subscribers offer themselves to the Inhabitants of this town and village, to receive and forward any gifts, for the relief of the suffering inhabitants on the Niagara frontier, and request the cooperation to this charitable end of the Washington Benevolent Society, and Masonic Lodge.
>
> F. A. Venderkemp
> A. G. Mappa
>
> Oldenbarneveld, Jan. 19, 1814.[11]

A month later the legislature passed a $50,000 relief act to augment the compassionate aid offered by private citizens such as Van der Kemp.

The sympathetic Van der Kemp had just recovered from a serious malady at the time he offered to send relief supplies to the Niagara country. He feared the infection might be the same as that which killed his father. "An odious swelling in my right upper jaw—rending my face so monstrous to frighten babes in their mothers' laps—aided with acute head ache and severe fevers" made death appear imminent. He had used a lotion of ammoniac and vinegar. His recovery by mid-January was signified by attendance at "a party of Quadrille" at Mappa's house.[12] He was well enough to dance—and also well enough to worry about political matters again.

The Madison administration had a staunch supporter in Governor Tompkins but Federalists and Peace Democrats had no confidence in either the state or national executive. Van der Kemp heard that Jefferson was in favor of Tompkins as next president and the idea revolted him. "It seems to me he [Jefferson] could not stoop so low—if this State must provide one— [let it be] a King [Rufus]— Platt [Jonas]—a Clinton [De Witt]—or any other one, whose little finger is bigger than the soul and body of that manikin . . ." [13]

As victories were won by the British and their allies on the European continent, peace with the United States seemed more desirable. Lord Castlereagh offered to negotiate directly and Madison agreed, appointing John Quincy Adams, James A. Bayard, Henry Clay, Jonathan Russell and Albert Gallatin as commissioners. The senate confirmed the appointments in January and February, 1814. Van der Kemp rejoiced: "God's blessings on the Peace Negotiations! May the Son [J. Q. Adams] be so successful as the Father —So their country shall be indebted to them—as their benefactors! hail—happy Peace!" [14] Sober second thoughts or discussions with more pessimistic citizens caused him, three weeks later, to ask Adams if he really thought the administration was sincere in negotiating for peace on a perfect reciprocity. He said a simple yes or no would relieve his anxiety. [15]

Adams replied that he did believe the administration wanted peace, but doubted that Britain would consent to a peace of "perfect reciprocity." [16] Van der Kemp had one more comment. He hoped that Adams was correct but why did not Madison allow John Quincy Adams and William H. Crawford to conduct the negotiations? The sending of five commissioners seemed a waste of money and a discourtesy to Adams. [17]

Another phase of the war delighted and enthused Van der Kemp. In November, 1813, the Dutch rose against their French masters and in a few months were able to re-establish their independence. The definite news reached Van der Kemp early in February and he wrote happily to Adams as follows:

Fill the glass to the brim—and empty it till the last drop. Now you rejoice with your friend on the reestablished ancient Dutch Government—My friends rule once more—The Almighty make them prosper, and confound their enemies, and humble them in the dust. Was John Adams now America's President—I would beg him, how ungracefully I may beg, to send me immediately on an extraordinary mission—to congratulate the government and renew the alliance, and treaty of commerce, which we owe to you—or—had I the hundred part of the confidence in our Administration, which you so imperiously commanded, I would offer it my services—persuaded that no individual—how far my superior in talents— could be so successful.[18]

The Dutch people at Oldenbarneveld rejoiced with Van der Kemp and asked him to prepare an oration. For three weeks he read nothing "except a few of Horace's Odes" while he worked from his own extensive notes. Congratulations on the freedom of the Dutch poured in daily, one accompanied by a cooked haddock. Van der Kemp said he stopped writing long enough to eat it all. He added, "I never dreamed that I should—so near the grand climacteric year [Napoleon's downfall] have composed an oration . . . in behalf of the Dutch, and meddle anew with their history and political concerns—" [19] The oration was read at Mappa's house.

He was requested to deliver the oration at Utica, and March 12 was set for the celebration. He asked if his friends James Kipp of Utica, Majors Benjamin Newkirk and Robert Cochran at Palatine and George Huntington of Rome could be invited. He would write personally to John Bernhard at Oneida Lake, "an old zealous friend of the Orange family." [20] Well did he remember the bitter political quarrel which had caused Bernhard to go out into the even more bitter winter weather in 1795—and the great relief with which he was welcomed back into the Van der Kemp cottage.

On March 8, the following notice appeared:

Pursuant to a previous arrangement by a number of Dutch descendants in this village, who are actuated by strong emotions of joy at the deliverance of Holland, the land of their Forefathers, from the shackles of tyranny and oppression, on Friday next, at ten o'clock A.M. Francis Adrian Van der Kemp, Esq. will deliver an Oration suitable to the occasion, in the Presbyterian Church. The descendants of Dutchmen, and such other patriotic citizens as may wish to partake of the Dinner, to be prepared by Mr. Welles, will please to send their names by Thursday noon to one of the committee.[21]

On the big day a procession led by a band made its way along the streets of Utica to the church. Doctor Azel Backus, president of Hamilton College, opened the meeting. Van der Kemp gave his oration with "pathos and rapture" and appropriate gesticulations. He outlined the Dutch history and praised the people for their sufferings, their endeavors and their recent glory. The Reverend Henry Dwight, pastor of the church, gave the closing prayer. Then they adjourned to dinner and to toasting and general rejoicing. The orator proposed one of the first.

The *County of Oneida*—May its inhabitants in emulating the Dutch in their patriotism, love of liberty, frugality, industry and activity, spur their fellow citizens to imitate their example, that the State of New York may obtain that rank and influence in our union, to which it is entitled by its wealth and population.

Peter Van der Kemp added a toast somewhat later:

Morris S. Miller, our representative in Congress—a cheerful friend at home—a firm supporter of our rights in Congress.[22]

Nathan Williams, prominent attorney, judge and former congressman, wrote a letter of congratulations to Van der Kemp but questioned one word, "miscreants," which seemed to apply to Madison's supporters in their opposition to the British.[23] Van der Kemp changed the wording for the printed version to avoid political wounds but asserted that "the alliance between the Dutch and English is founded upon the most solid basis—reciprocal Interest—" [24]

Abigail and John Adams raised a question of a different nature. How could the Dutch go back to a monarchy under the House of Orange after being a republic? Van der Kemp replied to Abigail, "To be frank . . . I would prefer any Monarchical form of government, did I reside there—than to remain a subject of the French empire—even if Bonaparte was out of the question." [25] To John he said, "I approve the Dutch invitation, and the Prince's acceptance— supposing him sincere— . . . If this house provides a wise constitution—then a greater share of Liberty may fall to the lot of every inhabitant than they ever enjoy'd since the abjuration of Philip II." [26]

The printed copies were distributed to Van der Kemp's friends and sold by booksellers. De Witt Clinton and Colonel Benjamin Walker appreciated their copies. Some were sent to Holland and to France. Clinton sent a note of thanks, one of the steps in the growth of his friendship with Van der Kemp.

The orator soon became involved in his studies again and in his garden. The latter became more laborious when his son, Peter, was ill for more than a month. Even though past the age of sixty the father worked in the hay in place of his son and recalled that if he had continued a military career he could have retired at sixty.[27]

When the word reached Oldenbarneveld that the city of Washington had been burned by a small British force in late August, Van der Kemp was shocked, and aroused anew against the administration.

Alas! City of Washington! This would not have happened under your [the Adams] administration! No President ought to be bullied by his ministers [probably directed at Secretary of War, Armstrong] and he who is too good natured or to weak—to controul the whole entrusted to his care . . . ought to resign the reins—[28]

The British had only retaliated for the unnecessary burning
of York and several villages of Canada. Van der Kemp did
not approve of any of the burning but he did believe in
good defense.

At Oldenbarneveld he saw more confusion in the movement of troops to Sackett's Harbor. Men and supplies passed
through and then returned because of counterorders. Such
confusion led to grave concern in a father whose son was of
military age. In September the Oneida quota was drafted,
in it Peter Van der Kemp. "He declined to volunteer—but
was determined to go at his country's call—" The boy's
mother and sister were quite upset but the father was proud
of his son. Betsy made Peter's knapsack and got his equipment ready. The company was ordered to be ready to march
the next day but counterorders during the night stopped
the departure and the whole outfit was discharged. Within
a day or two General George Izard passed through the village with four thousand men on his way from Plattsburg
to Sackett's Harbor.[29] Perhaps this was why Peter's company was not needed. This move was for diversionary purposes and actually weakened the American position at Plattsburg just before a British attack.

A month later Peter was called up under the new state
conscription law and this time marched to Sackett's Harbor.
Rumors reported the post to be in considerable danger. "The
English fleet is in sight—Ours is brave and commanded by
an expert, gallant and worthy officer—God give [grant] our
militia may be firm—but they are chiefly without arms, and
I doubt, that there is a sufficient supply." [30]

The new conscription law angered Van der Kemp and
Mappa. In October Van der Kemp began writing letters
and newspaper articles. A letter to Benjamin Walker gives
part of his activity.

As Judge [Morris S.] Miller and Mr. Varick [Abraham]
are absent, and I doubt if Mr. Jerh. v. Rensselaer is at
home—I send you enclosed [articles] *for the press*—requesting the publication with all possible speed. . . .
You shall I know agree with me about our critical sit-

uation, and that the only way to prevent disturbances
—and avert—perhaps—this deadly blow on our liberty
is to show the danger, and prepare the minds against
it. . . .

Friend Mappa urges immediate publication—a small
pamphlet in 8^e as the oration. It may then next week
be republished in the U. papers. It may be printed in a
day. Lothrop [editor of *Utica Patriot*] shall not decline
to correct the too great coarseness of Idiom. . . .

As *soon* it is published—I intend—to procure a town-
meeting in this place—to have the subject canvassed—

Tomorrow I shall send you another copy—to be forwarded to Albany, either for the N. papers of Websters
and Southwick—or for separate publication as may be
deemed best—Perhaps [Abraham] Van Vechten—or any
other acquaintance of us would charge himself with the
trouble.

We shall send a third copy to our friends in N. York
to have it inserted there likewise in the papers or published separately. . . .

Mappa was of opinion the signature of *an Exempt*
was preferable—if my name is prefered—upon maturer
consideration you are at liberty to use it. . . .[31]

The major article did appear in pamphlet form and occupied three columns in the *Albany Gazette* of November
17. It was titled, "An Address to the Citizens of Oneida
County on the Subject of the Late Law of this State, for
Raising 12,000 Men by Classification of the Militia." It was
signed, "By an Exempt." [32] A second article of similar nature addressed to the citizens of Madison county, was published through the arrangements of Peter Smith. Van der
Kemp also wrote a public letter to James Monroe, now secretary of war, intended for publication.[33]

The response was not encouraging. Van der Kemp could
not keep bitterness from his comment to Adams.

My son is yet at the Harbour—and I see him again—
in his Native State—doomed to conscription and the Con-

stitution violated by them who had sworn to be its guardians—If my fellow-citizens submit to this—they do not deserve the liberty acquired by their fathers blood—they deserve a Master—and the glorious deeds of the Heroes of 76—the example of an Adams had been for me an innocent lure—to throw my Offspring in Slavery—when I meant to save it from the fangs of European Despots.[34]

In December a bill was presented in Congress to provide for conscription. Representative Morris S. Miller, who had aided Van der Kemp in his work on the state level, made an able speech against it. This speech was published in pamphlet form early in 1815.[35] Miller and Van der Kemp were in correspondence at this time. Van der Kemp wrote that he approved Miller's reflections on the bank bill because peace seemed so doubtful, the administration not being "sincere in wishing it." He agreed with Miller that the cause of the nation was "desperate." The people of New York State were "in a deplorable torpor" and would not awake before the terrible "knife" of despotism was at their throats. Not a person was stirring besides himself. The address he had written had been "horribly mangled" by the press but he had written two more smaller articles. He did not intend to betray his country by surrendering rights "for whose preservation I crossed the Atlantic—I will live or die a free man." He implored the congressman to write something to rouse the citizens now suffering sickness and death from repeated unnecessary mustering of forces and "without a farthing of their promised wages." [36]

Whitesboro had a public meeting of more than two thousand citizens to consider conscription on January 27, 1815. They passed resolutions and sent a memorial to the legislature.[37] But peace had already been made. Reports came and with them a rumor that Madison refused the treaty of the commissioners. Van der Kemp said had it been true nothing could have prevented him from loading Madison "with a hearty curse." [38]

The peace was accepted and announced. Van der Kemp

with another Federalist and two Republicans arranged the celebration in Oldenbarneveld. He felt much better. Some two hundred villagers and others assembled for the reading of the treaty, and marched in procession with a band. Every house was decorated and lighted. Van der Kemp believed the day would bring greater harmony to the people and that now he could look forward to dying in peace.[39] War was over, conscription was over, Peter would return, all was well—for the moment.

⚜ XVII ⚜

Visit to Boston

THE trip to Boston in the summer of 1813 was one of the happiest events of Van der Kemp's long eventful life. It was an escape from unpleasant worries about the unhappy War of 1812, and it was almost a convention of educated, enlightened, and wonderfully pleasant people. In addition, he was the honored guest and the center of attention wherever he went.

The idea originated in his correspondence with John Adams and a growing acquaintance with Abigail. In 1809, two of Abigail's letters were published. Van der Kemp chanced upon them and read them with great pleasure. He praised her writing to John and thereby touched his friend deeply.

> There have been few ladies in the world of a more correct or elegant taste. A collection of her letters, for the forty-five years that we have been married, would be worth ten times more than Madame de Sevigne's though not so perfectly measured in syllables and letters, and would, or at least ought to put to the blush Lady Mary Wortley Montagu and all her admirers. So much you will say, for conjugal complaisance. So much, I say, for simple justice to her merit.[1]

Van der Kemp said he had been totally unaware of Abigail's writing. "Could it be known in the Western woods?" He was "buried in a corner of Oldenbarneveld" where

friends sometimes passed him by. He asked to be informed
when more of Abigail's letters were published. Van der
Kemp considered them far superior to Lady Montagu's
letters, in which he "searched in vain for that placid
modesty—that sweetness of manners—that pleasing timidity
and delicacy which adorn every female beauty and virtue,
and conquer our hearts involuntarily—" [2]

Early in 1811 Van der Kemp wrote that he would like
to go visiting for his health, and casually remarked that he
wished it could be to Quincy. Adams was pleased with the
idea. He thought Van der Kemp would enjoy his library
and some of the surrounding scenery. He assured him "the
comforts of life" would be offered; the Adamses were "little
concerned with the luxuries." Apparently he too was thinking of a trip, possibly to central New York. He asked how
far Van der Kemp lived from Lebanon in the vicinity of
Hamilton where Adams' daughter, Abigail Smith, had her
home.[3]

Van der Kemp learned from Peter Smith that the daughter lived in his general area of Peterboro and that he
understood Mrs. Adams planned to visit her daughter
during the summer. Van der Kemp said he would go to
Lebanon and pay his respect to Mrs. Adams, even if the
roads were bad,[4] but Abigail was not able to make the trip.

Later in the year Adams sent two volumes of the proceedings of the Academy of Arts and Sciences in Boston to
Lebanon to be forwarded to Van der Kemp, and Abigail
sent two volumes of John Quincy's lectures.[5] Van der Kemp
wrote a special note of thanks to Abigail, including a
prediction that John Quincy would become president.[6]

The correspondence between the two friends in Oldenbarneveld and Quincy showed an increasingly warm interest in each other's life and family. Early in 1813 Adams
wrote, "Oh! that my situation in Life would permit me to
undertake a Pilgrimage to Oldenbarneveldt!" He said he
would like to stop there both coming and going to Lebanon.
He would see and adore Mrs. Van der Kemp again and
would delight in the gardens of Mappa.[7] But Adams was

seventy-seven, and traveling by stage was too strenuous for him. He said if Van der Kemp would come to Quincy, he would show him "a pretty Hill, and what might be made a pretty Farm, the Athenaeum in Boston and a Botanical Garden at Cambridge; and a friendly heart." [8]

In the summer Adams wrote that both his philosophy and religion were being sorely tried. His only daughter, come from Lebanon, was in the next room on her death-bed. Abigail was worn down "with care, exertion and anxiety." In the midst of this a disease had struck his own eyes. Now he had just been informed Samuel Eliot had sent for Van der Kemp to come visit his son, Charles Eliot, who was dying of consumption. Samuel was wealthy and could pay the expenses.

In spite of their sorrows, Adams rejoiced at the prospect of seeing his old friend. "If you come this way, no Man will be more glad to see you than the Hermit of Quincy, though amidst all the Afflictions of his Household.[9]

Van der Kemp set out by stagecoach in the middle of August. It could have been a journey of sadness, yet Van der Kemp's encouraging manner, his wit and energy, his intelligent conversations, and his warm appreciation of the kindness of his friends left them all in better spirits.

Two letters to his daughter give some of the details of the enthusiasm and the pathos that enfolded Van der Kemp.[10]

Your letter afforded me an inexpressible pleasure—I was just returned from Cambridge. Judges, Lawyers, Ministers, Doctors come and see me as if I was indeed something, and know not that my goodwill is my prin-cipal merit, while it is to the partiality of my friends that I am indebted for the rest. . . . Saturday and Friday night Dr. Thatcher [sic], Channing, Holley visited me.

Samuel Cooper Thacher was a graduate of Harvard, one of the editors of the *Monthly Anthology* which Van der Kemp read, and at this time pastor of the (Unitarian) New South Church, following Dr. John T. Kirkland in that position when the latter became president of Harvard. He was a close friend of the late Joseph S. Buckminster, a correspondent of Van der Kemp. William Ellery Channing was pastor of the (Unitarian) Federal Street Church at this time. Horace Holley was also a Unitarian minister of Boston.

> Mr. Eliot [Samuel] took a walk with me to show me a part of the city—I must tell you in one word the city and the country and the inhabitants exceed far the most glowing and partial expectation—it is impossible to form of it an adequate concept. I must say come and see. Mr. Holley introduced me in the Athenaeum [private reading club and library of these educated men] and shewed the Library of John Quincy Adams of several thousand volumes. Sunday I heard Mr. Holley. After church Dr. Freeman and Mr. Carey visited me.

Dr. James Freeman was pastor of King's Chapel, Boston, from 1787 to 1826 and was the first to use the designation Unitarian. The Reverend Samuel Carey was his assistant and colleague at this time. Freeman wrote articles and sermons and was a member of the Academy of Arts and Sciences, to which Van der Kemp belonged, and of the Massachusetts Historical Society.

> Monday Mr. Eliot carried me with his carriage to Quincy—it was there a house of mourning indeed—I was received with affectionate tenderness as a beloved Brother could be—I was there at home again. Mr. Eliot returned. There again Adams brought me in the afternoon with his coach to a neighbouring Doctor and shewed me the environs.

When Van der Kemp stepped inside the Adams home, he failed to recognize Abigail, not having seen her since 1788. She was "a little mortified that he could not trace one line of a countanance he formerly knew" even though she knew "Grief had changed me since you saw me last and carefull —with Times deformed hand hath written strange the features o'er my face." But Abigail was well pleased with their guest.

For myself, I have so long known you, as the invariable Friend; and correspondent of my Husband; that every Sentiment of my Heart, was a veneration for your tallents, and respect for your Learning. I expected a feast of Reason—but that flow of soul, so nicely blended with a delicacy of perception, "which feels at each touch" was more than I had anticipated! and Mr. Vanderkemp now stands before me—not the recluse bookworm, but as the man of profound Learning as the polite Gentleman, whose modesty will not permit him to estimate his own worth.[11]

The moments and hours of good fellowship flew by and Van der Kemp found time to introduce only a few of the subjects on which he hoped to have Adams' comments. He had time only to glance at the Adams library and forgot even to look at his rare books. He apologized for talking too much and with too much spirit. "You know the impetuosity of my manhood—in my old age I am carried away by the same resistless torrent . . ."[12] They discussed their basic religious beliefs and found they were much alike.[13] Adams said, "In the heavenly doctrine of Christianity, reduced to its primitive Simplicity, you and I agree, as well, I believe, as any two Christians in the World."[14]

The morning after Van der Kemp arrived, John Adams got out his carriage and took Van der Kemp to visit the Josiah Quincys before going on to Samuel Eliot's house. Van der Kemp and Quincy were attracted to each other at once. Quincy was a studious man, only forty-one years old at the time of Van der Kemp's visit. He was a strong Federalist, and Francis had to promise to return to the Quincy home for a longer visit because they had so many ideas they were eager to share. Quincy had served in Congress where he was a member of the Essex Junto. He opposed the War of 1812 but supported the war effort. He confined his activities to Massachusetts after the war, serving in the legislature, in the Constitutional Convention, as mayor of Boston and as president of Harvard. Mrs. Quincy was the former Eliza Susan Morton of New York City.

Tuesday afternoon new visitants and invitation to see the pourtrait of Buckminister at Sam. Dexter's. Wednesday Mr. Tyng [Dudley], Brother in law of Mrs. Eliot, brought me in his carriage to Cambridge where I was introduced again to numbers, saw a large and exquisite Library, was placed in the procession [at the Harvard commencement] with distinction, in the church occupied no less honourable place, heard all the performances, dined at the college and drank tea by the President Kirkland who introduced me to the Governor, Lieutenant Governor, and a host of Doctors. I was present again at the solemnities in the morning, and dined at the President's, where among the guests was Judge Smith, late Governor of New Hampshire, several Judges, and a brother of Abbot [Abiel] of Coventry.

Van der Kemp was especially impressed with the cordiality of President Kirkland. He was the son of that Samuel Kirkland who had served with the Oneida Indians as a missionary and founded the mission school that became Hamilton College. John Kirkland was born in the Mohawk Valley in the old Herkimer mansion. He was educated at Harvard, became a clergyman and was called to the presidency of Harvard in 1810. Van der Kemp later wrote how President Kirkland called on him and persuaded him to go to the commencement so that he was able to enjoy his company for two days.[15]

Samuel Dexter was secretary of war under Adams and was otherwise a prominent lawyer, statesman and writer. Dudley Atkins Tyng was born Atkins but added the last name when he inherited the Tyng wealth. He was a lawyer, served as collector of Newburyport, and became reporter of the Massachusetts Supreme Court and editor of the *Reports*.

After dinner he [Abbot] too came to see me. Towards evening old Mr. Eliot came with his carriage to bring me to Boston. Norton had been my guide and companion.

Andrews Norton helped found the *General Repository and Review* to which Van der Kemp contributed. Norton became librarian at Harvard in 1813 and became a lecturer on theology through a bequest of Samuel Dexter. Norton was a close associate and friend of Charles Eliot.

Messrs. Savage, Abbot of Boston, Dr. Prince of Salem, another of Exeter, Messrs. Everett, Prof. Peck and Ware; (by the latter I breakfasted), were among the principal of my new acquaintances.

John Lovejoy Abbot was pastor of First Church in Boston and had been librarian at Harvard before Norton. Ashur Ware was a professor of theology at Harvard. Professor Peck had the wonderful botanical garden that Adams had promised to show Van der Kemp. Edward Everett had been graduated from Harvard in 1811 and was already a promising minister.

Charles [Eliot] was yesterday, as a mark of particular esteem, unanimously chosen at Cambridge a member of the P.b.k. [Phi Beta Kappa] Society an honour seldom or never bestowed out of the college. Today I must dine with Mr. Eliot's son in law—I had an urgent invitation of Dr. Morse [Jedidiah].

A week or so after the first letter, Van der Kemp wrote again to his daughter, picking up the thread of exciting events as before.

Tomorrow I leave Boston—Friday morning I left Mr. and Mrs. Adams. Col. Smith [Adams' son-in-law] brought me home. My worthy friend was much affected at my departure, as it is presumptive that we shall see one another no more. He failed not once to remember Mappa and your Mother at Olden Barneveld, and regretted more than once that you or she had not accompanied me.

After his return home, Adams wrote that if Van der Kemp had come as a traveler, the Adams house would have been his home and the Adams friends would have been the visitor's companions. He said that Abigail shared his feelings. Adams recognized that his wife had changed much since Van der Kemp last saw her in 1788. "Whatever changes in her en bon point, her bloom, her vivacity, her figure or her graces you may have perceived there has been none in her Friendship her Esteem her Affection or may I say Admiration for you.[16] He wrote to Jefferson:

> Theognis and Plato, and Hersey and Price, and Jefferson and I, must go down to posterity together; and I know not, upon the whole, where to wish for better company. I wish to add Vanderkemp, who has been here to see me after an interruption of twenty-four years.[17]

Abigail wrote to Van der Kemp "of the high gratification his visit to Quincy afforded his ancient Friends." They only regretted he could spare so little time.[18]

> Mrs. Eliot rejoiced at my return, it was a day later. My new friends renewed their visits, Chief Justice Parsons, Messrs. Lowell and Norton. In the afternoon Mr. Eliot ordered his coach to have me brought again to Cambridge with his brother [in law] Tyng to see Prof. Peck's cab[inet] of Nat. Hist. and Hortus Botanicus. In the evening I saw Charles. Saturday I dined with Mr. Eliot at his son in law's, Sunday morning I went with Mr. and Mrs. Eliot and daughters to Lowell's church and partook of the Lord's Supper, while I heard in the afternoon President Kirkland, who visited me during intermission.
>
> There is no longer any hope of Charles Eliot's recovery. I shall see Charles' sister at Springfield and stay there one day, after this visit I must stay one day with your friend Sophia Childs.[18]

Van der Kemp found his visit to Charles Eliot very sorrowful. He did not recover quickly from the experience, even though he knew his visit brightened young Charles and was deeply appreciated by his parents. Samuel Eliot,

the father, wrote to Adams that the short acquaintance
made him believe Van der Kemp's heart was as good as his
head was powerful.

> Your thirty years knowledge of him has not indeed
> deceived you Sir, & he is truly what you lately denomi-
> nated him—"a salt mountain"—& a few such would
> preserve a world! I bless God that I have the honor &
> happiness of knowing such a *man!* [19]

Charles Eliot died two weeks later.

On his return Van der Kemp was hospitably received at
Springfield, Stockbridge and Pittsfield by relatives of his
new friends and by the family of Dr. Timothy Childs. Van
der Kemp and these new acquaintances "canvassed and
reviewed" many interesting topics but not nearly all that
the visitor might have wished.[20]

The trip was a great success. Van der Kemp impressed
the Unitarian clergymen, the Eliots and their friends, and
above all the Adamses. John said the visit was "universally
agreeable" and that even "the disciples of Calvin, Sandiman
and Hopkins" preserved a "respectful silence." [21]

Abigail became very ill later in the year of a "pulmonary
fever," probably a result of all the sickness in the family
during the year and her efforts to nurse them all. She improved and Van der Kemp suggested she follow "Paul's
prescription." "Let her take a glass generous wine—this
shall renew the elasticity of the vital springs. We can not do
this by proxy—or I should not object to submit to this
penance in her place." [22]

In February Abigail was well enough to write to Van
der Kemp, chiefly about the status of learned women, a
subject which had been discussed by John and Francis in
their letters and probably again discussed by the three of
them in the Adams home.

> Dear Sir,
> Ever since your letter to the President, of December
> last, I have had a great inclination to address a letter to

Mr. Vanderkemp; and, being now confined to my chamber, by an attack of the rheumatism, I find a leisure hour to address my friend in his solitude.

And in the first place, to put him perfectly at his ease, I assure him that I make not any pretensions to the character of a learned lady, and therefore, according to his creed, I am entitled to his benevolence. I can say with Gay's hermit,

> "The little knowledge I have gained,
> Is all from simple nature drained."

I agree with Mr. Vanderkemp, that, in declaring his opinion, he has expressed that of most gentlemen, the true cause of which I shall trace no farther than that they consider a companion more desirable than a rival. In reading the life of Madame de Stael, I learn that it was her superior talents and learning, perhaps too ostentatiously displayed, which produced that coldness, estrangement, and unhappiness, which marred all her pleasure with the Baron de Stael, soured every domestic enjoyment and was the occasion of that sarcastic question to her by the Emperor Bonaparte. Upon some occasion, she had solicited an interview with him, and recommended to him some measure for him to pursue. He heard her, but made her no other reply than this: "Madame, who educates your children?"

I like your portrait of female excellence. . . .

There are so few women who may be really called learned, that I do not wonder they are considered as black swans. It requires such talents and such devotion of time and study, as to exclude the performance of most of the domestic cares and duties which exclusively fall to the lot of most females in this country. I believe nature has assigned to each sex its particular duties and sphere of action, and to act well your part, "there all the honor lies."

Have you seen John Randolph's letter and Mr. Lloyd's reply?

Present me in friendly terms to Mrs. Vanderkemp. Tell her, I wish we were neighbours. I should then have a pleasure which our residence in the country deprives us of, that of the society and converse of a gentleman of taste, science, and extensive information; and, although much of his learning might be above my comprehension, his benevolence, politeness, and urbanity would render it grateful, and be in unison with the good-will and friendship entertained for him by

Abigail Adams [23]

Of course, Abigail's modesty prevented her from being ostentatious about her learning, although she was an accomplished writer. Her letters to Van der Kemp include a perceptive discussion of the Dutch situation and a considerable variety of other topics, usually enlivened with anecdotes. Because Van der Kemp was also modest, she tried to assure him of his high standing. She reported to him that Mrs. Josiah Quincy was his "warm and respectfull friend" and ultimately it was to this lady that Van der Kemp gave Abigail's letters for proper keeping. When John was ill and Abigail needed assurance as to her husband's religion, Van der Kemp wrote to her that he was persuaded that "practice not Speculation makes the Christian."

When Van der Kemp suffered from his recurrent headaches and became very depressed, Abigail wrote that he should cultivate cheerfulness of mind since that acted like a medicine. Surely he was too much of a philosopher and Christian to let the "Nubs and stings of outrageous fortune" deprive him of his sense of humor. "Why then my good Sir do you so often suffer the glooms of imagination to take such fast hold of you?" Then she added a little poem in translation of one of Pindar's gems.

Care to our coffin adds a nail, no doubt
And every grin so merry draws one out
I own I like to laugh and hate to sigh

And think that risibility was given
For human happiness by gracious heaven
And that we came not into life to cry.
Enjoy, be lively, innocent adore
And know that Heav'n hath not one angel more,
In consequence of groaning nuns and friars.[24]

Of all the friends Van der Kemp saw on his visit, Abigail was the closest in understanding.

❧ XVIII ❧

Religious and
Historical Publications

WHEN Van der Kemp visited Boston, his warm reception
by the clergy, particularly the Unitarians, was due in part
to his religious writing. Some of the Massachusetts religious
leaders knew that Van der Kemp had helped to found the
Oldenbarneveld church and most of them had read his
defense of John Sherman. His learned contributions to the
religious magazines, *Panoplist* and the *General Repository,*
were known and appreciated.

It was natural for Van der Kemp to write on religion
in the western woods, as he had written and published a
great many sermons and religious essays back in Holland.
It was also easier, because he had brought with him to
America a large volume of religious notes as well as some
of his religious books. History gave a framework to his religious knowledge as it did to his political and scientific
knowledge. He used history extensively as a method of
studying religion.

The Panoplist, or the Christian's Armory was a religious
periodical that began in 1805. Van der Kemp read it regularly. Contributors included many well-known writers of
the day in the field of religion. In the early issues appeared
biographies of such divines as David Tappan, Archibald
Maclaine and Dr. Samuel Finley. Articles dealt with proofs
of the universal deluge, the wickedness of skepticism and

experimental religion. However, in October, 1805, two articles criticized John Sherman's book. Soon afterwards appeared "The Doctrine of the Trinity Universal," "Remarkable Conversion of a Deist," and a favorable review of Dow's *Familiar Letters to Sherman,* the same Dow whom Van der Kemp later castigated so severely in his *Wreath.* The "Life of Martin Luther" ran in several instalments. Then in October, 1806, came an account of Calvin's approval of the execution of Michael Servetus, taken from Jean Senebier's history.

This was as much as Van der Kemp could endure without expressing his strong opinions. He wrote to the editor of the *Panoplist,* Jedidiah Morse. First he offered his services in the projected revision of Morse's geography books, suggesting that Mappa would know the Black River country and that he might add some information on Europe, presumably Holland. Then he reacted to the *Panoplist* article:

> Having prepared for a friend a Short Literary Sketch of Servetus . . . I was engaged in giving him an account of that transaction of the deplored hate of that man at Geneva, when I received the last number of the Panoplist —in which I met an Extract of Sennebier by which—I candidly confess—my indignation was roused—You cannot approve it. I now intend to publish a genuine account of this transaction—and have pointed out the defects of Sennebier's relation. If you approve it, or rather I must say, if propriety and delicacy permits the Editors of the Panoplist, and I cannot see why not, the insertion of this Review—I am willing to prepare for them the next—and conclude all with the Litt. Sketch of the Restituto Christianismi—The whole shall thus be three articles of about the same lenght [sic].—[Signed "Candidus"] [1]

This letter was sent to an incorrect address and received no recognition until March, 1807, when a note appeared in the periodical, "Candidus is just received but is too late for this month." In the meantime, Van der Kemp had sent a "query" or "letter to the editor" commenting on a different article, which appeared in the February issue.

In a past issue of the periodical a set of rules for preaching had included the advice, "Discover no more of your plan than needs must." The author said that if "plan" meant system of doctrine, it was important to disclose it candidly. If "plan" meant the particular points to be treated in the development of the sermon, the preacher "*must needs* state them explicitly, if he would hope to gain the attention of his hearers." Van der Kemp had recently heard a clergyman begin with a statement that he should disclose no more of his plan than was necessary. After listening to the complete sermon, Van der Kemp concluded that the plan was still undisclosed. If the preacher took his method from the *Panoplist,* then that periodical should explain that the subject should be "placed in a lucid point of view" and discourage this "ambiguous mode of preaching." This also was signed, "Candidus." [2]

This insertion caused no evident stir among the editors or readers but the criticisms of Senebier roused a conflict. In the April issue the editors answered "Candidus" by declining to print his account of Servetus on the grounds that it was not concise enough and did not list sufficiently its authorities. They were not convinced that Senebier was wrong, especially since the extract had received the sanction of the late Dr. John Erskine. Two of Van der Kemp's remarks were quoted:

> It cannot be contested that the reformers were pretty generally ["we should say in too frequent instances," ed.] actuated by a blind, intemperate zeal against all, whom they suspect to be enemies of the gospel of truth, and embraced, too often, improper methods for its support, which by the more candid and Christian sentiments of our day, are disapproved. . . . It becomes us to state

historical facts fairly; then we may try, as far as truth will allow, to lessen *their* faults, who greatly sinned through ignorance. . . .

Had Sennebier, to extenuate Calvin's guilt, fairly acknowledged this instance of human weakness, and expatiated on Calvin's piety, . . . [writings and modesty]; had Sennebier delineated with few strokes, the turbulent spirit of democracy rankling in every breast at Geneva, Calvin's high authority in that city, with his uncontrolled power in the church, as president in the assembly of the clergy and ecclesiastical judicatory; had he shown this reformer exasperated by the virulent invectives of his haught antagonist, and urged his irritable temper unused to brook opposition, he might have induced his readers to deplore the frailty of Calvin, and to avert their eyes from a foul spot in such a bright character. . . .

The editors added that if the writer wished to submit further materials, they would be treated "with the respect due their author." [3]

Van der Kemp had recently read Hermann Venema's *Ecclesiastical History* in seven volumes, Michel de La-Roche's *Bibliotheque Anglaise ou Histoire Literaire de la Grande-Bretagne,* Johann Von Mosheim's *Life of Servetus,* and Frederic Samuel Bock's *History of the Antitrinitarians.* In a cordial letter to Morse, he asserted that these authors used authoritative documents rather than often unreliable secondary material. Van der Kemp hoped to send "Exegetical or Historical Scraps" to the *Panoplist* from time to time. He was "fully satisfied" with the remarks of the April issue but went ahead with comments critical of Senebier's history. He said he would prepare a life of Calvin with a short statement of "what *did* happen to Servetus." His closing lines classed Calvin as a demagogue.[4]

In the June issue the editors said the letter of Candidus led "into too wide a field of discussion" for the purpose of the periodical. They respected the writer and would wait for his comments on Calvin and Servetus before they wrote the life of Calvin for the *Panoplist*. They promised that Candidus would have no reason to complain of their treatment of the "transaction in question."⁵ Van der Kemp was disappointed with this answer. He believed he had given good sources and that only the approval of Erskine was given by the *Panoplist* for its support of Senebier.⁶ If the editors had withheld his "strictures" until he gave proofs, it would have been fairer than by trying to overwhelm him by the mention of Erskine.⁷

Van der Kemp finished the sketch of Calvin's life and sent it to Morse in October. He requested Morse's editing and offered the essay to the *Panoplist* in part if they could not use the whole. He believed that his sources were proof of the historical truth and the falsity of Senebier.⁸ The editors replied in the December issue with evident pleasure, thanking Candidus for his sketch which manifested his "learning, diligence and fidelity"; they hoped to use the sketch in a manner corresponding to his wishes. They also stated Candidus had sent an article on the authorship of the Epistle to the Hebrews which would be printed in the next issue.⁹

Van der Kemp was pleased and by the end of the year had the short essay on Servetus almost completed. It was composed chiefly of compilations from printed books and manuscripts and was valuable chiefly "for its authentic materials—brought together in one point of view." He was not afraid of Morse's rigidity against such a point of view, believing him to be liberal to outsiders even though he was a leader of orthodox Calvinism. Van der Kemp asked the *Panoplist* to give an account of the church in Marietta and suggested that one of the editors should expose the incoherence of the Unitarian constitution drawn up in Philadelphia.¹⁰

Van der Kemp's short article on the authorship of the Epistle to the Hebrews appeared in the *Panoplist* in January, 1808. It contained eight persuasive points taken from the works of Venema showing that Apollos wrote the letter. Although the editors accepted the article for publication, they felt their responsibilities called for a note of warning. The readers should use great caution because some of the arguments were "easily exposed" and some of the ideas tended "to diminish the authority of the Epistle to the Hebrews." [11]

Also in this number appeared the first instalment of "Sketch of the Life and Character of John Calvin," "taken from the *Religious Monitor,* with the addition of several extracts of a communication received from a learned and ingenious correspondent" (Van der Kemp).[12]

Francis waited for the magazine's publication of his material on Servetus with the description of his trial. Instead, only a repetition of Senebier's account was given. He wrote to Morse, "I am sorry that the nature of your work—perhaps your delicate situation too seems to prevent an insertion of my letters on Servetus—more so—as now you have sanctioned with your credit an indefensible account." He argued that a great man like Calvin did not need to have one error whitened. If Morse were writing about David, would he condone his murderous acts because he was great? On the other side, Servetus, too, was a great person. Though he was in error in some ways, he should not be painted black because of Calvin. The editors were also prejudiced and partial in saying the Socinians of old and the modern Unitarians had placed Calvin in an odious light. Van der Kemp knew that the Socinians opposed Calvin but also opposed Servetus, and that the latter was not the ancestor of Unitarianism. Again he insisted Senebier had misrepresented the facts of the Servetus case.[13]

After these sharp remarks Van der Kemp praised several recent articles in the *Panoplist* and commented extensively on a letter by "Timothy" on Van der Kemp's "Authorship of the Epistle to the Hebrews." He particularly thanked him for mentioning the work by Dr. James M. Macknight; he acquired a copy immediately. But "what matters it to a Sincere Christian, if Paul or Apollos or Luke was the writer —provided the book is convince [convincing]—the author

an inspired writer?" He offered to send some thoughts of
Venema on church government and some ideas of his
cousin, J. C. Van der Kemp, an orthodox Calvinist.[14] Van
der Kemp was too liberal for an orthodox publication. He
did not really belong in the *Panoplist*.

A comprehensive view of his generation of mankind had
been gradually forming in Van der Kemp's mind. Now it
came to light in a lengthy outline of a proposed history.
It never developed into more than a sketchy outline but
the title was descriptive of Van der Kemp's inclusive view:
"Moral and physical causes of the revolutionary spirit in
the latter part of the eighteenth century, with their probable issue on both continents." In the outline Calvin and
Servetus were not even mentioned and the Reformation
received only two lines.

The first draft of the outline was sent to Adams early
in 1811. Adams replied, "Lord! Sir, you have planned more
Work . . . than could be executed by any body in twenty
years: by me, not in 50 or 100." To a suggestion that John
Quincy Adams might write the work, the father replied
that he would never have the time or the means.[15] Adams
showed further interest by asking for the principal topics
and making a list of eleven topics as possibilities.[16]

In December Francis sent a more complete draft of the
"Sketch" to Adams. With a touch of humor, John asked:

What Title do you intend to give it?
An History of The Decline and Fall of Christianity?
   or
An History of The Improvement of the Human Mind?
   or
An History of The Progress of Society?

He added seven others, all in fun. He also asked why the
author omitted such characters as Tom Paine, Voltaire,
Luzac, Van der Kemp and a number of others.[17] Van der
Kemp replied that Adams' ludicrous titles would be in-
gredients only. He added that Mappa agreed with him that
John Quincy Adams should do the work.[18]

Van der Kemp also sent a copy to Jefferson and received a lengthy reply. The elder statesman said the outline was "a wonderful mass for contemplation" but that its author was best fitted to develop it. Jefferson hoped it would be "executed in the genuine republican principles of our constitution" including the "only orthodox object" of government—"the greatest degree of happiness possible to the general mass of those associated under it." Events listed in the outline would certainly prove the need for popular control of those chosen to govern, thereby preventing the rise of aristocracy and oppression, but the Constitution might not contain the "exact degree" of control necessary. Since distance from "the brigand governments of Europe" permitted America to experiment without interruption, Van der Kemp might encourage and nourish the project, might warn his fellow citizens "of the rocks and shoals on which other political associations have been wrecked" so that they might "direct theirs with a better knolege [sic] of the dangers in it's [sic] way." [19]

Van der Kemp also sent a copy to De Witt Clinton and asked if he could be persuaded "to embody this skeleton" and inspire it with life.[20] Later it was sent to LeRoy, Bayard & McEvers, an importing house of New York through which Van der Kemp sent and received communications and books from Europe. Van der Kemp wrote that he was including the *Sketch,* to be sent on to Dr. Joshua Toulmin in England. He wished the gentlemen of the company to peruse it first (probably William Bayard was closest to Van der Kemp), and perhaps show it to Rufus King. The author had no hope of executing the work but expected to copy the outline and send it to friends on the continent who might complete it. He said he would rejoice if a set of Europeans would "favour us with a grand Tableau." [21] At least two others, Paul Busti and Charles Eliot, had copies in 1813.

Adams asked what philosophy was intended for the work since "Every History must be founded on some Philosophy and some Policy." He said if he were writing a history, he would found it on the "Morality of the Gospel and leave all other Philosophy and Policy to shift for itself." [22] Other comments passed between the two friends having a bearing on the "Desired Work," such as Van der Kemp's interest in "the Negotiations of John Adams at the Courts of St. James, Versailles and the Hague" and Adams' reply that the documents were too scattered for either of them to collect. Later Adams said that his friend took a vast view of civilization and humanity, while his own was usually superficial and narrow. However, he would "guess" that all the wars of the previous fifty years were only a continuation of the wars of the Reformation.[23] And in turn Van der Kemp wrote that his idea of history was to compare the reigns of Louis XVI and Napoleon as to population, wealth, finances, arts, sciences, commerce, manufactures, agriculture, laws, police, constitution, liberty, exercise of power, army and navy.[24] John was asked to send his copy of the "Sketch" to John Quincy Adams, who was now the ambassador to England, for his perusal and to share with his English friends.[25]

The *Monthly Anthology* was published in Boston from 1804 to 1811. This literary and theological magazine frequently came to Van der Kemp's attention and he therefore was interested in its successor, the *General Repository and Review,* edited by Andrews Norton. In the first year of publication (1812) Van der Kemp undoubtedly read such articles as "Defence of Liberal Christianity," "An Important Question Examined" [doctrine of the Trinity], and "Extracts from Madame DeStael's Memoirs." In various issues of the magazine were Abbot's statement on his removal from his church at Coventry, "Lectures and Essay on Comets," and "Account of Expeditions to the Sources of the Mississippi" by Pike.

The "Sketch," with a few changes suggested directly or indirectly by Jefferson, Adams and others, was sent to editor Norton and was published in the October, 1813, issue with a short but appropriate introduction.

We insert the following at the request of a very respectable correspondent, who says—"If this sketch deserve your approbation, I shall be gratified if you procure it a place, under the article of Intelligence, in the next number of the Repository. I am tired of copying it, and in my opinion it would be a valuable work if well executed."

The sketch was eight pages in length, was truly a sketch outline, and encompassed introductory developments in the Middle Ages, the Renaissance, and the Enlightenment through the Revolutionary Period up to "18—." Ideas were prominent as well as institutional, social and political developments.*

After his failure to have the materials on Calvin and Servetus properly presented in the *Panoplist,* Van der Kemp kept these writings on the shelf for a few years. In 1812 he asked Adams if he would "peruse" them. Adams said *No.* He cared "not a Farthing about either" and he was annoyed by all bigotry.[26] However, the crusty and outspoken old gentleman (Adams was now seventy-seven) relented and said he would get one of his granddaughters to read them aloud if Van der Kemp would send them.[27] The essays were sent with the request to send them on to Abiel Abbot or Andrews Norton.[28]

A few weeks later Adams wrote, in a gleeful tone, "I advised you, before you embarked for America, to beware of Religious Prejudices. . . . Yet you have forgotten them [warnings] again and are becoming the most renouned Heretick and Schismatick in America; . . ."[29]

Adams knew well that the religious interest of the "Mennonite preacher" could never be killed, and his liberal views never shaken.

In 1812 the sketches on Calvin and Servetus were pub-

---

* A recent book which approaches this outline is R. R. Palmer's *The Age of the Democratic Revolution.* Van der Kemp would have been fascinated by it and it is belated justice that Palmer attributed a good share of the revolutionary spirit of the Netherlands in the 1780's to Van der Kemp.

lished in England. Norton saw the British periodical about the same time that he received, from Abbot, Van der Kemp's essays and some sermons written for his family.[30] In a few months Van der Kemp was informed that his essays on Calvin and Servetus were at last to be published, and that the editors of the *Repository* would correct them.[31] They appeared in the publication in 1813, though not in their original form. With this introduction, Van der Kemp became a frequent and well respected contributor to the *Repository*.

The magazine was unable to use the sermons and Van der Kemp sent them to the Reverend Henry Dwight for his criticism, also sending the account of his "jaunt in this Western district." He wrote that his sermons had been intended to impress his children and spur them on to further inquiry.

> The polished Thacker [sic] knew that a rigid examination was the only powerful mean to discern truth from falsehood, to confound error and imposture and place truth on an unshaken basis. These means can never be discountenanced, or rejected as insufficient but by those who mistrust the solidity of their principles, intend to profit by the ignorance of others, and are thus interested, that their machinations—artfully concealed from the human eye—remain enveloped in darkness.

Samuel Thacher was one of the editors of the *Monthly Anthology*.

Dwight was asked to send both sermons and *Tour* to his brother Edmund, who would deliver them to Samuel Eliot to be placed with his collection of Van der Kemp's papers.[32] Samuel had asked long ago for copies of Francis' writings, and the scholar had spent much time in copying works destined to go elsewhere to oblige his valued friend.

Henry Dwight was not well and had given up his pulpit in Utica to move to Geneva. He wrote briefly that he did not agree with Van der Kemp's conclusions on baptism but hoped him success.[33]

In the April, 1813 issue of the *Repository*, Norton had
an article of controversy in which he stated:

> Concerning the manner in which Calvin spake of the
> sufferings of Servetus, I will give a passage from a man-
> uscript account of the whole transaction, which I have
> received from a most respectable and very learned cor-
> respondent, whose name, with all, to whom he is known,
> it will do me honor to mention, Fr. Adr. van der Kemp.

A quoted paragraph from Van der Kemp's manuscript
followed.[34]

In the next number was a long article entitled, "Life of
Michael Servetus" taken largely from Van der Kemp's
works on Servetus and Calvin. Most of the credit for the
article was given to Van der Kemp and frequent citations
were made directly to his manuscripts. The editor criticized Senebier as strongly as did Van der Kemp but added
several good authorities to the list used by him. Van der
Kemp was asked to put the original articles in the Harvard
Library.[35]

The October issue of the quarterly carried an article by
one of the editors that included remarks on Samuel Crellius. One of the sources reported Crellius to have been a
Socinian. The editor said he had raised this question with
Van der Kemp, "a gentleman every way qualified to give
correct information on the subject." Van der Kemp's con-
vincing reply in the negative was quoted, about one page
in length.[36] Van der Kemp's information about Socinianism
appeared in the last issue of the *General Repository*, as the
publication failed. Adams was disturbed and wrote to Van
der Kemp, "The Repository cannot live. And why? Thousands of cartloads of Trash foreign and domestic circulate
freely and sell well." [37]

At about this time a book was published attacking the
Christian religion. George Bethune English, a young clergy-
man, told his reasons for renouncing his ministry. William
Ellery Channing and Samuel Carey wrote critical reviews.
Van der Kemp, eager to read both the book and the re-

views, was grateful to obtain them through the Eliot family. He wrote a reply to English, sending one copy to the Eliots and one to Adams with the remark,

> If it is deemed by better judges, that the publication might do good by unwary youth, they are welcome to it —provided the idiom is corrected and my name secreted —as I cannot wish to be compromitted with a man of such a character.[38]

Adams read the reply hurriedly and did not like it. He said it was too sacerdotal in style and too Calvinistic in spirit. "Free discussion must not be browbeaten: Rail not! Rave not!" [39] Van der Kemp decided not to publish it, and Adams was pleased. He knew that English was a fine young man, "from his childhood, Sober, Studious, and without a Stain on his moral character." If a serious public controversy were aroused, it might well get out of control. He said America had too many such controversies already.[40] Edward Everett was not so fearful. He published a reply to English, and English responded with a rebuttal. The young man did not return to the ministry, but turned to the military instead. He joined the Marines and later enlisted in the Egyptian army.

This was not the end of Van der Kemp's interest in religion and history but his serious efforts to write for publication were near an end. His *Sketch of a Desired Work* inspired additional reading and study from time to time, first on one point and then on another. He probably did not give up hope of doing the work himself until 1818 when his time was completely taken up by his work as a state translator.

In the religious field he was instrumental in publishing Jefferson's "Syllabus"; this effort will be related in another chapter. Otherwise he conceived the idea of writing a life of Christ, inspired in part by his correspondence with Jefferson. His interest went as far as sketching an outline. A copy to De Witt Clinton was very brief, but another copy to John Adams was more detailed and four pages in length.

Part I, "Preliminary discussions," contained the general principles of natural religion, an inquiry into the authenticity of the Sacred Scriptures, a history of the Jewish nation with its theism and morality, a general view of the heathen world before the Christian era, and a comparison of heathen and Jewish civilizations. Part II included a scholarly examination of the many questions which had arisen about the life and doctrine of Jesus. Van der Kemp inserted a "general observation" in this part which repeated his previous basic assumption: "All what is necessary to believe and to do to secure our happiness must have been *so clearly* revealed, as to be understood without any difficulty by any one of a sound judgment and a sincere heart." At the close of the section was a corollary: "The fundamental part of the Christian Revelation is the *divine mission* of Jesus—not his person—character." Part III was the relation of the earthly life of Jesus under four headings; his person, character, views and doctrine, and success of his enterprise. In the last section Van der Kemp considered prejudices among "the great," the scientific and the vulgar, and pointed out that the doctrine was committed to illiterate disciples. Was Christ an enthusiast and an impostor? [41]

If Van der Kemp had written this proposed work on the basis of the outline, he would have redeveloped his natural history discussions of the origin of the earth and the deluge. The treatment of ancient history and philosophy would have been fair and generous. He would have accepted the divinity of Christ but would have rejected or passed quickly over the idea of the Trinity. Van der Kemp would have accented the character and doctrine of Jesus with probably some open criticisms of particular church officials down through the ages. And without doubt he would have digressed here and there.

At about the same time that he wrote the first draft of the outline of the *Life of Jesus,* Van der Kemp also copied in English for the first time his *Tour through a Part of the Western District of New York in 1792.* His notes and letters had been in Dutch but well organized. Now he did it in

English with an idea that the New York Philosophical Society might publish it. Van der Kemp sent it to De Witt Clinton with this in view and it went on to John Adams. Both enjoyed it. Adams wrote that he read it with "as much Interest Pleasure and Instruction as Coxes or Moores or Crusoe's or Gullivers," and added later that it surpassed Scott's *Lady of the Lake* which he enjoyed greatly.[42] The *Tour* was published in the Seymour *Centennial Address* in 1877 and again in 1878 in Durant's *History of Oneida County*. Van der Kemp accepted the praises of his friends as sufficient reward for those writings which were not published in his lifetime.

❧ XIX ❧

Publishing
Jefferson's "Syllabus"

DURING the American Revolution, Van der Kemp admired
Thomas Jefferson as a political leader and writer. As secretary of state under Washington the political philosopher
was respected. When Van der Kemp read the *Notes on Virginia* and fragments of other scientific writings, he wanted
to probe further into the great man's ideas. For a scholar,
respect for Jefferson was in no way inconsistent with opposition to his political leadership during the Napoleonic
threat.

Jefferson's "Syllabus" was a small essay on religion which
he had sent to Benjamin Rush with an explanatory letter
on April 21, 1803. The essay recalled "delightful conversations" in the evenings of 1798 and 1799, with the Christian
religion as one of the subjects. In spite of reports to the contrary, Jefferson claimed to be a follower of Christ, "sincerely
attached to his doctrines, in preference to all others" and
ascribing to Jesus "every human excellence." He had just
read Joseph Priestley's little essay on "Socrates and Jesus
Compared" and had decided to draw his own ideas together
in writing an estimate of Christianity. The essay was written
midway through his first term as president, and he wished
the document to remain private; he feared publicity would
bring attacks which would weaken freedom of religion. He
felt a man should never betray "the common right of inde-

pendent opinion, by answering questions of faith, which the laws have left between god and himself." [1]

Although Van der Kemp did not know of the "Syllabus" until later, he had had contacts with Jefferson, and knew many of his writings. Through a mutual friend Jefferson had given him letters of introduction to America in 1788. When Van der Kemp applied for official intercession for his funds in the Netherlands, Jefferson as secretary of state answered the request. Van der Kemp knew and appreciated Jefferson's part in the Revolution, knew the Declaration of Independence and the act for establishing religious freedom in Virginia. In the *Notes on Virginia,* he had read not only the parts on natural history but also the part on religious freedom and freedom of conscience, where Jefferson wrote, "The rights of conscience we never submitted [to government], we could not submit. We are answerable for them to our God." Van der Kemp believed this too. Likewise he accepted as his own feeling another statement: "Reason and free inquiry are the only effectual agents against error. Give a loose to them, they will support the true religion by bringing every false one to their tribunal, to the test of their investigation."

Jefferson read Van der Kemp's *Researches on Buffon's and Jefferson's Theories in Natural History* and his *Sketch of a Desired Work.* The great man appreciated Van der Kemp's education and recognized that he was unafraid of ideas.

Van der Kemp first saw the "Syllabus" when he visited John Adams at Quincy in 1813. Jefferson had loaned it to Adams, who showed it to Van der Kemp during one of their religious discussions. Shortly after returning to Oldenbarneveld, Francis asked Adams for the "Syllabus."

Shall I not receive the Syllabus of the Philosopher of Monticello? or, must you ask his leave? I think I was entitled to it, having in my *Philos. Researches*—which I now think, stand no chance for Publication, but are intended for Cambridge's College[—]have been so profuse in his

deserved praises—defending his one and twenty gods
against the cants of scholars, as [likewise] I lashed his
pantheistical boat in one of his mem.[oirs] in the *Philo.
Trans.*[2]

But Adams returned the "Syllabus" to Jefferson. Adams,
himself, was afraid to publish anything on religion, afraid
of the calumny "worse than Death: worse than the stoning
of Stephen." He said he would be held up in the pulpit
and the press and circulated in private letters and in whis-
pers as "a Deist an Atheist, and the Devil knows what." He
said that Jefferson would be unwise to let a copy of the
sketch be taken. "Repose is all that he or I can desire.
Neither Monticello nor Mount Wollaston [Adams' home]
are ambitious of being quoted as Authorities in the Science
of Theology." [3]

Before Van der Kemp received this letter, he asked again
for the "Syllabus." Adams replied immediately that he was
honor bound to return it without making a copy. Van der
Kemp regretfully accepted this course of action; he was
quite intrigued with the sketch, adding that "the contents
of that paper imbued me with some less unfavorable opinions about the moral principles of that man." [4]

For two years Van der Kemp thought from time to time
about the "Syllabus" and at last on March 24, 1816, wrote
to Jefferson for it. Jefferson replied that it was only an outline sent to Rush and later to Adams. Both had been asked
not to publicize it. The author was unwilling to draw on
himself "a swarm of insects, whose buz is more disquieting
than their bite." However, he told Van der Kemp there
would be no objection to anonymous publication. It might
even "do good by producing discussion and finally a true
view of the merits of this great reformer." He had also ex-
tracted from the Bible the text of the morals of Jesus, "as
distinguishable from the matter in which they are imbedded
as diamonds in dunghills." He thought that the "Extract"
with improvements and the "Syllabus" combined with a life
of Jesus to be written by Van der Kemp would at last show

the world "the immortal merit of this first of human Sages."
If the material were published in England there seemed
little likelihood that Jefferson would be suspected of authorship.[5]

Van der Kemp read the sketches with enthusiasm and
prepared the "Syllabus" and the letter to Rush for publication, being careful to copy them by his own hand. Then
he sent the work to the *Monthly Repository of Theology
and General Literature* in England. When he informed
Jefferson of the disposition, the latter replied that he was
"entirely satisfied." He hoped for a full and fair discussion
of his major grounds but doubted if it would come to pass.
He did not want to become involved in the discussion however.[6]

After concluding the correspondence and after trusting
Van der Kemp with the "Syllabus," Jefferson asked Adams
about him. "There is a Mr. Vanderkemp, of New York, a
correspondent, I believe, of yours, with whom I have exchanged some letters, without knowing who he is. Will you
tell me?"[7] Adams replied with a laudatory sketch:

The biography of Mr. Vanderkemp would require a
volume, which I could not write if a million were offered
me as a reward for this work. After a learned and scientific education, he entered the army in Holland, and
served as a captain with reputation; but loving books
more than arms, he resigned his commission, and became
a preacher. My acquaintance with him began at Leyden,
in 1780. He was the minister of the Mennonite congregation, the richest in Europe, in that city, where he was
celebrated as the most elegant writer in the Dutch language. He was the intimate friend of Luzac and DeGyselaer. In 1788, when the king of Prussia threatened Holland with invasion, his party insisted on his taking a
command of the most exposed and most important post
in the seven provinces. He was soon surrounded by the
Prussian forces; but he defended his fortress with a prudence, fortitude, patience, and perseverance, which were

admired by all Europe, till, abandoned by his nation, des-
titute of provisions and ammunition, still refusing to surrender, he was offered the most honorable capitulation.
He accepted it, was offered very advantageous proposals,
but despairing of the liberty of his country, he returned
to Antwerp; determined to emigrate to New York, he
wrote to me in London, requesting letters of introduction. I sent him letters to Governor Clinton and several
others of our little great men. His history in this country
is equally curious and affecting. He left property in Holland, which the revolutions there have annihilated, and
I fear is now pinched with poverty. His head is deeply
learned, and his heart is pure. I scarcely know a more
amiable character. A gentleman here asked my opinion
of him. My answer was, "he is a *mountain of salt* to the
earth." He has written to me occasionally, and I have
answered his letters in great haste. You may well suppose
that such a man has not always been able to understand
our American politics. Nor have I. Had he been as great
a master of our language as he was of his own, he would
at this day have been one of the most conspicuous characters in the United States.[8]

John exaggerated the facts of his friend's early life a little
but did not exaggerate his feeling for Van der Kemp.

Although Van der Kemp specified that the publication
should conceal the source of the "Syllabus" when he sent
it to England, the editor of *The Monthly Repository* was
not cooperative. The writing was ascribed to "an Eminent
American Statesman" who would "probably be recognized
by such of our readers as are acquainted with the characters of the leading men in the American revolution." The
editorial introduction, Van der Kemp's covering letter, Jefferson's letter to Rush and the "Syllabus" all appeared in
the October issue of 1816. When John Quincy Adams saw
the material in the English publication, he had no doubt it
was the work of Jefferson and Van der Kemp. He sent a
copy home on November 19 and repeated the names of the

authors on November 26.[9] In February, in all innocence, Adams sent the copy to Van der Kemp with permission to send it on to Jefferson. Abigail explained its origin. Van der Kemp hurriedly explained Jefferson's desire for anonymity, and Abigail wrote to John Quincy not to disclose the authors. Van der Kemp had cleverly dated his editorial letter O——d which could have been Oxford and did not say a statesman had written the "Syllabus" but even insisted that no guesses or hints should be made. Before the manuscript arrived in England the friend to whom it was addressed died and the editor of the *Monthly Repository* reported the author as a statesman and spelled out Oldenbarneveld.[10]

Jefferson became alarmed by a similar report that his authorship was known. He wrote to Van der Kemp that he had learned "with real concern" that the editor had the name of the author of the "Syllabus" and was coyly withholding it. He feared that with coaxing, the editor would disclose Jefferson's name and let loose upon him "the genus irritabile vatum [the irritable genus of soothsayers]" on both continents. Jefferson declared:

be it so. I shall receive with folded arms all their hacking & hewing. I shall not ask their passport to a country [area of learning] which they claim indeed as theirs, but which was made, I trust, for moral man, and not for dogmatising venal jugglers. Should they however, instead of abuse, appeal to the tribunal of reason and fact, I shall really be glad to see on what point they will begin their attack. for it expressly excludes all question of supernatural character or endowment. I am in hopes it may find advocates as well as opposers, and produce for us a temperate & full development. as to myself, I shall be a silent auditor.[11]

Van der Kemp's explanation to Jefferson was satisfactory, as he thought all editors pretended to greater knowledge than they had. He was not afraid of strife but had reached an "age of quietism" when he did not wish "to be kicked by the asses of hierophantism." [12] The rumors of Jefferson's authorship caused no great attacks upon his character, quieting his fears. He and Van der Kemp enjoyed a pleasurable correspondence thereafter.

Van der Kemp made some efforts to follow through on Jefferson's suggestion that he write a life of Christ. His sketch was sent to Adams but his friend discouraged the project. He replied, "What! Why! Wherefore! Is not the Life of Jesus in the Four Evangelists? Where else can you find it?" He had seen half a dozen modern lives of Jesus which Jefferson might not have seen but to no loss on his part. They were of no value to Adams and he expected nothing from Van der Kemp's biography. Van der Kemp had suggested that Andrews Norton or Edward Everett might be persuaded to do the job. Adams insisted it had already been done.[13]

Jefferson was discouraging, but for a different reason. He called the sketch "a magnificent skeleton . . . of what would indeed be a compleat Encyclopedia of Christian Philosophy." He felt the magnitude was such that it would require a Newton in physics, a Locke in metaphysics and a historian with great judgment, candor and many years ahead of him. He hoped that Van der Kemp would do a part of it himself, the mortal biography of Jesus. "[T]his candidly and rationally written, without any regard to sectarian dogmas, would reconcile to his character a weighty multitude who do not properly estimate it, and would lay the foundation of a genuine christianity." [14] Jefferson suggested some German works which might be useful and commented briefly on Italian sources which Van der Kemp had mentioned.[15]

Adams had suggested that Van der Kemp read and answer Charles François DuPuis—but that it would take him twenty volumes. Van der Kemp replied that the Christian system could be explained in a few lines and no human power could crush it. "The Gospel Doctrine is from above— the purest—the most perfect morality—proved by an irresistible evidence the resurrection of Jesus—with the fullest display of the mercy of our Beautiful Father." His tremendous sketch "aimed to examine and destroy the sandy foundations on which the bigotry of orthodox believers" as well as infidels built their various systems.[16] These sentiments were similar to a short statement by Jefferson:

The doctrines of Jesus are simple, and tend all to the happiness of man.

1. That there is one only God, and he all perfect.

2. That there is a future state of rewards and punishments.

3. That to love God with all thy heart and thy neighbor as thyself, is the sum of religion.[17]

The full title of the essay as published in *The Monthly Repository* was, "Syllabus of an Estimate of the Doctrines of Jesus Compared with those of Others." Van der Kemp wrote that the "most virulent and artful attacks" of infidels had done less injury to the religion of Jesus than had some reputed friends with "bigotry and false zeal." The "Syllabus" had the "stamp of candour" in the design to place Christianity in a clear view. The author of the "Syllabus" proposed to treat the ethics of the ancient philosophers, the Jews and Jesus as they were formulated. When Jesus appeared "his parentage was obscure; his condition poor; his education null; his natural endowments great; his life correct & innocent; he was meek, benevolent, patient, firm, disinterested, and of the sublimest eloquence." He was executed before he had a chance to develop a full system of moral duties. Therefore, the fragments are defective and have been further disfigured by schismatizing followers who engrafted on them "the mysticisms of a Graecian Sophist, frittering them into subtleties, & obscuring them with jargon." However, with care one can construct the system of Jesus. He emphasized one God with just attributes. He taught universal philanthropy. He demanded purity of thought as well as action. He taught emphatically the doctrine of the future life.[18]

Both Van der Kemp and Jefferson hoped that the sketch

would be stimulating to readers and would arouse discussion and further writing. No evidence appears in *The Monthly Repository* that readers were either antagonized or excited. However, further contributions to the magazine by Van der Kemp may have been encouraged because of this outspoken sketch.

In the November issue a letter from John Sherman and the Reverend Isaac Bliss Peirce asked aid for the church at Trenton. This letter was followed by a copy of the articles of association sent by Van der Kemp. In the same issue was a reprint of Van der Kemp's article on Crellius, first printed in America in 1813, and a translation of a journey of Crellius done by Van der Kemp.

In August, 1817, *The Monthly Repository* published a five-page article by Van der Kemp entitled, "Some Account of Dr. Balthasar Bekker and of the Mennonite Baptists." Bekker had written a book, *The Enchanted World,* trying to expose the common belief in devils. Van der Kemp surveyed the book, gave numerous collateral writings, and indicated the repercussions ending in Bekker's removal from his pulpit. The last part of the article described the Mennonite Baptists, particularly Dutch, and pointed out their liberal-conservative division. He hoped that his comments would inspire the leaders of the liberals to write the complete history of Unitarianism in Holland.

At about this same time Van der Kemp became enthusiastic about another liberal religious effort. He acquired a copy of the book, ΑΙΡΕΣΕΩΝ ΑΝΑΣΤΑΣΙΣ: or, *A New Way of Deciding Old Controversies,* written under the pen name Basanistes. The "New Way" was an attempt to explode the doctrines of the Trinity by showing that the arguments in support of the divinity of three, by the same arguments, could be made ridiculous by the inclusion of Moses. Van der Kemp thought an American edition would do good, especially among the higher class who might therefore be lured by it to become patrons of liberal sentiments and supporters of liberal writers. In America, with no state church, such patronage would overawe "an intolerant

Clergy" and the mob would then be swayed to support freedom of religious thought.[19] Van der Kemp loaned his copy to Adams, who also enjoyed the clever presentation.

In the fall of 1817 a Dutch lady, Miss Halshoff, visited America in behalf of world peace. She had written a pamphlet called *Peace Republican's Manual*. She had been imprisoned twice for her activities. Van der Kemp was impressed by the pamphlet and sent copies to both Adams and Jefferson. The latter was also impressed, saying the *Manual* was full of the "soundest principles of human independence" and that he commiserated with "her sufferings in so holy a cause." [20]

At about the same time Van der Kemp sent his little essay on "Incestuous Marriages" to both his friends. Adams laughed at it but Jefferson took it seriously. He thought Van der Kemp had proved without question that a man might make a second marriage with his first wife's sister under both natural and Mosaic law. Adams said it was legal but inexpedient. Jefferson wrote that during the Revolution he was on a committee to revise the laws of Virginia. They had copied the very words of Levitical law which allowed marriage with a sister-in-law. After some years the Virginians decided that such marriages often produced heartburnings, jealousies and even crimes. But, as Jefferson explained, that part of the law was later repealed.[21]

Jefferson was asked to publish more of his writings but insisted he had nothing worth publishing. When Van der Kemp brought up the subject of the cycles of nature and the question of species becoming extinct, Jefferson replied at great length to some of Van der Kemp's arguments in his earlier *Researches*. He commented particularly on the heavenly bodies and Van der Kemp must have been delighted. The movements of these bodies had been considered erratic and potentially destructive of the earth under certain movements. But Pierre Simon de Laplace, French astronomer, demonstrated that these supposed irregularities were strictly in obedience to the laws of motion and should continue forever. This eternity did not seem to be contrary to the Christian religion inasmuch as the God who created the bodies and laws might stop them. Jefferson opposed the theory of an evolutionary development of both land and life and reiterated his doubts as to the possible extinction of any species.[22]

Jefferson's health was not sufficiently good for him to carry on extensive correspondence. A stiffening wrist handicapped him in 1820 but he wrote about his condition, about the worthlessness of his papers, and a blast about the concealing of true Christianity by religious leaders. He hoped that education would dissipate the "clouds of darkness" but thought he would not live to see it.[23] In 1823 he had to dictate a short letter to Van der Kemp merely thanking him for his letters and apologizing for being unable to answer properly.[24] He was better in 1824 and wrote in some detail of a book by Pierre Jean Marie Flourens who had experimented with removing the cerebrum from animals, particularly chickens. This resulted in the loss of purpose, direction and memory. The conclusion was that the seat of thought was the cerebrum. Jefferson raised the question as to whether a human being would still have a soul if his cerebrum were removed. And if the soul left the body with the cerebrum, did it go directly to heaven? He seemed to hope these questions would confound the strict creed holders.[25] Van der Kemp was stimulated by such considerations but at the age of seventy-two was unwilling to seek a strong controversy.

The last letter from Jefferson was on November 30, 1825. He was more and more disabled but wanted to thank Van der Kemp for having Peter Vreede's book on commerce sent to him. He was unable to write a review of it. His health was poor and, at his age, he much preferred to read and study the classics. He said he was spending most of his time organizing the University of Virginia. He was proud of the faculty, obtained mostly in England, and the first year was drawing to a successful close. More applicants were expected for the second year than they could accommodate but they planned to enlarge the facilities as fast as possible. Jefferson considered the institution to be "on the most liberal plan" and very inexpensive.[26]

Van der Kemp won Jefferson's friendship through their mutual interests in natural science and liberal religion. Van der Kemp was the more aggressive of the two in the correspondence but Jefferson wrote with great interest. The influence on one another at their advanced ages probably was a matter of encouragement in their set interests. The publication of the "Syllabus" was the high spot.

❦ XX ❦

Friendship
with DeWitt Clinton

Van der Kemp first knew De Witt Clinton as a promising
young man visiting his uncle, George Clinton, governor of
the state. George received the Van der Kemps in his home
and tried to help them get settled. After Van der Kemp
moved to Oneida Lake, he saw little if any of George Clinton. The careers of both uncle and nephew were followed
and generally supported by Van der Kemp but not until
1812 did he make an effort to get better acquainted with
the younger man.

Van der Kemp was impressed with De Witt's rise in politics and wrote a letter reminding him of the former good
relations with the Clintons. He included his *Sketch of a
Desirable Work,* asked De Witt to read and criticize it and
perhaps to complete it.

> Could you who so boldly planned, to enrich New-York
> State with a Magnificent canal-navigation—whose execu-
> tion done would immortalise a Weston [British engineer
> employed on the New York waterways]—Could you Sir!
> be induced to embody this skeleton . . .[1]

From this time on the friendship between the two men developed along three major lines, their interest in natural
science, their approval of a canal and the project of translating the Dutch records at Albany. The interests in these

three areas were never separated in a time sequence and other common interests of lesser import frequently supplemented the three. The best way to examine the friendly ties seems to be to look at the concurrent developments separately but with realization of the overlapping.

When Van der Kemp made his oration in celebration of Dutch independence in 1814, a copy was sent to Clinton. De Witt thanked the orator and said, "An event of so much importance to the cause of national independence, involving the destinies of a people so intimately connected with many of us by consanguinity and commemorated in such an able & eloquent manner must make the deepest impression upon every intelligent & elevated mind." [2]

The next manuscript sent to Clinton was the *Researches in the Theories of Buffon and Jefferson*. Clinton was greatly impressed. Van der Kemp said he had done the work "on the entreaties" of his worthy friend, Chancellor Livingston, and had submitted it in embryo state to Jefferson. He had worked on it further with their approval and Charles Eliot had agreed to edit it, but died before he could do so. Now he also wanted Clinton to read and criticize it so that improvements could be made. Then he asked Clinton if he might borrow a copy of his recent speech, *Introductory Discourse, Delivered before the Literary and Philosophical Society of New York*.[3] The request was timely and tactful. Clinton had been deposed as mayor of New York City and had retired from active politics. The letter came from a respectable scholar, a man with friends in high places, and a man who had supported Clinton for the presidency in 1812. The request was non-political at a time when Clinton was avoiding open politics.

There is a possibility that Clinton discussed Van der Kemp's scientific interests with other people. He seemed to know more than was in the letter. He wrote back that he would read the treatise with "most respectful attention" when it came from Boston and that he was glad Van der Kemp had devoted himself "to the illustration of the Natural History" of central New York. Clinton agreed to send the requested *Introductory Discourse*.[4] This spurred Van der Kemp to send his *Tour* to Clinton since it contained so many observations of natural wealth and wonders (largely omitted in the account in Chapter VIII) in central New York. In the accompanying letter Van der Kemp also discussed the canal, as Clinton had just been made head of the canal commission. The *Introductory Discourse* had pleased Van der Kemp immensely. He commented in a highly favorable way on the whole production and then commented on some details.

> Your observation pag. 36 of Lakes dried up—can be placed in these Western parts beyond doubt—I write this moment [in Oldenbarneveld]—on the bottom of one—or large pond of water certainly—after the high lands were drained—if I can obtain leisure—I shall prepare the outlines of a short excursion last summer as an appendage to my tours to Oneyda Lake.

Van der Kemp asked Clinton if the president of the Philosophical Society should not have made an answer to the "slanders" in the *Quarterly Review*. Livingston would surely have done so when he was president of the Society for Promotion of the Useful Arts. Clinton was asked for copies of the *Transactions*.[5]

Clinton enjoyed reading the *Tour* and in time received the *Researches* from Boston. He raised questions about the fish Van der Kemp had seen and asked if he should not prepare an essay on the catching, preparing and curing of salmon in the Netherlands. Clinton said he would be glad to convey such an article to the Society for the Promotion of Useful Arts. He asked about Frenchman's Island in Oneida Lake and had spied an item in the *Researches* of great interest. If the petrified animal in Peter Smith's petrified honey-comb could be distinctly recognized as the honeybee, it would go far toward settling the controversy in favor of its American nativity. He said also that he had proposed Van der Kemp for membership in the Literary and

Philosophical Society and that his admission was certain. His closing words sealed the friendship.

> I have only to add that it will always afford me pleasure to hear from you and that if my humble efforts to promote the cause of science and the prosperity of our Country shall receive the approbation of such men as you, I shall feel amply rewarded. Laudari a laudato viro is surely a *laudable ambition*.[6]

Van der Kemp explained at some length about the fish of the Oneida Lake area with additional comments on the eel flies. He had received from a friend in Holland all the details of catching and preparing salmon and if Clinton could make it known in America it would prove lucrative and a blessing to the country. He gave an interesting account of Des Wattines on Frenchman's Island, how he had lived and of his return to France. Van der Kemp was pleased at membership in the society but wondered about the expense.[7]

Some pamphlets, perhaps political in nature, were sent to Van der Kemp by Clinton, one apparently signed Atticus and the other Williamson. Van der Kemp enjoyed them and said that the brother of Abraham Varick and Jonas Platt would bring from Albany any publications De Witt was willing to dispose of in his friend's favor. He recalled a passage from Clinton's *Introductory Discourse* predicting "that our country will be the chosen seat—and favorite abode of learning and science." He mentioned a few lines from the English poet, George Herbert,

> Religion stands on tiptoe in our Land
> Ready to pass to the American strand—

and a quatrain from the Bishop of Cloyne,

> Westward the Star of Empire takes its way
> The first four acts already past
> The fifth shall close the drama with the day
> Time's noblest offspring is the last . . .

Van der Kemp told Clinton that it was in his province to assist in the realization of the "pleasant dream." [8]

In the November elections Governor Daniel Tompkins was elected vice president of the United States and the control of the legislature proved to be largely in the hands of Ambrose Spencer. Three of the four elected members of the new Council of Appointment were friendly to Spencer and also to Clinton. The legislature then provided for an election in April, 1817, to choose a successor to Tompkins. Before these things were evident to the public, Van der Kemp wrote to Clinton on December 27, 1816, about the latter's return to Albany on business:

> You go then to brave our cold climate at Albany! Art thou not apprehensive to feel some inconvenience from this change?—to meet unexpectedly—some chilling coldness? Why not rather armed yourself in time with a Spencer by which a northern blast might be blasted—and an eastern lukewarmness heightened to a blaze. I know fear is not your predominant weakness—but even some precautions may often be admissable to men armed cap-a-pie.

Further advice was given in regard to the canal with the thought that if all went well there would be a demand for Clinton to be governor. [9]

A month later Van der Kemp asked for Clinton's speech to the Philosophical Society in 1811. He had recently seen a reference to it in a work by Elias Boudinot entitled, *Star in the West, or an Attempt to Discover the Long-Lost Tribes of Isreal.* Van der Kemp suggested that if Clinton knew Boudinot, he could inform him that Van der Kemp's *Researches* would be of assistance in his thesis that the ten tribes plus other casuals peopled America, perhaps by way of Asia and Bering Strait. (It is interesting to note that the Mormons accepted the Lost Tribes into their tradition.) Van der Kemp's treatment of the Arab invasions as promoters of migrations should be helpful. [10] Clinton had read the *Star in the West* but had grave doubts about the thesis. He said Boudinot got his system and many facts from James

Adair's *History of the Indians* (published in 1775) and that Adair was adept at mangling, distorting, stretching and lopping traditions, customs and facts connected with the thesis. He intended to write more about the peopling of America in a few months and also would comment on Van der Kemp's own writings. He was sending by Jonas Platt two volumes on canals, one of the transactions of the Literary and Philosophical Society, two volumes of the Collections of the New York Historical Society and one of Clinton's published addresses.[11]

Van der Kemp's somewhat favorable opinion of Boudinot was reduced. He said he awaited impatiently Clinton's views and that he was welcome to use any of the material in the *Researches*. Apparently Van der Kemp had read all the books which Clinton sent because he commented at length on various parts, particularly on the canal and on fishing. Van der Kemp was something of a conservationist in wanting the catching and curing of salmon to be efficient. He also wanted restrictions to prevent the catching of salmon in the improper season.

Clinton's satirical political article on Abimelech Coody puzzled Van der Kemp. Gulian C. Verplanck had written a series of articles attacking Clinton from an independent-Federalist position at a time when some of the Republicans were demanding Clinton's removal from his office of mayor of New York City. Van der Kemp was a Clinton supporter but also had been an independent Federalist himself. If he read the Verplanck articles, he must have been disturbed. Now Clinton had characterized Abimelech Coody (Verplanck) as

the head of a political sect called the "Coodies", of hybrid nature, composed of the combined spawn of Federalism and Jacobinism, and generated in the venomous passions of disappointment and revenge, without any definite character; neither fish nor flesh, nor bird nor beast, but a nondescript made up of "all monstrous, all prodigious things." [12]

Van der Kemp asked, "How can a western woodsman decypher the mystic rights of N. York Politicians—without you condescend to give a clue?" [13] Perhaps Van der Kemp was trying to find an intellectual justification for his support of the shaky and uncertain Clinton party.

Clinton was elected to the governorship in the fall of 1817 with a tremendous majority. Clinton had won support by his canal stand and by an appeal of "good feeling." It looked to Van der Kemp like the decline of bitter factionalism and the improved operation of the republican system of government. He was delighted and commended Clinton with flattery—then opened up the subject of sunspots. This led into a consideration of the universe and the origin of the earth. He wondered if the Mosaic account was a re-creation of an earth that had existed in some form some time before. This would be orthodox, not subject to the charge of heresy. He also said his *Achaian Republic* could not be published in America because a general cry might be heard against the author, "Brekekex-coax-coax"—the derisive croaking of the frogs of Aristophanes.[14]

The re-creation idea was stimulated in part by the *Protogoea* of Gottfried Wilhelm Leibnitz which Van der Kemp owned and now loaned to Clinton. This introduction to modern geology treated the earth's evolution from the creation to the deluge, and included the idea of a re-creation. Before reading it, Clinton indicated his acceptance of the idea because "all the phenomona which we witness proclaim that this world is the wreck of a former one." The Mosaic accounts certainly fitted all the evidence of geology.[15]

Both men were interested in local applications of science, for the sake of the local research and for economic development of central New York. Van der Kemp suggested a divisional study—"1) the alluvial part—2) the Highlands—considered before a passage was opened to [for] the western waters 3) from the Cohoes—to the Little Falls, 4) From these to Rome 5) from there to St. Laurent—& Lake Erie." Van der Kemp had seen branches and leaves of trees taken from a considerable depth of Colonel Colbrath's well at Rome.

He knew also of the finding of a squared log, charcoal and ashes in a cut on Wood Creek. On the way to Rome from Oldenbarneveld he had seen an old river bed at the village of Floyd. With Clinton's guidance, superintendence and encouragement, the nature of New York could be discovered and made known.[16]

Sometime during the winter of 1817–18, Van der Kemp wrote an essay and made extracts from a Dutch journal on the growth of papaver (poppy) and on a disease of the hooves of neat cattle which resembled a disease of sheep in Holland. These sketches were sent to Clinton.[17] Van der Kemp also translated within the next year Nicolas Cornelis Lambrechtsen's *A History of New Netherland*. Lambrechtsen had sent a Dutch copy to the New-York Historical Society and Hermann Bleeker sent it to Mappa to get Van der Kemp to translate it.[18] The translation was not published until 1841.

A different interest recorded in the correspondence was a suggestion to the governor regarding the growing dairy industry in Oneida County. Van der Kemp wrote:

> The quantity of butter in this district is immense—It is preferred at York Market—Col. Mappa shall communicate a correct statement—Would it be proper—it would contribute to improve and increase this branch—to appoint either here or in N. York—an inspector of butter.[19]

How many times Clinton visited in Oldenbarneveld would be impossible to determine. Van der Kemp invited him to stop at the village in 1819 and it is certain that he stopped in 1820 and 1822. Clinton wrote the *Hibernicus Letters* as of 1820. The letter about Van der Kemp is literary in style and therefore was not intended to be accurate in detail but only in the picture it presented. It shows Clinton's appreciation and affection for the scholar in the wilderness.

The letter was dated September, 1820, from the "Western Region" and described Clinton on a hunt coming upon two successful anglers, Van der Kemp and Mappa. A conversation of great interest and good will began and ended with an invitation for Clinton to go home with them for a feast on the fine trout. They went to Mappa's "elegant house" and "enjoyed a treat worthy to be compared to the Symposium of Plato." A highly complimentary statement of Van der Kemp's attainments was followed by the conclusion that in the secluded village of Oldenbarneveld was *"the most learned man in America"* cultivating "his beautiful and spacious garden," and enjoying the study of literature and science. With the virtues of the "fireside and the altar" and the "esteem of the wise and good," he was a great contributor to all who shared his conversation or his correspondence.[20]

The *Hibernicus* letter was published and Van der Kemp secured a copy for himself.

The correspondence continued and the two men saw each other in Albany a few times for business and pleasure. Comments and questions on natural history continued to pass between them and each continued to send materials to the other as gifts or loans. Political matters sometimes entered the discussions but chiefly as they affected the two big projects, the canal and the Dutch records.

In 1822 Clinton wrote, "I shall go to the West early in June to visit the whole line of the Canal—and if possible I will make a diverging visit on my return to the most learned man in America." [21] Van der Kemp replied, "I expect Your Exc.[ellency] does not intend to feed me with smoke—thus I shall expect him here on his return—as I presume—I am the man—designated by you." He assured Clinton that he and his wife, if she came, would meet a cordial and respectful reception and that the scenery of Trenton Falls would compensate for his own humble cottage.[22]

Clinton made the visit, apparently a pleasant one, although without Mrs. Clinton. In his diary was recorded the following notes.

When I slept at Oldenbarneveld [I] heard mine host in fervent prayer—very loud—the custom of the country.

Van der Kemp is a man of pure morals & unaffected piety—His family agreeable but ugly—something fascinating in personal beauty—his house clean—his furniture convenient—his library well chosen and erudite—his position charming—his neighborhood agreeable. Col. Mappa & Dr. Guiteau gentlemen of education.[23]

The two men discussed the canal in particular because that was the guest's greatest concern of the moment. Then they passed to the political and economic growth of the state, science, religion, and education. Within two months Van der Kemp invited another visit, this time with Mrs. Clinton. He suggested that the Clintons come by way of Amsterdam through Johnstown to Fairfield where Clinton could inspect the medical college. If he did so, Professor Westell Willoughby would be his guide and his host. From there he could come by the old Military Road to Oldenbarneveld and journey northward to Sackett's Harbor, Kingston, Montreal and Ogdensburg.[24] Van der Kemp was a good friend of Willoughby and probably wanted to do his friend and the young Fairfield college a good turn.

Clinton and Van der Kemp shared their griefs as well as their intellectual interests. In 1822 Van der Kemp told his friend how ill Sophia Mappa was. She had developed the tic douloureux, a facial neuralgia. The Mappas had "exhausted all the poisonous remedies" of the physicians of Oneida County, of Boston and New York City. Then they took her to Philadelphia where she became bedridden but at last started a recovery. She convalesced at the home of John Van der Kemp. Mrs. Busti was ill at the same time.[25] Mrs. Busti died in April as did also John Lincklaen at Cazenovia. In 1824 another grief was disclosed to Clinton. John Van der Kemp's wife, Julia, died. Clinton was asked to put the death notice in the Albany paper.[26] In the summer Paul Busti died as did also Adam Mappa's sister.

Clinton, too, had his woes, personal as well as political. Van der Kemp supported him in both. In the summer of 1824 Clinton wrote to his friend that he was greatly afflicted by the loss of his son. The young man was an officer in the Navy and died of yellow fever in Havana. Clinton said sorrowfully that the son "possessed a noble heart—intelligence courage—professional skill and the promise of a life of continued honor & usefulness but alas he has gone—" [27] Clinton noted Van der Kemp's sorrows and reminded him of his enjoyments—"Mens sana always and generally in sano corpore—a worthy affectionate family—excellent neighbors—the possession of universal respect—and the consciousness of an honorable well-spent life." He added another loss of his own, the death of P. S. Van Rensselaer, former mayor of Albany.[28]

The two men seldom wrote to each other about religion but one example illustrates their differences of approach. Van der Kemp wanted to read *Ecce Homo,* an anti-Christian, semi-scientific work. Van der Kemp said such attacks could not penetrate the "shield of Religion." He said further:

> We may humbly inquire allways with due reverence to a first cause—a Being all wise and good—and I can not see—while it is as impossible to penetrate as to develop his wonderful creation—yet we may unravel a part—more so when it increases our ideal of his almighty power and wisdom . . .[29]

Clinton replied:

> *Ecce homo* is a book highly blasphemous—The Trinitarians believe in the divinity of the person as well as of the Mission of Christ—The Unitarians only in the divinity of the Mission—both creeds ascribe the utmost purity to Jesus and consider him with the highest veneration—but Ecce Homo assails his moral character and treats him as an imposter. This book is not for sale and I cannot ask the author for a perusal—It would be indirect encouragement.[30]

Van der Kemp was the more open-minded, willing to read the anti-religious in order to assess the scientific parts. However, there were so many other topics more congenial to Clinton that no arguments arose between them on religion. The canal was a tremendously attractive topic for ten years and the Dutch records only a little less so. However, the friendship between De Witt Clinton and Francis Van der Kemp was well established on an intellectual and perhaps political basis some time before either canal or records became an absorbing common interest.

❧ XXI ❧

The Erie Canal

IF MORE Dutchmen had moved to the upper Mohawk Valley and beyond, perhaps New York would have had canals sooner and with less political trouble. The Dutch knew canals but did not need them in the Hudson Valley. When Van der Kemp made his way over bad roads and across shallow streams to Lake Ontario in 1792, he naturally thought of canals; he pictured them in his enthusiastic letters to Adam Mappa. At one time De Witt Clinton thought Van der Kemp was the first to write of the through route. Probably Elkanah Watson deserved the credit because he wrote articles about it. Van der Kemp's letters to Mappa (originally in Dutch) may have been passed around, but were not translated and published until many years later. Van der Kemp's influence on consideration of the canals was more likely through his enthusiastic conversations in Oldenbarneveld and Utica and contacts with important friends, De Witt Clinton in particular.

Early in 1810 Jonas Platt, one of Van der Kemp's closest friends, began an active interest in a canal. Through his efforts and for political reasons Clinton's aid was enlisted. Clinton was a member of the legislative committee set up to examine the possibilities for a canal. The committeemen traveled through the probable areas of location and made a favorable report in 1811. Platt presented a resolution, which was passed by the Senate, to print five thousand copies. Congress considered the canal in 1812 but let it die in committee. The political situation in New York State, with Clinton running for the presidency, and the onset of the war, caused the canal commissioners to withhold a report in 1812. With so little accomplished Van der Kemp still praised Clinton for "so boldly" planning "to enrich New-York State with a Magnificent canal-navigation." [1]

During the war nothing was done except that the legislature repealed the commission's powers. After the war Platt and others organized a mass meeting in New York City for December 30, 1815, with William Bayard in the chair. Platt was the main speaker and called for action. A committee of four, including Clinton, was set up to draft a memorial to the legislature and a persuasive document resulted. Newspapers noted the meeting and the memorial.

When Van der Kemp sent his manuscript of the tour to Lake Ontario to Clinton on January 8, 1816, he wrote:

> Well shall I have been rewarded . . . if it could spur a de Witt Clinton, to use his powerful influence with his friends next Legislature—to have an act passed—to open a canal between Lac Erie and the Mohawk—or to incorporate a company for the purpose. New-York can do it— Amsterdam built its Magnificent State bourse under less favorable circumstances.

In a postscript Van der Kemp added,

> I can scarce express the pleasure I felt in seeing a notice of the New York meeting so my wishes have been anticipated—God prosper it—be it thro your influence and unrelenting activity! and posterity will bless the name of de Witt Clinton—No New-Yorker ought to wish to obtain it from the fed. government—it would claim the benefit—and exact the profits—[2]

The next day Van der Kemp wrote to John Adams, "I am stirring again every man's soul with whom I have some connection to rise in their strength in behalf of our Western Canals." [3] Whether the word *again* meant he had supported the action of 1810 and 1811 or perhaps only that he was in general favor dating back to 1792 is in doubt. The rest of the statement shows that he took an active part in the local movement and perhaps, by correspondence, with other parts of the state.

The Federalist newspaper of Utica, *Patriot and Patrol,* reported the New York meeting favorably on January 12. Beginning in the January 19 issue the paper printed the complete memorial in three instalments. On February 1 a group of interested citizens met in Bagg's Hotel, Utica, and approved the canal project through a petition to the legislature. Other communities in the state did likewise.[4]

The state legislature received a flood of petitions and memorials for the canal and found it impossible to ignore the sentiment. However, some of the leaders were dubious of the scheme and fearful of political developments that would favor Clinton. After much wrangling a new commission was approved on April 17 with a $20,000 operating account but with little power. De Witt Clinton was one of the five commissioners. Van der Kemp assured the commissioner that the canal was certain of success. Clinton sent to his admirer a copy of the New York memorial.

The commissioners were busy the rest of the year directing surveys, making estimates, determining locations, and considering financing. They traveled along the route, inspected, conferred and made speeches. Clinton came through Utica from the west in August and discussed the project with the editor of the *Patriot.* Clinton's optimism inspired the editor to write an enthusiastic report that the construction was practical and without undue difficulty. The story was repeated in other papers.[5]

Van der Kemp was pleased with the article. Yet he realized the financing might be difficult and politics might interfere. He wrote to Clinton in October that the practicality was "above doubt" and he hoped the project would meet no further "pusillanimous obstructions." Van der Kemp opposed putting a special tax on the areas adjacent to the canal and thought it was bad politics. He believed a loan could easily be obtained in London or Amsterdam if the state guaranteed it. A small general tax could pay the interest and tolls would pay the principal.[6]

Van der Kemp was even more uneasy in December. In addition to favoring the alliance between Clinton and Ambrose Spencer, he went so far as to recommend political plums to ease the opposition.

> Your great project stands in my opinion on an unmoveable basis—but I know what powerful engines can be set at work by malice and self-interest—It might answer a good purpose—if in the detailed report was proposed the appointment of a committee of four—one from each district—with a *competent* salary—to superintend the construction of the canal—*till* it was finished—This might be the means to stop the mouth cerberus—never minding to what party he belonged—provided he was an influential dog and I need not tell you—that few can withstand this magic spell—and I would not scruple to make use of this enchantment—when a grand praiseworthy object might have failed without it.

This was probably the lowest that Van der Kemp ever stooped in his moral principles. The question of expediency for a great undertaking seems to have been uppermost in his mind. He urged again a loan as the basis of financing and emphasized the great destiny of New York State through the canal.[7]

The commissioners were not neglectful of the financial aspects. Clinton had procured a promise of support from the state of Ohio, and applied to Congress for assistance. Paul Busti for the Holland Land Company promised a thousand acres plus the right-of-way through their lands. The report to the legislature was impressive. Van der Kemp read about it and asked Clinton for a copy. He added to his request the hope that the legislature would not only accept the report, but also lay plans for another canal from Oneida Lake to Lake Ontario through Little Salmon River.[8] Clinton sent by Jonas Platt "the Reports Maps & Documents relative to the Western & Northern Canals also a book on Canals." [9]

Clinton became a candidate for the governorship in the midst of the consideration of the canal by the legislature. Support for Clinton and the canal grew, even for the financing. The project was passed and was accepted by the Council of Revision on April 15. On April 25, Van der Kemp reported to Clinton his comments on the report:

> All what I did see thus far effected no change in my opinion—I confess—many sacrifices must have been made —to obtain—so far as it is granted—and when Clinton shall be at the head of our state—many obstacles shall be gradually removed—and new energies created—This at least I prognosticate—and God forbid—that I should be disappointed. Had I possessed power equal to desire—I should have ambitioned to execute it alone—at least I would not place my state in a condition of dependency to the general government—I would not allow it a entrant in our domestic concerns. This should appear of no less deleterious influence—as if our Executive was chosen by —or became actually an officer of the General Government. The canal is practicable—it can be executed—and money is obtainable on the credit and guarantee of this State—in England—in Holland—David Parish will procure it in the first—Paul Busti in the later place—You must effect it—and compell us to say—"muneris id tui etc—"

Van der Kemp thought a short canal to Salina a very good idea because a shaft some forty to fifty feet would reach the real salt bed, "an inexhaustible treasure." He was sorry about the extra taxation on the lands within twenty-five miles of the canal. He thought it should be twelve and a half miles with more of a burden on Troy, Albany, Waterford and Lansingburg.[10] Oldenbarneveld was about fifteen miles from the canal line!

Clinton became governor on July 1, 1817, work on the

canal was officially inaugurated on July 4, and progressed smoothly. In December, 1817, Van der Kemp commended the governor for re-establishing Thanksgiving, wrote of sunspots, the creation, serpents, and *The Achaian Republic*.[11] Early in January Van der Kemp sent some of his Dutch publications to Clinton to be given to the New-York Historical Society, sent the "Outlines on Christ," asked if Clinton had written the proposed essay on the peopling of America and further asked if the "Symposium" ("Dutch Conviviality") had a chance of publication in the *American Monthly Magazine*.[12] Clinton said he was so busy he had little chance to write. He had received the *Protogoea* of Leibnitz sent by Van der Kemp, and promised to read it carefully. He sent the first volume of De la Plaine's *Repository of the Lives and Portraits of Distinguished Americans* and said he had delivered Van der Kemp's publications to the historical society "with respectful notice of the author." He had also sent some "transactions" for his friend.[13]

At this time the business of the translation of the *Records* came up to share their attention with the canal. Digging was going on between Utica and Rome and politicians were maneuvering constantly to support or to block Clinton and his "ditch." The elections for the legislature in 1818 continued a favorable majority for the governor, insuring one or two more years of support.

Early in 1819 Van der Kemp thanked Clinton for sending the canal commissioners' report and commended him for the proposal to set up a Board of Agriculture. Then he asked assistance from the governor for an aged couple of his acquaintance, saying, "the humble cottager deserves as well the attention of a governor—if he can be made happy—as arts and sciences—agriculture and commerce [deserve] his all powerful protection." [14]

Late in October the section of the canal from Rome to Utica was completed and filled with water. After a small breach was repaired, the section was deemed ready for trial. Clinton and other commissioners, engineers and prominent citizens boarded the *Chief Engineer* and one horse towed the boat easily and gaily to Rome and back in only eight hours and twenty minutes traveling time. The trip was a huge success and was witnessed by "almost the whole neighboring population." Morris Miller and Benjamin Walker were on board. If Van der Kemp was not on shore watching he received full reports from friends and neighbors who were present. The reporter of the *Utica Observer,* who was on board, was oratorical in his description and his praise of the project. If anyone missed the event, he could have had the spirit and the color from the paper.[15]

Van der Kemp was so impressed with the progress that he made arrangements to have the official reports sent to Gerrit Boon at Rotterdam in the Netherlands. He was especially anxious for these to reach Holland soon because three new canals were being undertaken and he wished the Dutch to "see that their Brethren in N. York State do not sit idle —in contemplating their unrelenting exertions—but have actually undertaken, and for a great part accomplished—a far more gigantic enterprise." [16]

The canal was opened as far as Montezuma on May 20, 1820, and two packet boats left Utica to make the ninety-mile trip west. Officials boarded the boats at Utica and this section was successfully inaugurated. Freight from the west moved into Utica to be sent on down the Mohawk and Hudson rivers. But all was not well politically. The forces against Clinton led by the Tammany organization were making gains under the guise of being more interested in the canal as an economic project than Clinton was. The governor was re-elected to another three-year term in 1820 but by a very small majority and with the opposition in control of the legislature. The Council of Appointment removed from office many of Clinton's friends. Yet, work on the canal continued.

Cognizant of Clinton's mounting troubles, Van der Kemp wrote: "Your Exc. has raised three gigantic monuments— which party-spirit can not shake, and on which envy's gnashing teeth shall be broken." He referred to Thanksgiving, the *Records* and the canal, assuring Clinton that, "The Canal shall remain when obloquy is buried in oblivion." Then reiterating his interest in lateral canals—an interest on the increase at the time—he asked, "Is a lateral canal from Lake Ontario between Salmon River and Bruce's Creek at Oneyda Lake . . . entirely obliterated?" He considered it worthwhile, probably thinking of the maze of canals in Holland. He let his enthusiasm and his imagination run free when he added, "Did I possess as much wealth as good will, I would make a canal—easily achieved—from this village [Oldenbarneveld]—along the West Canada Creek to the Mohawk—" [17] The maze of canals that he and many others envisioned was not absurd in a time before railroads and a time when turnpikes were often in disrepair, including the Utica Turnpike to Oldenbarneveld.

In this period Clinton made his visits to Van der Kemp and wrote the *Hibernicus Letters*. Van der Kemp now considered Clinton deserving of the presidency or perhaps vicepresidency with John Quincy Adams. He believed the best people of the state would be "cheered" if Adams or Clinton became president. However, he recognized the Tammanies as dominant and thanked God that he could refrain from action and "not *longer* be drawn in this dreadful Political vortex" (this to John Adams).[18] Clinton philosophically wrote that when the "opus basilicum" was finished the state could be as prosperous as she pleased but "wealth and prosperity, my friend, are too often the parents of folly—and the more opulent the state the greater the temptation to the enterprises of faction." [19] The attacks on Clinton continued. Colonel Robert Troup published a pamphlet in vindication of the claims of Elkanah Watson to the original idea of the canal. Clinton published in 1821 *Public Documents Relating to the New York Canals* and at the close of the year *The Canal Policy of the State of New York*, the latter being an attack on Watson's claims and signed "Tacitus." Van der Kemp read these with interest, probably with approval. When he asked the bookdealers, Charles and George Webster of Albany, to send the latest *Canal Commission Report* to Gerrit Boon, he asked them to send "any other interesting

Publications—as Tacitus Letters in answer to the Surmises of Col. Troup." [20]

The growth of political opposition was more than Clinton could overcome and he was not renominated for the governorship. Joseph C. Yates was named and elected along with an overwhelming majority of anti-Clintonites in the legislature. By the new constitution, now in effect, Clinton's term came to an end on January 1, 1823. In the last weeks Van der Kemp wrote him a letter of praise and consolation, particularly stressing the canal and its present and future contributions to the economy.[21] Six weeks later when Clinton was no longer governor, but still head of the canal commission, Van der Kemp wrote to John Adams that the Yankees could "never press the odious steps of the New-Yorkers —in paying eminent public services with the foulest ingratitude." [22] He feared that Clinton would be removed from the commission.

In April, 1823, Van der Kemp wrote, "I remain yet full of anxiety about the canal board—they who would stoop to humble themselves to cast away our Judges—might be inconsiderate enough to change the canal board." [23] The change in the high court by the Tammanyites in the constitutional convention was a sore point with Van der Kemp and he had told Nathan Williams that he opposed the elimination of the old judges who had been chosen in good faith for life terms.[24] He feared that the same political forces might upset Clinton and interrupt progress on the canal.

Van der Kemp had a friend, Henry Seymour of Utica, on the commission, and to some degree he served as Van der Kemp's connection with the new administration. He told Seymour with glee that the Tammanyites had threatened the officers in Trenton, who had reacted by eliminating every last one of them, down through fence viewers. However, the appointment of justices of the peace put the nearest one three miles away from Oldenbarneveld, a great inconvenience. Personal matters were discussed (in the one letter available), including a visit by Mrs. Seymour to the Van der Kemp cottage. As a friend to Seymour, Van der

Kemp concluded, "I feel for you if Clinton, [Stephen] Van Rensselaer and [Myron] Holley should be removed, but shall not be surprised." [25]

However, the three men retained their posts on the commission during 1823. But Holley's accounts were irregular, causing political controversy. Newspapers on each side made attacks, counterattacks and appropriate defenses for Holley's accounts. When Clinton's enemies were unable to damage him in this manner, they became determined to remove Clinton, but were unable to do so until 1824. In the midst of this wrangling Clinton told Van der Kemp, "The Canal Commissioners have escaped the sword of destruction. I made no advance or effort to retain my place . . . but as it now stands, I shall endeavour to close the great operation as soon as possible." [26] Van der Kemp replied:

> I thank my God, that no unhallowed hand was stretched out over the canal-commissioners, . . . I fostered no doubt . . . that the canal would have been accomplished—but now I rejoice—and—perhaps—I may yet see the day— when at the junction of it with the North-river, a splendid monument shall be erected with the names of the men, so much deserving the thanks of Posterity.[27]

Early in October there was a gala celebration for the laying of the first stone in the last lock near Albany. Van der Kemp called it a glorious day and said if he had wealth he would join in the "orgies." [28] After the celebration Clinton told his friend, "The laudari a laudato viro is more pleasing to me than the huzzas of thousands or the pageantry of public celebrations." [29] No doubt the huzzas of thousands convinced the Tammany party to end Clinton's office. He was removed by vote of the legislature in the middle of April, 1824.

The indignant Van der Kemp wrote to his friend at once. He called Clinton's departure, "A glorious exit—equal in renown to that of Aristides." He declared, "Those fellows cannot beat the lustre of your deeds—it humbles them in the dust—I should prefer the most outrageous removal above a vote of thanks of a similar gang." [30] In the correspondence Clinton said little about his removal but much about friends, books, ideas and family. Even when he was renominated for the governorship, he merely wrote, "You see that I am again before the public for an elective office—I feel no other anxiety on this occasion than as it may affect the prosperity of our beloved country." [31]

Clinton was elected with a comfortable majority and the canal work went forward to completion. In October occurred the grand opening with the trip from Buffalo to New York. On October 30, the governor's flotilla reached Utica where public speakers welcomed and praised Clinton. There was great celebrating all over the county, including Oldenbarneveld, though the village had its main celebration on October 26, the same as at Buffalo.

Immediately after the firing of a national salute at twelve o'clock, a procession was formed in front of the house of Elisha Burchard, under the direction of Major E. Backus as Marshall, and Lieut. Joshua Storrs, as deputy Marshall of the day; and moving from thence to the Church, in the following order, viz.:

1. Band and martial music
2. The Military Companies in their uniforms
3. The Musicians of the Choir
4. Committee of Arrangements
5. Clergy and Orator of the day
6. Revolutionary Patriots
7. Officers of the militia in their uniforms
8. Citizens in general

The whole procession consisting of a large concourse of citizens from the neighboring towns, was altogether more numerous than anything of the kind ever before witnessed in the town of Trenton. On arriving at the Church, an eloquent and highly impressive oration was delivered, by Doctor Frederick [Francis] Adrian Vanderkemp; and other exercises adapted to the occasion were performed—after which the procession returned, . . .

marching up the road by the house of Judge Vanderkemp,
. . . [and on to the two official banqueting places]. After
the cloth was removed, the following toasts were drank
interspersed with appropriate music from an excellent
Band.

1. The day we celebrate—It commemorates one of the
proudest events in the annals of our history; its recollection will be as durable as the waters which are this day
united.

2. Our beloved Country—. . .

3. The President and Vice President of the United
States—. . .

4. The State of New York—Abundant in resources and
powerful in strength—May she ever be as conspicuous
for her magnanimity and patriotism, as she is celebrated
for her public spirit and her enterprise.

5. Internal improvements of every description—. . .

6. The Grand Erie Canal—A splendid triumph of human integrity and art over the obstacles of nature, and
an adamantine chain of union among the members of
our great confederated republic.

7. The Canal Commissioners—Their perseverance, industry and economy, are above praise.

8. The Governor, Lieut. Governor and heads of department of the State of New-York.

9. General LaFayette—. . .

10. The memory of Washington, and the departed
heroes and patriots of the Revolution—. . .

11. The three surviving patriots . . .

12. The Orator of the day—An ornament to science,
venerable in years, and irreproachable in life.

13. The American Fair—. . . [the ladies] [32]

In the oration Van der Kemp proudly addressed his
"Fellow Citizens." He said the celebration was a "dutiful
act of Thanking a bountiful God for a blessing" and that
their posterity would regret missing it. He spoke of his
selection as orator "at the decline of my days—at the brink

of the grave—my eyes dimmed with age—in the possession only of an incorrect idiom and a harsh pronunciation." Van der Kemp had acceded to the request of his townsmen for an oration as he had done twenty-five years before for a eulogy of Washington.

He said it would have been wonderful if all of them could have been at Lake Erie to enjoy the pageantry of the great opening. However, in their own village their tribute could only be construed as the language of their hearts.

He spoke at length on the lack of freedom and economic opportunity in Europe while "in this happy land, every mechanic, every labourer who is industrious, active and frugal, may, with God's blessing, be independent if he will." He reminded the people how they had acquired freedom and prosperity—through the battles of Bunker Hill, Saratoga, and Monmouth, where some members of the audience had been engaged. The great Washington had been commander-in-chief, but had needed La Fayette, Von Steuben and De Kalb to train the men. The Americans had been without arms until John Adams secured a liberal supply from the Dutch. After we had won our independence, the two nations had been friendly and since had been "the refuge of the persecuted sons of liberty in every part of Europe." Religious liberty was hailed by the speaker and the clergy was called successful, beloved and respected "without the support of civil authority, without the inquisition or the rack."

"Our astonishing population, our wealth and industry" increased day by day. "We levelled the mountains, and destroyed the woods, smoothed the waves [of rapids and falls], and grasped, now and then, successfully at the skies," all for the improvement of the country.

When I visited the western wilderness in 1792, and examined its waters, their Union with those of the Hudson appeared to be practicable by this State—by the city of New-York *alone*, guided by *Philip Schuyler, Stephen Van Rensselear* and *Jonas Platt*. This was called a dream and yet De Witt Clinton contemplated the great scheme and it was executed. Clinton—and I am not over partial to this great man—Clinton was the father of that great and stupendous undertaking, the Erie Canal, although many worthy individuals, as he often avowed, had considered such a project would be beneficial to the state if practicable. Clinton manly and fearlessly struggled against the obstacles opposed by prejudice, and which were countenanced by many of his zealous friends. Clinton could not be shaken by antagonists, nor daunted by the scurrilities which they called to their aid. He was neither discouraged nor intimidated by refusal of assistance from the general administration at Washington, but marched successfully on, combatting every impediment, and triumphing over every obstacle, to the execution of this gigantic plan. Unbiased in his heroic course, he hesitated not to stake upon the result of the undertaking his fortunes, his great future prospects, and his so gloriously acquired fame. . . .

He mentioned the work of the other canal commissioners and the plaudits to New York and to Clinton from many of the other states. He said the "name of the illustrious Clinton was re-echoed in Europe from shore to shore."

The benefits of this great Canal to the state of New-York are already immense, and cannot be sufficiently appraised, and shall increase from day to day for many years to come. Albany, New York [City], nay, the vast population of our state are already gathering incalculable advantages from the Grand Erie Canal. Agriculture, commerce, manufactures, are now striving together for the highest prize. Unrelaxing activity, honest persevering industry and economy, must regulate the steps of each individual, and comfort, and affluence, and wealth, shall be his final reward. Our state will become the glory of the Union, a bright example to her sister states, and an irresistible lure to the oppressed, wise and good of every country.

. . . Your silence, your eyes, your throbbing breasts—
my own feelings, all these united, make me confident that
this day shall not have been celebrated in vain.

The God of our fathers, Our God, pour out upon us
and our children the choicest of his blessings, and merci-
fully avert the dangers incurred by our wanderings: Farewell! Be happy! [33]

The venerable orator's vision of 1792 had been fulfilled.
The obstacles and delays could be forgotten. Rejoicing and
thanksgiving were in order.

❧ XXII ❧

Translating
the Dutch Records

THE first indication of Van der Kemp's interest in Dutch
records of early New York was his attempt to obtain some of
the colonial documents from Amsterdam with the intent
of giving them to the New-York Historical Society. He first
requested copies in 1814 or 1815 when the Dutch nation was
restored and his friends were in high places. He wrote again
in 1817, telling De Witt Clinton of the correspondence. Van
der Kemp said the best Dutch historians, Jan Wagenaer and
Petrus C. van Hooft, contained very little about New Netherland.[1]

Clinton was impressed with the possibilities of filling in
the blank spots of New York history. When he became aware
of how little had been done with the great mass of Dutch
records in the office of the secretary of state at Albany, he
thought of Van der Kemp as a translator. A small beginning had been made by a previous translator and then was
stopped. With the approval of the legislature for a renewal
of the project, Clinton offered the position to Van der Kemp
on January 21, 1818, saying that he should come to Albany
for the arrangements and that he might do a part of the
work at home.[2] Van der Kemp was doubtful about the status
of the position. He wrote to Clinton that by strict economy
and aid from his son he had preserved his independence so
far and could not now part with it "as with the last breath

of life." He suspected that a translator might be very insignificant, something of a menial servant in the secretary's office. Nor would he come to Albany as "an humble suppliant" to beg the members of the legislature for a job. However, he thanked Clinton cordially and indicated that if most of the work could be done at home there was a possibility of his doing it. He said that Jonas Platt, Henry Seymour, Nathan Williams, Abraham Van Vechten and Congressman Joseph Kirkland would all vouch for him so that there need be no doubt of his faithful execution of the trust.[3]

Clinton immediately assured Van der Kemp that the office of translator was confidential and honorable and he had been appointed because a man of undoubted capacity and leisure was needed. Probably he could do most of it at home in hours when he had nothing else to do. Friends urged Van der Kemp to go to Albany and look into the situation. There he was treated with the greatest respect, was told to name his own conditions of work, and was offered a reasonable salary and expenses. After looking over the forty volumes of bound documents, he agreed to undertake the work of translation. His friends and relatives were pleased to see Van der Kemp, now sixty-six years old, embark upon the work with his normally great enthusiasm and vigor. He agreed to do as much as he could by fall and take it to Albany for a decision on a continuation of the project. Adams congratulated him for the "honourable Usefull and profitable Employment and Amusement for Life" and added facetiously that it was a rescue from his writing "metaphysical and delirious" cosmogonies.[4]

Thinking of the project on a grand scale, Van der Kemp wrote to a friend in Philadelphia for the records of the Swedes and their relations with New Netherland. He also wrote again to Holland to get the Dutch government documents from 1614 to 1648.[5] By May he completed one volume, equal to about two of the originals, amounting to 460 pages. He was pleased but admitted to John Lincklaen that his uncouth English and the scrawl of the Dutch made the work difficult.[6] He suffered from eyestrain, but expected that working in his garden in the growing season would rest his eyes and restore their strength. While he gardened during the summer, he thought about the translations and wrote about them in his correspondence. Rather proudly he informed Adams that as early as 1660 the Dutch sent seeds, plants and equipment for the beginning of a botanical garden, that they established potash and salt works and set up a Latin school in New Amsterdam.[7] Adams was impressed but asked if the Dutch had banished or hanged Quakers and if they had executed witches as had the Yankees. He believed errors should be investigated as well as progress.[8]

Some of the documents in the next group were partially effaced or blotted and very difficult to read. They contained the minutes of the governor and council and appeared to be very dull. In regard to Adams' question on Quakers, he found one Quaker had been exiled, and suspected persecution because of the documented persecution of Lutherans. However, the director of the West India Company had commanded free exercise of religion in the private homes. He had found no records of witches as yet.[9] In October Van der Kemp renewed his translating and in one document found mention of a Thomas Adams. He asked John if Thomas were one of his ancestors; if so he wished to include the fact in his annotations. In the same letter, Van der Kemp reported that word had come from Europe that Napoleon had carried away to destruction the original documents of the West India Company. However, he had been notified he could have copies made of the documents in the archives of the king of the Netherlands if he paid for the expense.[10]

Clinton now requested Van der Kemp to come to Albany so that the arrangement for the translating could be officially approved. He went, perhaps in January, 1819, having sent his translations on ahead for official perusal. At this stage Van der Kemp admitted he would be mortified if Clinton was not pleased with his work. He was eager to complete the task and said he ought to have all the documents in his home so that they could be taken chronologically, rearranged where necessary, and be readily available in annotating the work. He also requested that the state procure the documents from Holland.[11] His trip to Albany was largely successful. He received one hundred dollars for expenses and five hundred for salary. It was agreed to 'send all the documents to Oldenbarneveld and the plan of procedure was entrusted to Van der Kemp. He started translating again at the end of January and told Adams he would relay bits of interesting information such as the fact that Negroes were used for farming by the Dutch on Manhattan as early as the 1630's.[12]

When Van der Kemp picked up his work again, he found the papers most difficult. Some were muddy and some were moldered away. Much seemed to be perfectly worthless in content. Yet here and there he found "a pearl," particularly information about the economy of New Netherland. He was impressed that the colony was something of an emporium of all North America, supplying goods to New England and Virginia and taking their products to Europe. Especially notable in volume and value of products exchanged, was the trade with New Haven where the Dutch took in pay peas, wheat, beef, pork and sewan (wampum). He found that New Netherland was chiefly a tobacco colony up to the time of its conquest by England. "Could it be that it was curbed and extinguished to favour Virginia?" By the first of March he completed almost six hundred pages and the farther he went the more surprised he was that these potentially valuable records had lain so long unused.[13] In another month he completed two hundred pages more, admitting that although the work was arduous and hurt his eyes he had found it highly interesting. The prudent and energetic business practices of the Dutch comprised a complete instruction book of how to operate a successful mercantile colony. Commerce was the soul of the operation but agriculture was not neglected. They handled almost exclusively the trade in furs, tobacco and salt with the Netherlands and other Dutch colonies. However, the government was aristocratic to an excess and "bigotry tainted their religious establishment." [14]

By the end of April his eyes were so weak that he had to give up the work by order of his physician. In June the treatment by "blistering" was considered unsuccessful and sublimate of mercury was used. His eyes allowed some work and when he got through the dirtiest documents, the "Augis stabulum," he was rewarded by finding the next documents clean and clear.[15] When John Adams asked for his eye remedy, Van der Kemp reported that he had consulted three physicians, Guiteau, Willoughby and Coventry, and all were apprehensive of cataract. They suggested the blistering, then changed to the mercury—a solution of four or five grains in an ounce of brandy with several drops to be taken internally morning and evening. The Eliots had consulted their doctor and his opinion was similar. However, because of Van der Kemp's vitality, Guiteau prescribed a stronger solution and up to ten drops as a dose. The same was weakened with water and dropped into the eyes as often as he could think of it. If this did not work, "electricity" must be tried. If a cataract developed, an operation would be necessary. Van der Kemp recommended that Adams consult his physician for a proper solution for his weak eyes.[16]

Van der Kemp's eyes improved to some extent, and he worked on the records more, before breakfast, in the evening, on rainy days. This, plus vigorous gardening, was more than his sixty-seven years could stand. As he worked in his garden in late July, muscular spasms seized both his knees, giving excruciating pain for an hour and a half. Another spell followed the first after a brief interval and when it was over he was too worn out to move at all. Great weakness and loss of appetite kept him incapacitated for two weeks. He recovered and was in the garden again by the end of August and working on the *Records* even sooner.[17] He was only one month behind his schedule when he completed the eighth volume in September.

By this time the De Witt Clinton political fortunes were less promising and Van der Kemp wondered if Clinton's enemies would be successful in the elections and then proceed to stop the translations. The scholar declared he had not sought the position and if politicians wanted to save a few dollars by discontinuing his project he would be "pretty indifferent about it." [18]

Perhaps the political situation made him more observant of the politics reflected in the *Albany Records,* as they came to be called. He commented on the despotic power entrusted to the governor and his council, yet found no case where the power was abused. In critical situations the governor had called a goodly number of the respectable inhabitants together for advice and then executed their resolves. Van der Kemp noted with interest that at one time twenty-five families had come from their "delightful abode" in New England to settle in the Dutch colony for the sake of liberty of worship. The *Records* contained the negotiations.[19] In December he sent four more volumes, containing about five hundred pages each, to Albany. He was given fresh inspiration when he was told that the first seven volumes were neatly bound, lettered, and available for scholarly use. In spite of his declared indifference, in December he said he hoped his work might be approved in the new year when Clinton would start another term, even though he was without much support in the legislature.[20]

In January Clinton wrote for Van der Kemp to come to Albany and a few days later Jonas Platt urged that he come immediately. He went. Clinton made the correct approaches to the right people in the legislature, impressed them with the scholarship of Van der Kemp, and all was well. He was received as a distinguished person, the secretary of state had recorded a notice of his work in the journals of both houses of the legislature, and the pay was liberal. The money was enough to meet his expenses of the past year, to purchase some things needed by his family, to pay three hundred dollars to his son as part payment on the property which John had finished paying for in 1819. There was even enough money left for Mrs. Van der Kemp to go to Philadelphia to visit John and his family. He enthusiastically declared his intention to work another year at the translations if his eyes held out.[21]

The money from the translations was followed by a legacy of a thousand dollars from Van der Kemp's wealthy friend, Sam Eliot. The scholar repaired his cottage, paid the last four hundred dollars to his son, and had enough left over to plan another visit to Boston and Quincy.[22] John Adams was pleased at the prospect of seeing Francis again and said he would be welcomed by all.

The translating continued although hindered by Van der Kemp's weakened eyes. His daughter, Betsy, helped with some of the writing. By July he had three more volumes finished. In addition, the copies of the documents in the Hague were promised. When the state of New York hesitated to pay for the copying, David Parish, a wealthy merchant of New York City and friend to Van der Kemp, offered to pay all the costs. This gift to the state made Francis exclaim, "May I not indulge a little pride in possessing such friends!" [23]

With some of the legacy Van der Kemp had two new rooms built to his cottage, a small guest room and a room for his library and study. These filled out his needs for scholarship and for friendship, parts of Van der Kemp's life that were very nearly on an equal basis. He was appreciative of the legacy, as he had always felt kindly toward all the Eliots. While the house was being remodeled, young Sam Eliot stopped at Oldenbarneveld to see Van der Kemp and to discuss the scholar's projected trip to Boston. He was cordially invited to make his headquarters at the Eliot home. In July one of the Eliot girls in a small party stopped and planned all of Van der Kemp's travel arrangements. Near the middle of August he set out by stage, probably stopping briefly at Albany and Pittsfield.

The visit was as pleasant and stimulating as his first trip to Boston. He conversed and dined with officials, clergymen and scholars. He was treated as a member of the Adams family again and was once more welcomed into the home of Josiah Quincy, soon to be mayor of Boston and after that president of Harvard. William Ellery Channing, unofficial leader of American Unitarianism at the time, received Van der Kemp graciously, while President John Kirkland of Harvard sought him out. Nearly all of his Boston friends were connected with Harvard in some way. The high point of the trip now came, the official adoption of Van der Kemp by these Harvardites through the ceremony of conferring on him an honorary degree of doctor of laws.

Though Van der Kemp was appreciative, perhaps it took some coaxing by the Eliot clan, by Kirkland and by Quincy to persuade him to accept the honor. Only two years before, Van der Kemp had written disparagingly of the granting of such degrees to any but "men of supereminent deserves," and his feeling was, "Throw not the pearls to the swine." Yet how could he refuse this mark of esteem from friends he respected highly—especially when he learned that Channing was to receive the same honor at the same time? They were sincere and all felt as did John Adams, "We all rejoice that Harvard University has done itself honour by enroling your name among its adopted Sons, most eminent for science and learning." [24]

Van der Kemp accepted the title of "Doctor" thereafter but seldom mentioned the conferral of the degree. He apparently found the more common acts of friendship to be more to his liking, especially his reception by Adams. When he returned home he wrote back:

> I cannot express my feelings for the affectionate reception which I met with at Montezillo—You honour me not only with your distinguished and partial regards to which I am indebted for all the attentions which I received —but you treated me as a Brother—as a Friend—with cordiality—which was followed by each member of your family. . . .
>
> What delightful time I spend under your roof—in your presence and that of your Family! I shall a long while feast upon it. When I walk in my garden—and see your plumb trees growing and your lilies in full flower—my

imagination will transport me to Montezillo—and then I shall listen, if I do not hear the voice of John Adams—[25]

Dudley Tyng took Van der Kemp to Worcester, where they visited the Antiquarian Society, and then continued to Lenox. Van der Kemp started the homeward journey from there, making a stopover at Pittsfield. The perfect trip was marred by only one small incident. In descending from the stage at Utica, Van der Kemp fell and injured his legs, though not seriously. As soon as he was settled at home again and had given full reports to family and friends, he gathered some garden seeds to send back to Adams in return for the plum trees and flowers. He sent some "Salada" seeds of the "excellent Frankforter" variety and a few Brussels sprout seeds. The field salada was recommended for spring and fall served with oil and vinegar, and, in season, with chopped beets, butter and vinegar. He recommended boiling and stewing of the Brussels sprouts with a little butter and nutmeg.[26]

Van der Kemp went back to his translating with renewed vigor, perhaps too much so. He completed his twentieth volume but with more eye trouble. He considered the next batch of documents to be in the worst condition of all but knew if he could do them he could say, "Rubiconem transii." In November he made a trip to Albany to arrange some details and went on to New York City for medical treatment.[27]

The re-election of Clinton had been fine but his plans were often upset by having the majority in the legislature against him. The national election was satisfactory but European affairs were more threatening than usual. Adams wrote that he feared more European troubles, "the leagues, holy and Unholy," and regretted that progress was so often interrupted by "frenzikal Monarchs, deleterious Nobles, and ferocious blind Ignorant Sans Culottes, and Radicals."

"Then Adams added a comment that could be made only by one old friend to another. "All the above is fustian—now for something of real use to mankind—You once men-

tioned to me a remedy for corns, will you have the goodness to send me a receipt . . . ?" [28]

Ven der Kemp shared Adams' fears about the troubles
of Europe. He thought the United States should surpass
Europe in civilization within a hundred years even if there
were troubles in America over race, political power and
education.[29]

Van der Kemp continued to work on the *Records* and
had three large volumes ready to send away by October.
He admired most of the acts of the Dutch but deplored
their encouragement of the slave trade. He particularly
noted that the Dutch had encouraged education of Indians in the colony schools.[30] Van der Kemp had hoped to
finish the translations during Clinton's administration, but
the Constitutional Convention had shortened the governor's term by a year and a half. He feared the work might
not be finished by January 1, 1823.

Late in 1821 Van der Kemp sent a summary of his work
to Clinton with the suggestion that it be included in his
message to the legislature. Clinton received it too late for
his regular message but promised to use it and also to pass
to the legislature Van der Kemp's suggestion of an index
for the translations.[31] Van der Kemp had also suggested
the index to Secretary John van Ness Yates, who sent his
approval of it to Clinton, saying, "The act of 1804 is silent
in this respect—and Mr Vander Kemp probably did not
feel authorized to proceed further than to make translations literally and faithfully from the originals." [32]

As part of a special message of January 22, 1822, Clinton
reported to the legislature Van der Kemp's progress and
recommended the index. His praise of the work was enthusiastic. He said the translations contained "much valuable information . . . illustrating an interesting period
of our colonial history, hitherto, in a great degree closed
against us." Van der Kemp had performed a great service
"among all the difficulties involved in deciphering, explaining, and translating ancient and mouldering manuscripts,"
and he had "successfully performed a work, which perhaps

no other man, in this country, was capable of accomplishing." [33] Clinton sent a copy of the message to Van der Kemp with the notation that he had endeavored "to render justice to a very worthy gentleman." [34]

The index was approved by the legislature, but when Van der Kemp pushed for appropriations to get more documents from Holland, Clinton advised caution. Van der Kemp wrote again to a cousin in Holland who passed his request on to the Advocate General of the High Court. In December he wrote yet again to get records copied but it was in vain.[35] In the meantime he continued the work on the last few volumes, and in May told Adams he thought he could finish and be able to say "without boasting, that I procured to this State, what she could not have obtained without me." [36]

As the work approached completion Van der Kemp began to consider ways of promoting its use. An initial suggestion was that, as soon as the index was completed, the historical society should offer a prize for the best essay on Peter Stuyvesant. Van der Kemp said he would give twenty-five dollars to it.[37] The *Albany Gazette & Daily Advertiser* accepted for publication several columns entitled, "Scraps for History, from our Dutch Records." [38] Van der Kemp wrote to the editors that he was very pleased and hoped they would continue publishing extracts.[39]

In July Van der Kemp wrote to remind Secretary Yates of the proposed general index to assist "Scientific inquirers." He asked if the completed volumes had been lettered and numbered. He also requested that the few remaining documents be sent immediately to Oldenbarneveld, so that he could include them in the last volumes.

Then came the first recognition of trouble. Van der Kemp offered to have conveyance of the papers and some paper and quills charged to him if the secretary hesitated to pay it. The expenses of the project were heavier than he had expected. He had been allowed one hundred dollars for trips to Albany and contingent expenses the first year. Now he had had to hire some of his gardening done, as he had been working on the *Records* from half after four until late in the evening. He also felt obligated to reward his son and daughter for copy reading. He reminded Yates that the first year's payment, six hundred dollars, was described as for labor and expense and that the administration of the project to completion should call for something further.[40]

On September 16, he reported the completion of the twenty-fifth volume, his last, and noted he had translated over 3,000 pages since the November before. The entire project comprised a total of well over 12,000 pages. Now State Comptroller John Savage rejected Van der Kemp's claim for contingent expenses. The scholar, mindful of his hours of labor and the value of his work, could not contain his wrath. He wrote to Clinton:

> That man does not know me, if he assumes, that it is in his power to humble me—He is digging a grave for himself—while he rashly endeavours—to undervalue one of your Exc. most glorious undertakings during your administration—I now nearly regret, although prudence and your interest in my behalf directed your Exc. step —that my answer was not plunged in his throat—I expect that by all means your Exc. can not stoop to a compromise. As I would *now* not consent to receive 99$ and 99 cents per year . . . Platt . . . approves my answer. . . .

In a postscript he said another volume of documents had belatedly arrived at Oldenbarneveld. "I shall not touch—not even try to decypher a single line" lest the legislature refuse to pay the postage.[41]

Clinton tried to arrange a fair financial settlement for his friend, but without success. Shortly after his term of office expired on January 1, 1823, he wrote that he would be in New York for a few weeks. He added that the usual uproar about offices when a new administration came in would make it unwise to raise the Van der Kemp claim yet.[42] In March Van der Kemp told William Bayard that except for the hundred dollars the first year as allowance,

he had received nothing but clerical wages for his work
and that the state owed him at least three hundred dollars.
He declared that when Justice was deaf he would not
humbly beg for what was justly due even if he was "craving a crust of bread." [43]

Van der Kemp sent the untranslated volume back to Secretary Yates and asked plainly if the secretary had forgotten
him. Van der Kemp asked for all correspondence relative
to the matter, including the Yates letter of approval for
contingent expenses. He said they could let someone else
finish the last set of documents as long as the great state
of New York was the debtor "of a Recluse in the western
woods." The absence of malice in the character of the
amiable "Recluse" was indicated by the closing sentence,
when he invited Yates to come with his wife for a visit to
the Van der Kemp home and Trenton Falls.[44]

Appropriate action in Albany may have made it unnecessary for Yates to send copies of the papers to Van der
Kemp, as the claims were adjusted and paid by April. The
total cost of the project amounted to $7,754 for translating
(including trips to Albany and other incidentals) and
$140.37 for stationery and binding. Much of this had al-
ready been paid to Van der Kemp. The total may have been
fair payment for three years of scholarly effort, inasmuch as
the secretary of state was getting $1,500 per year and the
comptroller $2,381.81,[45] but the state's reluctance to settle
the final claim was a bitter blow.

In February, 1824, Van der Kemp noted that Governor
Joseph Yates (not the secretary) was having trouble. He
tried to reappoint the same judges, including Jonas Platt,
but was obliged to name new ones when the legislature rejected the experienced judges. He had voiced approval
of the canal, even recommended a branch to the St. Lawrence River, but had given Clinton little credit for the
canal and for having the Dutch records translated. He
stood on the unpopular side of the presidential elector
question and seemed to have fallen from public favor. Van

der Kemp had mixed emotions about his fall. He said that he himself would now pay for any documents which came from Holland and would give them to the New-York Historical Society.[46] Fighting for his payments from the state for his long months of arduous work was a humiliation not easily forgotten.

The break between the party factions which had supported Yates, and the canal politics, returned Clinton to the governor's chair on January 1, 1825. Early in April Clinton told Van der Kemp that he had called on Secretary Yates for a full report on the translations and hoped Van der Kemp would do that last volume.[47] Van der Kemp was disgusted. "Better Yates should finish the translation. My eyes are bad; I'm old & tired." [48] Van der Kemp was now seventy-three.

The translations were used by scholars of his day, but not by historians in time for Van der Kemp to appreciate it. John Romeyn Brodhead in his *History of the State of New York* had hundreds of references to the *Albany Records*. Other writers used the *Records,* although with fewer citations. In 1865, Edmund Bailey O'Callaghan used some of Van der Kemp's translations, even as he criticized the translating as unidiomatic, incorrect, unreliable and incomplete. Some forty-five years later, A. J. F. Van Laer, archivist of the New York State Library, classed the translations as "worthless for critical historical work" because of inaccuracies and free translation.[49] Whether Van Laer, with his European training in the "scientific" pursuit of history, was too harsh a critic, or whether Van der Kemp was carried away by his enthusiasm for making his translations immediately available and interpretive in nature, will probably never be known. A fire destroyed his translations of the *Albany Records* in 1911, and only fragments quoted in Brodhead and elsewhere remain.

Nevertheless, the work represented a significant achievement for Van der Kemp in his declining years. Clinton, in his message to the legislature of 1827, commented on the work of the New-York Historical Society and followed these

remarks with praise for Van der Kemp's accomplishment.
"The translation of our Dutch Records, at the public expense, by the learned Doctor Vanderkemp, have opened
sources of historical information, which were before locked
up in a language little known and in manuscripts scarcely
legible." [50]

❧ XXIII ❧

Family Life

FRANCIS Van der Kemp was a typical European patriarch in his family and usually seemed to have the last word. He did not consider himself an autocrat, however, but the intelligent male head of the family who made the decisions after due consideration and what he called free discussion. Being an enthusiastic talker, he no doubt stifled discussion at times without realizing it. His wife understood him, and deferred to his opinions. Only twice did she want to "have her own way" on major decisions; she would not leave Holland when Francis first suggested it, and hers was the determining voice in the move from Oneida Lake.

Bartha considered that her position of wife and mother required her to be economical and efficient in running the house. Francis praised her for this and as a gracious hostess to their guests. She admired his gardening efforts, and appreciated a fine head of cauliflower as much as a lovely rose. She also catered to the whims of her husband. When he grew exotic vegetables, she cooked them. When he caught fish, they had fish for dinner. When he considered the poor state of his health required veal chops three nights in a row, that is what she prepared. Of course, Francis could and probably did wax eloquent about the exquisite taste of the food she prepared and even more so about the improved state of his health after the veal chops. If she discounted some of his compliments, she at least accepted them as a pleasant way of life.

Apparently Bartha never delved into the intellectual pursuits of her husband. She did not read the histories or science or even Scott's romances. She no doubt listened to his frequent "loud thinking," said yes at the right time, and tried to calm him when he became excited—a frequent occurrence. She also knew that housecleaning chores did not include tidying his desk. And she left his library alone, "every book of which he could identify in the dark." [1]

Francis admitted that he was frequently carried away in conversation and writing to the point of bluntness. He was a champion of free speech and free thought and seldom failed to exercise it. He had a loud voice which must have carried beyond the walls of his cottage and probably by its volume carried many a point within the family circle. He never expected members of the family or others to resent his booming opinions or his bluntness.

The Van der Kemp children went to public school when they lived on Esopus Creek and probably attended the little school in Oldenbarneveld. Francis took a great interest in their education, attending personally to religious training and teaching fine principles of living. He wrote essays for them and conducted family devotionals. The three children had access to his extensive library of excellent books.

John was the most promising of the children. He apparently learned easily and had the desire to excel in the pattern laid out for him in the family and in the community. He was an obedient son, accepting parental guidance without great frustration or rebellion. As a teenager he became clerk to Adam Mappa and learned well both the mechanics of land company business and the perplexities of handling personal income. When he was twenty-one he received the appointment at the Holland Land Company's main office in Philadelphia where he was equally successful. Francis was proud of John and confident that he would fulfill his responsibilities.

In 1809 Van der Kemp joyfully told Adams of John's approaching marriage:

My Eldest Son John at Philadelphia did ask me two days past for my consent in his marriage with a Miss Julia Taylor, of a respectable family and connections with a moderate fortune, adequate to his wishes. His former prudent conduct made me not hesitate one instant to comply and grant him this boon. You are father, and can place yourself in my situation. My decline of life is crowned with happiness. What can I wish more in my retirement—your exalted distinguished friendship, the friendship of a few worthies, the happiness of a beloved son—the certainty that in all events He will be in Gods hands the tutelar angel of my remaining family! What a rich fund of gratitude towards a good God! Now I can lay down my head in peace.[2]

John Van der Kemp had respectfully followed the old custom of asking his father's consent, even though he was twenty-six years old and had been in an independent position in Philadelphia for almost five years. He worked for Paul Busti, one of his father's good friends. Busti considered John his protégé, and demonstrated his fondness for the Van der Kemp family in many ways. The success of his son banished fear of poverty and dependence from Van der Kemp's mind, "soothed by domestic enjoyments and remaining literary amusements" in his "humble cot." [3]

Cuneira, or Betsy, was also a conformist to the family organization, although she had wider interests than her mother. She was a dutiful daughter, a religious liberal like her father, and intellectual enough to help her father when his eyes began to fail. In addition, she acquired a good knowledge of domestic arts from her mother. Perhaps her conformity was to her disadvantage in backwoods America; she seems to have attracted few beaux. John Mappa accompanied her a few times to various places but married someone else.

A story about a honey party may be sufficiently true to indicate why Van der Kemp, referred to as "the Old Judge," was considered stern and extremely careful about his daughter and her associations. The young people of the area often went in sleighs to Garrett's Tavern to have hot biscuits and honey. One of the young men of the village ventured to invite Betsy to go along to a honey party in his cutter. Betsy said she would like to go if the young man asked permission. Van der Kemp consented but on the condition that she be brought home by twelve o'clock sharp. The party was successful and the couple started home. On nearing the village the young man looked at his watch and reported, "Four minutes to twelve." Betsy replied, "I hope we will be on time." The horse was encouraged to a faster pace and they drew up in front of the cottage at twelve. There stood the judge on the outside step waiting. The youth saved his "bacon" and his "credit for promptness." [4]

Peter Van der Kemp did not seem to be as intelligent as the two older children and probably was less of a conformist. He had the same education as his brother but made little impression in the village life with his industry. Father and son discussed vocations without agreement. Farming had not the scientific appeal to the son which it had for Francis. At last, when he was twenty-one, Peter decided to try commerce. Francis wrote to John in Philadelphia, to Paul Hochstrasser in Albany, and to Benjamin Walker, hoping he could survey possibilities in New York City. Van der Kemp told Walker, "His intellectual endowments are rather indifferent—his moral character without a spot—without any vicious propensity thus far—his manners decent—his affectionate regard towards his mother and superiors has thus far unequivocally been exemplary—" [5]

John had written that his brother ought to start in "a good store above a Merchants Counting House." John and Francis presumed that Peter "might make a good storekeeper but not a merchant." However, in such a position over a counting house the boy, "by uninterrupted assiduity perhaps," might become a merchant. If efforts to get a place failed in the cities, Francis would try in Utica and Whitesboro although he thought these places "too near his old abode." [6]

These prospects did not materialize, as Peter was conscripted by the militia and marched to Sackett's Harbor in 1814. He returned home, apparently taking up again the tasks of helping his father on their ten acres of land. Peter had an easy-going, amiable disposition, and earned the reputation as a joker, perhaps in his youth. He may have had a few tries at store jobs, but no work is mentioned for him after the war except on the little home farm and a one-year appointment as poundmaster (to take care of stray animals) in the town of Trenton in 1824.[7] Both Peter and Betsy lived at home, and neither married. Though Peter may have tried Francis' patience, his fatherly affection never wavered. Peter's death by drowning in the Erie Canal at Syracuse in 1857 was an ironic aftermath to his father's interest in "Clinton's ditch."

Benjamin Walker, to whom Van der Kemp applied in behalf of Peter, was an influential businessman of Utica. He originally came from England but served in the American Revolution under Von Steuben. Later he took over the care of Von Steuben's lands near Oldenbarneveld. Walker had a good library which Van der Kemp was welcome to use but borrowings were limited to the infrequent visits of the two men and to an occasional request for a book to be transported by a friend. Among those borrowed were some of the works of Laurence Sterne which Van der Kemp reread with "fresh pleasure," no doubt reading choice excerpts to his family.[8]

In one letter Van der Kemp asked for an article from the *Quarterly Review* or the *Edinburgh Review* on looning, the ability of seafaring people to sense the arrival of ships at some distance away. Van der Kemp was intrigued with this early treatment of extrasensory perception and wanted to recheck the article. Later he asked for *Lee's Memoirs* if Walker had it.[9] When the allies captured Paris, Van der

Kemp congratulated Walker for the safety of his daughter there. Van der Kemp had corresponded with her a few years earlier. Then he asked Walker to get him some sherry wine.[10] Toward the end of 1814 Walker made plans to leave Utica for retirement in Madison County. Van der Kemp suggested that maybe Varick would get that keg of wine for him—sherry, not above $2 the gallon. Very sincerely he told his friend, "I hope as soon as you are settled—and can leave home—that you will come and see us—was it even only for one or two days." [11]

When John Mifflin died in 1813 Van der Kemp was oppressed with grief. Not only had the man been a good friend to him, but he had also assisted John Van der Kemp when he first went to Philadelphia. John helped to bury Mifflin and Francis notified one of Mifflin's close dependents. Francis thought how few of his oldest friends still lived— Adams, Cau and DeGyselaer. He had heard it said that one grows insensitive in old age. He declared he felt sorrow and grief and happiness to the same excess as when he was young.[12]

Perhaps the keen sensitivity to grief, frustration and other stimuli common to his life caused some of the numerous headaches through the war years and thereafter. He complained to Adams of violent headache in April, 1814, and again in June. His daughter thought it was because of overwork. She scolded him that he went too fast and could never rest until nothing remained to be done.[13] The headaches plagued him through the fall, and by December he had become despondent. He turned to reading. It was ineffective. He sketched a history of plagiarism, being the only one of the times who realized that the Latin phrase about Franklin—*Eripuit caelo fulmen; mox sceptrum tyrannis*—attributed to various contemporaries, was stolen from Manilius. He grew tired of this sketch and put it aside to immerse himself in ancient history. Yet he found nothing to relieve his anguish except chatting with friends or family or leading family or neighborhood devotionals.[14]

Some of Van der Kemp's trouble may have been caused by the frustrations of the war, as he improved rapidly after peace was declared. He wrote happily:

It shall give you some pleasure—that this is the third day I am relieved by my unrelenting Antagonist—He called this morning—but I stopt my ears—unwilling to admit him—although in a heavy snow storm—and at length tired and disappointed he must have sneaked of[f]. So that I have preached this morning for my family —and read and wrote the remaining part of the day—A guard of kind interesting letters—and a barrel of cyder —from my old friend Scriba . . . must have intimidated the fellow. . . .[15]

His headaches did recur, though not so intensively, but he now also suffered from pain in his shoulder. John Adams added his scolding for Van der Kemp's overwork and worry and closed one letter with "Vivamus, Scribamus, bibamus, atque amamus"—Let us live, let us write, let us drink and let us love.[16] A few months later to a remark by Van der Kemp "alas! what avails me now this vain knowledge—" Adams replied with encouragement and the words,

You have a Talent, at the Pathetick, which I could never equal, if I would; and which I never would equal, if I could. Who can read your excursion to Oneida Lake without Tears? I could give you histories too, of do-mestic separations! But I forbear. "That way Madness lies."! . . .

But your endeavours to do good will not be in vain. Neither your Letters nor mine will be lost.[17]

Adams' reference to "domestic separations," when duties to his country took him from his Abigail for extended periods of time, was kindly intended to remind Francis of the blessings of his own family life. He appreciated his friend's concern and once said, "It shall be a part of my Sunday's devotion to give you my sincere thanks for your kindness, which I received in your letters. . . ." [18]

In the summer of 1815 Bartha went to Philadelphia to visit John and his family and the Bustis. She traveled with Adam Mappa and his daughter, Sophia. John Van der Kemp, with help from Paul Busti, had offered to pay his mother's expenses. Francis said it was a great satisfaction to see her "obtain an object, for which, I doubt not, she secretly wished, although her delicacy prevented its utterance, when she deemed it unfeasible." Then Francis received both a payment for translating and a legacy and was proud to be able to pay the expenses himself.[19] Mrs. Van der Kemp undoubtedly had a wonderful time. However, she found that at her age (69) she could not always cope with two "sprightly boys," her grandsons, particularly the younger. Mrs. Busti declared that the visit had contributed greatly to her convalescence from a long illness.[20] Francis and Betsy made a little trip, too, towards the end of the summer to Oneida Lake. Mrs. John Bernhard wanted to see them because she thought it might be her last summer. The Scribas and many other old friends also lived in the area. The Bernhards had prospered, chiefly by their hard work and that of their son.[21]

The garden still demanded Van der Kemp's time, frequently to his annoyance, but he kept some interest in specialties. He sent Brussels sprouts seeds and Egyptian rye grains from his own farm to his friends in Massachusetts. In the fall he worked in the rain and his shoulder pain came back.[22] He caught a bad cold after that but said he cured it with "good roastbeef and an excellent Sparerib." Cider or wine was included—"wine is the medicine of life for old age." [23] He called this cold influenza in another letter and said that if he got his shipment of herring and Bordeaux wine from Holland, he would either "pickle or drown" the disease.[24] His cures were so excellent that for the next two months he accomplished more work than in the preceding two years. Only occasionally did his bursitis and headaches recur.[25]

John Van der Kemp's younger son died of an unknown disease in early April, 1818. The loss plunged the Van der

Kemps into deep sorrow, particularly the grandmother and aunt "who doated upon the boy." Francis knew John and Abigail Adams would sympathize and sought relief in telling his sorrow to his friends.[26] Abigail, who had already exchanged several friendly letters with Van der Kemp, sent a wonderful letter of consolation praising the family for their firmness under such heavy trials.[27]

In the fall of 1818 Abigail herself was ill. She became progressively worse, and asked Harriet Welsh to write to Van der Kemp and return some of his papers. Shortly thereafter she died. Van der Kemp consoled John Adams not to "mourn without hope" of a future life when they would be reunited.[28] John replied, "I wait for my Summons with resignation—You may rest assured that you will never be forgotten—though I have lost my dearest Friend who frequently reminded me of you—and who never forgot you." [29]

Van der Kemp's ailments and pains continued to come and go. He hurt one of his legs while working in his garden in late October, 1817, and during part of the winter was confined to a chair. Betsy was sick at the same time but recovered and nursed her father.[30] By spring he was in his garden again planting some of his crops for the third and fourth times because of late frosts and early worms. He found time, however, to complete his autobiography for his son and his friends. In July, while he was weeding his garden, he was pleasantly surprised by a visit from the Guilds of Boston. They dined at his cottage and renewed the friendship begun at Boston in 1813.[31]

Betsy made a trip to Philadelphia in the summer and brought back the demand by Paul Busti that her father come down.[32] Francis decided to go and set out in late September. As the stage descended Triphill (Tribeshill), something went wrong and the vehicle upset, injuring six passengers, Van der Kemp the worst. He received bruises on his forehead, left thigh and shin, his right elbow was somewhat mangled and his right shoulder was dislocated. For an hour the pains were excruciating until a doctor was secured to set the shoulder and dress the wounds. In his

typically philosophical manner, he considered himself
fortunate that the horses were quiet until released from
the stage, probably saving them all from much greater
injury. The journey continued without ill effects except
for the slow-healing shin. He stopped a few days at New
York where he renewed a number of old acquaintances,
some going back to the months the Van der Kemps lived
there on arrival in America. One visit at least he paid to
a library to peruse the travels of Ledyard in manuscript.[33]
On his safe return home he recalled for his friends the wonderful trip:

> The courteous and distinguished reception I met with
> exceeded far my most sanguine expectation, and my chil-
> dren shared in their father's enjoyments. Often it seemed
> a dream, and brought the days of a former epoch to my
> recollection. My friend Busti, who . . . charged himself
> with the expenses of my journey, made me a handsome
> present of Italian writers—old and new. L'Abbe Corea,
> Dr Whistar, John Vaughan, Dr Collins vied with an-
> other to render my residence agreeable, while Mrs. Miff-
> lin with her amiable Daughters and Mrs. Gibson formerly
> Miss Bordley—with a few female connections of my chil-
> dren, made me loose sight of the attention I owed in re-
> turn to scientific men. In New York this happiness was
> continued—De Witt Clinton—Drs Hosack and Mitchell
> filled up several gaps in my Library and even Dr Romain
> paid a visit to his Father's friend—while several of my
> Utica neighbours—then in the metropolis charged them-
> selves with the burthen of seeing me again home in safety.
> But I have, in recompense for all the favours—bestowed
> with such a liberal hand—be loaden as the ass of Tek-
> hunen—with solicitations and demands which I could not
> decline, but for whose accomplishment one winter shall
> scarce be sufficient.[34]

Apparently Jonas Platt and his wife enjoyed the friendship and the intellectual pursuits of the Van der Kemps
fully as much as did the Adams. However, there are only

scanty records of their relationships, as most of the correspondence between them concerned business. Van der Kemp first met Jonas in Whitesboro when he made his "Western jaunt" in 1792, with a letter of introduction from George Clinton to bring them together. Forever after the two were close friends; Van der Kemp once classed Jonas as one of his two very best friends. When Platt had occasion to go to Oldenbarneveld, he stopped to see Francis, and they sometimes met in Utica or Whitesboro. Jonas often corrected the writings of his friend.

One visit to the Van der Kemp home occurred in the summer of 1817, when Jonas and his wife stayed overnight. The conversation led to the Adams family. Jonas thought Abigail's letters should be published (as indeed they later were). Some of John Quincy's poetry was read aloud, including "Lines to a Mother on the Death of Two Infants." "Both [the Platts] were all attention—and—at last—tears bedewed their cheeks—perhaps from the recollection of their own similar situation." Van der Kemp ascribed Platt as "a man of uncommon worth—and a bright ornament of the Bench." [35] Again Van der Kemp said of him: "Judge Platt is one of the noblest characters I have become acquainted with—I knew him since 25 years—I love & respect Him—to Him alone in this State I communicated the Biographical Sketch—He is my warm Friend." [36]

Adam Mappa and his wife were like members of the Van der Kemp family. The Mappas lived in the beautiful Mappa Hall with its stately columns, its delightful fireplaces and grand stairway. The spacious gardens and lawns were just across the road from the Van der Kemp gardens. The families went in and out of the two homes without hesitancy, sometimes held religious services together, and exchanged garden produce. Sophia Mappa and Betsy Van der Kemp enjoyed a warm, close friendship that lasted throughout their lives. When Mappa was in severe financial trouble because of the business inefficiency of his son, Van der Kemp consoled his friend over a period of months. He knew it was a "hard trial indeed for a man in his advanced age—so much—so deservedly respected—so sociable—and possessing, all it did seem, what a mortal could wish." Through the son with many good qualities but not "energetic ability and commercial prudence," Adam was held for debts. Van der Kemp said, "I will not complain and rather endeavour to sooth—where I cannot heal." [37] Van der Kemp charged items in New York City to Mappa's account and he and his son always paid.

Van der Kemp never tired of old friends or of making new friends, among them the granddaughter of John Adams. John once wrote:

> You have many friends whom you justly celebrate. I have a few to whom I can never do Justice. You have no Enemies. I have many, and have had more, among the most mean insidious and dastardly of whom have been some of your confidential Friends and Correspondents.[38]

John was afraid that the infirmities of his old age would reduce him to insanity, complete invalidism, "a Sniveling Baby." [39] Ven der Kemp feared isolation and loneliness more than invalidism. He wrote to John,

> I ardently pray, that my days may not be so far prolonged—that I should stand—mournful helpless—alone, even poverty is not so dreadful. This may be soothed, may be ennobled by kind affectionate regards—but betray'd by friends—or who stated themselves so—or forsaken by relatives—by children—what horrible situation! God forbid—that a similar lot fall to . . . [me].[40]

In 1819 Van der Kemp made a visit to Oneida Lake where he went "to bid a last farewell, to a friend decaying in mind and body"—John Bernhard. They had been fast friends since the winter when the Van der Kemps had shared their log house at Kempwick with the Bernhard family. He also visited George Scriba, no longer a wealthy man but happy and contented, enjoying the respect of all who knew him. He thanked Francis cordially for the visit and Francis was so warmed by it that he wrote, "What a blessing! to possess friends." [41]

If Van der Kemp had remained on the lands at Oneida Lake, he might have become as wealthy as Bernhard. But it would probably have been at the expense of his intellectual contacts and to the detriment of his own health and that of his family. Ultimately he sold his Oneida lands, apparently at a profit, to add to family comfort in their cottage at Oldenbarneveld (after 1833 named Trenton). The village had its stores, taverns, church, and a doctor— but best of all were neighbors and friends.

The Van der Kemps earned an honored place in the village, sharing in its excitements, its joys and its sorrows. Francis was sometimes the leader and spokesman for the village, but he was always the leader and spokesman for the Van der Kemps.

❧ XXIV ❧

The Rewards
of Scholarship

WHEN Van der Kemp finished the translations, he deserved
a rest, an easy life for his remaining years. He was seventy-
three years old, his income was sufficient, and his home was
comfortable. His eyes were too weak for extensive efforts
as a scholar. Yet he could not have enjoyed sitting under a
shady tree or by his fireplace for the rest of his days. He
needed to be active, and he was. His land still required
gardening and his correspondence required the composing
of letters.

Perhaps these activities prevented vain regrets that his
estate was small, with a cozy cottage, ten acres of land, and
his library comprising the dreamed-of inheritance for his
children. He may also have regretted that his academic
seclusion had prevented more success in publishing his
literary efforts. Yet his major speeches had been printed in
the newspapers and also in pamphlet form. In addition to
his early religious writings in the Netherlands, his more
recent religious essays had been published in England and
in extract in America. Editorials and editorial comments
appeared in magazines and newspapers in unknown number. Though some of his longer works written in recent
years were unpublished and his sketches of important works
unfulfilled, he had to his credit the completion of the
voluminous research on military law back in the Nether-

lands, and his translations of the *Albany Records*. Through the years in the Oneida wilderness and his "corner" in Oldenbarneveld, he and his friends had suspected certain factors holding him back. His "uncouth" English had resulted in some rejections. Adams had warned him his scholarly topics, requiring deep thought, were not often to popular taste. He lived far from the centers of the publishing world, and research materials often had not been available in the wilderness. His efforts toward publication had been accomplished almost entirely through correspondence, and the long months when his carefully handwritten copies made the round-robin circuit from helpful friends to prospective publishers had sometimes caused material to be outdated before it was ever set in type.

Perhaps Van der Kemp should have attached himself to one of the educational institutions. The idea never seems to have occurred to him, even though he was well-acquainted with President John Kirkland of Harvard, whose father had founded Hamilton College, and also with Dr. Azel Backus, president of Hamilton for some years. At Fairfield Medical College he had a good friend, Dr. Westell Willoughby, with whom he exchanged materials and ideas, and from whom Van der Kemp received advice on his eyes.

In addition to his warm associations at Harvard, he was in correspondence with Professor Benjamin Silliman of Yale who was founder and editor of the *American Journal of Science,* and had enlisted Van der Kemp's assistance in its beginning.[1] Dr. David Hosack of Columbia University was an admirer of the scholar of Oldenbarneveld over a period of years and gave him a copy of his *Memoir of De Witt Clinton,* published in 1829 and inscribed to Van der Kemp "from his friend the author." [2] However, these associations did not draw Van der Kemp to college teaching. Perhaps he knew he would have been too impatient with students who exhibited less than his own drive and thirst for knowledge.

In the 1820's he renewed his friendship with a man of scholarly ability and political eminence—John Quincy

Adams. Francis had first met him in Holland, when John
Quincy had attended the University of Leyden. In recent
years, Adams had known Van der Kemp was one of his
most ardent supporters and well-wishers. Van der Kemp
had followed his career as a politician, a professor, a diplomat and as a writer of both prose and poetry. He con-
fidently predicted the presidency for John two years before
he was a candidate.

When Monroe appointed Adams secretary of state, Van
der Kemp was very happy. When the secretary sent him a
copy of his treatise on weights and measures, he was delighted and honored. He thanked the author through his
father "for this distinguished mark of attention—to an old
friend of his revered Parents." He approved the weights
and measures proposal to Congress wholeheartedly.[3] A few
months later John Quincy sent a copy of his Independence
Day address. Van der Kemp liked it, though he was sorry
it aroused slander, and felt the treatise on weights and
measures far outshone the address. Van der Kemp was
pleased to write to the elder Adams that Judge Platt and
his friends had praised the treatise highly.[4]

Francis' pleasures in his years of "retirement" did not
depend entirely on correspondence. He occasionally saw
Jonas Platt, Peter Smith or other friends on his travels to
Utica and elsewhere. When visitors came to his cottage, he
was proud to show his garden, particularly his flowers, and
to offer a sip of his wine. He had good wine, most frequently imported through the firm of the Bayards, and his
year's supply was usually a quarter cask of sherry and a
case of bottled wine. To get it from New York to Oldenbarneveld was not easy but possible. Once he wrote to the
Bayards that the sherry arrived in safety, likewise the
"Rhine cavaliers" but only nine "Redcoats," three having
died "broken hearted on the Road." He had the sound
ones "confined in close custody" until he should issue
orders "for their execution." Then he would judge their
"intrinsic worth." [5] In ordering his supply for 1822 Van
der Kemp asked for the oldest and best sherry obtainable

and a supply of good Bordeaux or Hermitage because "old men require some good old wine." [6]

Van der Kemp continued to handle his Dutch correspondence through the Bayards and frequently sent and received books, preserved herring, and flower and vegetable seeds. Sometimes he charged the expenses to his son or to Adam Mappa. Sometimes he sent a sum of money to be drawn on as long as it lasted. As Van der Kemp's financial agent, William Bayard was drawn into a misunderstanding which distressed Francis. Gerrit Boon had criticized Mappa's handling of the Holland Land Company's business and apparently threatened Mappa. Van der Kemp tried to clear the matter between his friends but in vain. Now Sophia Mappa had written to Boon to end their friendship. Van der Kemp asked Bayard to intervene with Boon to give Mappa more time.[7] Perhaps he did. But a year later Van der Kemp was again concerned. He asked Bayard to place the last four hundred dollars from Albany to Mappa's credit and with Mappa's approval send it to Boon. The latter had ordered prosecution of Mappa and Van der Kemp was sure this transfer of funds would prevent it.[8] This was a strange echo of the occasion many years before when Van der Kemp had come to Boon's rescue by swift repayment of a loan from the company, after Boon had been criticized for his handling of company funds and the extending of personal loans.

In the summer of 1822 Van der Kemp happily sent Boon a twenty-five pound keg of superior maple sugar from Fairfield to prove that Boon's idea of commerical production of maple sugar was possible. The friends remembered the days when this long-ago project had failed on the Holland Patent lands. Mappa, Boon, and Bayard were as important to Van der Kemp in their ways as were Clinton and Adams.[9]

With Adams he continued the discussion of current topics, one of which was the success of Wesley and Wesleyanism in America. Van der Kemp related the phenomenon to his whole picture of civilization, as usual:

Wesley's appearance is certainly a wonder in the moral world—and yet—how awkward—how terrible such appearances are—they contribute finally to ameliorate and enlighten the moral world—as earthquakes and Volcanoes and Inundations the Physical, or Revolutionary convulsions and the hurricanes of Despotism do on the Political State of mankind.[10]

Although Van der Kemp made no mention of the appearance of the great revivalist, Charles G. Finney, over in the neighboring village of Western, he must have been impressed by Finney's Wesleyan-like success. In his own village Van der Kemp could observe revivalism also. However, the most pressing religious problem to the Unitarians in Oldenbarneveld was the series of sermons by the minister of the Presbyterian church, the Reverend David Harrower, in defense of Trinitarianism. In 1822 the series was published. In 1826 the Reverend Oliver Wetmore, also Presbyterian, led a revival movement which he directed toward the complete destruction of this "stronghold of Socinianism" (the Unitarian Church). Van der Kemp's friend and fellow churchman, Ephraim Perkins, wrote a pamphlet in reply. Attacks and counter-attacks grew acrimonious. Apparently Van der Kemp counseled moderation and freedom of conscience to both sides. Wetmore wrote:

It becomes me to state that in the opposition which has been made to the revival from Unitarians, there are honorable exceptions; and without being invidious, I will mention the Honorable Adrian Vanderkemp, whose talents and affability of manners I highly esteem.[11]

In 1822 Adams commented on the influence of New York State in national politics and how its vote would probably swing the balance in the next presidential election. Adams was perfectly aware of his son's availability but was brutally realistic. "All I have to say is that whoever is chosen he will be but a President with a crown of thorns upon his head." [12] Van der Kemp was apprehensive that the "growling hurricane" at Washington would upset his hopes for the election. On the international scene he was interested in "South America's regeneration." [13]

From time to time friends asked Van der Kemp for recommendations and he complied when possible. In 1821 he recommended Joseph Salter, a brother-in-law of John Mappa, to William Bayard and also to Frederick Gebhard. The young man was a fine, able clerk and wanted a position with a future in business.[14] A few months later Van der Kemp recommended Philo Birdseye, a neighbor boy, as a printer's apprentice.[15] In the same year he proposed to John Quincy Adams the name of George Stroutbridge as consul at St. Thomas.[16] Adams replied that no vacancy existed but he would hold the recommendation. He added a friendly and respectful paragraph as an invitation for Van der Kemp to write again.[17] In a few months another letter was sent asking Adams to look at his manuscripts *On the Use of Copper* and the *Achaian Republic*. He was advised that his (Adams') niece, Caroline Amelia De Wint, might send two others, the *Tour to Oneida Lake* and the *Symposium*.[18] On his way to New York for an eye treatment Van der Kemp had spent a few days at Caroline's home on the Hudson, enjoying her company and that of her children immensely.[19] If Adams had had the time to criticize these manuscripts, perhaps Van der Kemp would have made another attempt at publication.

De Witt Clinton told Van der Kemp that the historians Van der Donck and De Laet were being translated and asked if Megapolensis were sufficiently interesting to publish in translation.[20] Van der Kemp doubted the value of the first two as to their entirety. He had translated Lambrechtsen and it was collecting dust. He had not seen Megapolensis and did not indicate a desire to translate anything.[21]

Van der Kemp was not able to keep his hand from another matter. In late 1822 a meeting was held in Albany in support of Greek independence. The orator, Joseph Yates, made an erroneous allusion to the Dutch during the American Revolution and the oration was printed. Van der Kemp read it and immediately wrote a letter to the editor explaining the actions of the Dutch and the great work of John Adams at the time. The letter was printed on December 4 and resulted in a controversial correspondence between Yates and Van der Kemp and Yates and Adams.[22]

Adams chuckled about being drawn into such a controversy at the age of 88 and told Van der Kemp that a committee had even contacted him. However, he was convinced that the opposition of the Dutch to England, the cooperation of the Netherlands with France and Spain and their treaty with the United States was the turning point of the Revolutionary War. He hoped it would be recognized some day.[23] Van der Kemp joined to this sentiment the wish that Americans would come to appreciate the Dutch contributions in New Netherland, perhaps through the *Albany Records*. Holland had received from Americans first neglect and then scurrilities. Perhaps John Quincy Adams would come forth and "do justice to the Dutch." [24]

In February, 1823, John asked Van der Kemp if he would give to the Quincy library his extra copy of Manilius and inscribe it. Van der Kemp sent Manilius and Virgil but had to ask that one of his friends give them proper hard bindings. Adams was pleased and wished he had begged the Manilius when he could still see to read it.[25]

Van der Kemp's interest in books for his own entertainment and enlightenment, as well as for others, is attested by the books he acquired in these years. At the time of his death, his library consisted of nearly 1,400 books. Clinton sent numerous volumes including *Memoirs of the Board of Agriculture, Statistical Account of the County of Albany, Silliman's Tour to Quebec,* Stephen H. Long's *Expedition from Pittsburg to the Rocky Mountains,* Sir James Prior's *Life of Burke,* and *By Ways and Highways.* Van der Kemp mentioned to Adams Niebuhr's *Roman History,* Morse's *Revolution,* and in general Italian and German literature. Van der Kemp indicated interest in numerous subjects

which probably were inspired by periodicals or newspapers. His religious interest was as strong as ever, one of
his concerns at this time being getting a fine Bible for Peter.
He sent two back to the Websters because they were not
what he had requested. He wanted engravings and the
Apocrypha, and he wanted a short address from father to
son bound in the front.[26]

Clinton sent Van der Kemp some anti-slavery pamphlets
in 1823. They were quite welcome not only to the recipient
but to his friends. Van der Kemp had been disturbed about
the slavery which existed in early New Netherland when
he was translating the *Records* and his feeling was intensi-
fied by the Missouri Compromise debates. He told Clinton
that the institution "must cause finally the ruin of the
Southern States" if an "heroic medicine" were not applied
soon. He supported gradual emancipation and suggested
that the best slaves be put on small farms with a small
rental and that they receive freedom after a definite period
of "good conduct." [27]

His national concern of deepest interest was the presidential election of 1824. He thought Clinton would be a
good president, and he said in early 1824 that he respected
General Jackson "as a man of original worth and energy." [28]
Since Clinton was tied up in the New York governorship,
John Quincy Adams was the one he wanted most. John
Adams hesitated to say that John Quincy wanted the presidency. He contended that his son was not playing politics
but was defending himself from hypocritical, insidious,
imprudent and brutal attacks.[29] Van der Kemp said he admired John Quincy Adams as a great statesman, an accomplished scholar, and as an honorable son, husband and
father. "He may in my opinion *ardently aspire* at the Presidency, because he may, under God's blessing promote the
welfare of his country." [30]

New York had as much politics and confusion in its
selection of presidential electors as it did in the choice of
governor. There was a great demand for the electors to be
chosen by the people instead of the legislature. Governor

Yates called a special session of the legislature on August 2, 1824, to provide for this change. The majority of that body was controlled by anti-Clinton forces who expected to name the electors, and they voted adjournment without action. The People's party called a convention at Utica for nomination for governor which was a popular change such as the change in the electoral choice. De Witt Clinton was chosen at this convention in late September. He favored Jackson for the presidency, though not with great vigor. The state legislature met on November 2 to choose electors, with the old guard for Crawford and strong support for Adams and Clay. Much electioneering took place. The final decision came with general revolt in the lower house against the old guard. The result was a divided vote, Adams 26, Crawford 5, Clay 4 and Jackson 1.

Van der Kemp was wholeheartedly for the revolt but gave up immediate hope a few days before the results were announced. He said to John Adams on November 18 that he had delayed writing until the legislature should choose. But "the current cabal" disappointed him although he still had "some faint hope." [31] A few days later he heard the results and was pleasantly surprised, although he would have preferred a unanimous vote for Adams.

The electoral vote was counted in the United States Senate on February 9 without a majority. This was expected. It took a few days for the House to come to a decision and again Van der Kemp became impatient. He started a letter about the recently published letters of Adams and again urged publication of all his important papers. He then asked for a copy of George Washington Adams' orations which had been mentioned in the *North American Review*. At this point the news came and he sent his congratulations to the father.[32]

Van der Kemp also wrote a warm letter of congratulation to the son, saying, "It is listening to a deep sense of duty—that I take the Liberty—at this momentous period of congratulating you and My Dear Country at the long desired election of a man of your character and talents to the

Presidency of the United States." He made a wish for the promotion and expansion of prosperity in a manner that would reward the new executive's services and mentioned the great pleasure the election must give to John Adams. Then in a postcript he asked for the return of his manuscripts inasmuch as the president-elect would now be too busy to criticize them.[33]

John Adams was touched by all the letters from his friends, including one from Adam Mappa, but said none was "more cordially welcomed" than that from his friend Van der Kemp. He said he had only one copy of George's oration left but he sent it. He ended his letter with comments on the fine administration of Josiah Quincy as mayor of Boston and the poor state of his own health, the latter as a reason for so short a letter.[34]

In December Van der Kemp wrote to John again, particularly commending his grandson, George, and praising the recent presidential address. He approved strongly the proposed monument to Washington and the establishment of a national university, but had qualms about the strengthening of the standing army.[35] One more letter Van der Kemp wrote to John, on the following July 5, not knowing John had died the day before. Francis wrote of their long friendship and of his own infirmities which required special efforts to make his letter legible. He had just about given up the faint hope of ever going to Montezillo again. He asked for the loan of a new book on the human nervous system if John had it or could get it. Otherwise he extended his best wishes for the continued success of the new Adams administration and for the happiness of the whole Adams clan. When Van der Kemp read the news a few days later, he wrote letters of condolence to both John Quincy and Thomas Adams. The president replied in a few weeks with a warm letter recognizing the long friendship between Van der Kemp and the Adams family and closing with a statement of his own friendship.[36]

In his last years Van der Kemp had to rely more and more on the members of his own family for stimulation and companionship. It was a close-knit family, even with John living in Philadelphia. The son made frequent trips (frequent for those days) to Oldenbarneveld and on at least one occasion took his sister with him on a business trip to western New York. She stopped off to visit the Lincklaens in Cazenovia and then returned as he came back from Batavia. All the Van der Kemps had visited John in Philadelphia at some time. In 1824 they were saddened by the death of John's wife, but grateful for the growing boy, Adrian, John's only living child.

When Adrian was born in 1810 Francis had written in the family record a blessing for the infant.

> May this boy grow up in wisdom and virtue and inherit the piety and intellectual endowments of his old Uncle Adraen s'Gravezande—then he shall be the delight of his parents & the ornament of Society, a firm Supporter of the Gospel—and a blessing to the age he lives in.[37]

Now the boy was ready for college, although he was not sure which one. Apparently Union College in Schenectady was his first thought, but his interest dropped when Francis could not furnish full, immediate information. Harvard was next considered, a pleasant thought to Francis, but the final choice was Yale. Adrian took a two-hour entrance examination, passed, and was admitted in September, 1825.[38] In November all was going well and grandfather Van der Kemp had scholarly hopes for the boy.[39] *

The grandparents, Aunt Betsy and Uncle Peter continued a comfortable existence, marred from time to time by sickness or infirmities but made happy again by birthday and other celebrations and visits from friends and neighbors. Their finances were satisfactory although Francis was careless in a scholarly way with his accounts. On one

---

* Adrian did not live to fulfill his early promise. He died young, as did all but one of John's children by both his first and second marriages. John was survived by a daughter, Mrs. Bernard Henry of Philadelphia. She had no descendants, and the Van der Kemp line came to an end.

occasion De Witt Clinton endeavored to handle some personal business for him in New York City and clear his account with the Bayards. First, Van der Kemp wanted a meat thermometer ($10) for his friend, Dr. Willoughby; then he wanted a case of surgical instruments ($6 to $8) for Dr. Coventry's son; next, a lamp for Mrs. Guiteau and a few flower bulbs for Betsy; and last a lottery ticket for himself—"the last tribute I can pay to that Literary institution." [40] After purchasing these things Clinton was to pay Van der Kemp's account with Bayard and send the balance of his money. Clinton had difficulty and delays in taking care of the matters but made the purchases. Then he found that Van der Kemp's indebtedness with Bayard was some forty dollars more than the whole payment.[41] Instead of $180 as Van der Kemp thought, it was $290.40. Van der Kemp said he was "mortified" and "utterly disappointed"; when he had asked Bayard a few months back about his account, the man said not to worry because it was not much over fifty dollars. Van der Kemp suspected he had "consulted with his generous heart; not with his Books." [42] Either Clinton or Bayard took care of the deficiency until Van der Kemp could get the sum from his son. A few years later he forgot that he received a payment of $140 interest in December and expected it again in April.[43]

Such difficulties were always adjusted without loss to anyone and then Van der Kemp would resume his interests in the higher things of life. In 1827 he wrote to Abraham Varick in Utica about some business matters, then told about the "brightening" prospects in Oldenbarneveld. Two stores and two new houses were under construction and two pieces of property had been purchased by Captain James Douglas. He invited the Varicks and Mrs. Morris Miller to visit and hoped he might see them in Utica. Mrs. Van der Kemp was recuperating from an illness, but he was "vigorous as ever" although he had suffered recently from working too long in his garden "in a severe blast of wind." Betsy added a note to the letter that her mother had run out of knitting cotton and needed some to make "a pair handsome fine stockings" for the grandson, Adrian. A half pound of number 18 was desired and could be sent by the stage driver.[44]

The year 1828 was a year of sorrow. Van der Kemp relied heavily on religion for consolation and many times wished for release from the cares of life. On February 11 of that year De Witt Clinton wrote him a warm letter about a political appointment and a book he intended to send.[45] Clinton died later in the day of a heart condition. In April, Adam Mappa died, the oldest friend he had since the death of Adams. In September Mrs. Van der Kemp died at the age of eighty-one, "bewailed at her death—beloved and re-spected by all her Relatives—friends and acquaintances here and in Europe." [46]

By this time Van der Kemp's correspondents had dwin-dled to just a few people, John Quincy Adams being one. However, their letters were not as intimate as those be-tween his father and Francis. Van der Kemp sent some Dutch papers to Adams and received in return a paper on the life of John.[47] In a letter of 1829 Adams wrote of his return to Quincy and his "delight" in Van der Kemp's correspondence. He was sorry Van der Kemp's eyes troubled him and hoped they would strengthen as did the eyes of his father.[48]

In April Van der Kemp wrote the last letter that is avail-able. It was a happy letter to Abraham Varick that indi-cated he still knew how to live. In addition to matters of business, he added a note to the wife of his friend saying he was preparing "a few general remarks" illustrating the Holy Scripture. He intended soon to send the first parts to her for criticism. The essays had been written for his Betsy. If Mrs. Varick liked the papers, she might pass them "to Mrs. Susan Lansing—Mrs. Seymour and Mrs. Miller —Mother and Daughter." A postscript requested the return of an address by Josiah Quincy's son on the life of his father. Bryan [?] Johnson and Dr. Coventry should have it and Coventry should return the April issue of the *North American Review* together "with a long affectionate letter." [49] Early in August Van der Kemp visited Scriba at Oneida Lake once more.

In the middle of August John Van der Kemp visited his father and found him in good health. By this time John had remarried and a son, John Jacob, had arrived. Adrian apparently stayed at Oldenbarneveld while John made a business trip; when John returned his father was dead. He wrote in the old book, "My venerated father Fr. A. Vander Kemp died at Oldenbarneveld, Town of Trenton Oneida Country New York with a violent attack of cholera morbus on the 7th September at 15 min past 7 o'cl. P.M." [50] On September 10, 1829, the Reverend Isaac B. Peirce delivered the funeral oration in Van der Kemp's church and Francis was buried in the village cemetery south of town. The minister eulogized Van der Kemp for his good works, his enduring friendships, and for a strong religious faith combined with a remarkable tolerance for the differing views of others:

> While true to his own faith he conceded to others their equal right to differ from him, with a cheerfulness that to the eye of bigotry might at times have appeared the offspring of indifference. But where religion was concerned, nothing was to him indifferent. No man searched deeper for truth, his faith was the fruit of honest, enlightened, just and laborious research.[51]

In his lifetime he was honored in many ways. Tributes by the governor were printed in the newspapers and spoken to the legislature upon several occasions. Some years before his death, a tribute appeared in *A Gazeteer of the State of New York,* published in 1824. In the section on Oldenbarneveld the *Gazeteer* says:

> The venerable Mr. Van Der Kemp, a fine classical scholar and a volunteer patriot in the cause of America, while struggling for Independence, resides on the border of this Village. This gentleman is now employed in decyphering and translating the old Dutch Colonial

Records, of the Colony of New-York, appertaining to the Secretary's office—smoothing the way for the labors of the Historian, whom, it is much to be wished may soon appear.[52]

Molded from European stock and from European strife, Van der Kemp had become a patriotic American, eager to contribute in any way he could to the advancement of his adopted country.

John Quincy Adams wrote the warmest letter of their correspondence to Van der Kemp on September 10, not knowing of his death. He commented on Van der Kemp's new grandson and other family interests, wrote of his own family, and told of the elevation of Josiah Quincy to the presidency of Harvard.

The rewards of Van der Kemp's scholarship, and what John Adams called his "vast view of civilization," were many and varied. He never aspired to a position of power, recognizing early in life that his contributions to his fellow man could best be made through the written word.

He used this medium in his youth, not only to provide religious inspiration, but especially to advance the cause of freedom in the Netherlands. There his writings brought to the people an awareness of lost liberties and the need for eternal vigilance. He achieved significant advances toward freedom of the press, and brought about changes in the court system. Though the cause for which he labored seemed to have been lost when he was imprisoned, he actually had helped to pave the way to freedom. His writings had kindled a "revolutionary spirit" in his countrymen and hastened the day when Dutch independence became a reality.

When Van der Kemp came to America, he turned his back upon the old world and looked forward. Taking Adams' advice, he gave up his calling as a minister. While wresting a living for his family, he pursued his literary career in a new language and a new land.

In Oldenbarneveld he was a recognized leader. He was

chosen as town orator for special occasions and respected as an official in various capacities, including that of judge. He was revered by his townsfolk as a man of wisdom and beloved as a friend.

Van der Kemp was known in Oldenbarneveld as "the old Judge," at Harvard as an honorary doctor of laws, in Albany as a state translator; but to the world at large he was recognized as a man of letters. His contributions to the learned societies and to the scholarly and religious journals of his day were well received.

However, his influence was most often at the grass roots level. He had contacts but not power. He advised but did not command. He was able to relate the past to the present and future in a comprehensive fashion envied by John Adams as a sharp contrast to his own admittedly "superficial and narrow view." His legacy might best be measured in terms of his influence upon the thought of the early leaders of America, who valued his opinions as a historian and astute political scientist.

Notes

NOTES TO CHAPTER I

1. *Autobiography of Francis A. Van der Kemp*, a manuscript in the form of a letter to his son in 1817. Historical Society of Pennsylvania. This manuscript is extremely valuable to a reconstruction of Van der Kemp's life in Holland. Material not otherwise cited is generally taken from this source. The *Autobiography* was first published in England in 1837.

2. The Adams Papers, Letters Received and Other Loose Papers, January 18, 1809, Microfilm, Cornell University, Film 469.

3. Frederick A. Pottle, ed., *Boswell in Holland, 1763–1764* (New York: McGraw-Hill Book Co., Inc., 1952), p. 28.

4. *Ibid.*, pp. 32 and 68.

5. Helen Lincklaen Fairchild, *Francis Adrian Van der Kemp, 1752–1829, An Autobiography together with Extracts from his Correspondence* (New York: G. P. Putnam's Sons, 1903), pp. 190–1.

6. Adams Papers, September 26, 1812.

NOTES TO CHAPTER II

1. Adams Papers, May 9, 1817.

2. J. M. Robertson, *A Short History of Free Thought, Ancient and Modern* (New York: Russell & Russell, 1957), p. 334.

3. Petrus Johannes Blok, *History of the People of the Netherlands*, Part V, *Eighteenth and Nineteenth Centuries,* Translated by Oscar A. Bierstadt (New York: G. P. Putnam's Sons, 1912), pp. 174–6.

4. *Ibid.*, pp. 181–3.

5. Professor Wyttenbach came from Switzerland in 1770 to teach at Amsterdam. Van der Kemp wrote in 1815 that Wyttenbach taught him most of what he knew of the learned languages. He added: "I was accustomed to treat him with reverence—but our characters were too disparate to love him—or court his intimacy—" (Adams Papers, Letter to John Adams, March 7, 1815.)

6. Blok, pp. 181–3.

7. *Oeuvres complètes de Voltaire* (Paris: Baudouin Frères, Editeurs, 1826), XXXV, 40.

8. *Oeuvres de Voltaire*, LVIII, 317–18.

9. *Oeuvres de Voltaire*, XXXV, 58, 62.
10. Adams Papers, May 5, 1813.
11. *Ibid.*, October 4, 1813.
12. *Ibid.*, August 16, 1815.
13. Adams Papers, Sept. 26, 1812. Part of this letter is on reel 416, July–Dec. 1813, by error.
14. Hendrik Willem Van Loon, *The Fall of the Dutch Republic* (Boston: Houghton Mifflin Co., 1913), pp. 325–6.
15. Adams Papers, September 26, 1812.

NOTES TO CHAPTER III

1. Adams Papers, Letter to John Adams, January 18, 1809.
2. *Ibid.*, November 14, 1816.
3. *Ibid.*, October 6, 1815.
4. Genealogical MS, Oneida Historical Society.
5. Adams Papers, Letter to John Adams, August 16, 1815.
6. MSS in Oneida Historical Society.
7. *Ibid.*
8. Adams Papers, February 16, 1813.

NOTES TO CHAPTER IV

1. Samuel Eliot Morison, *John Paul Jones, A Sailor's Biography* (Boston: Little, Brown and Co., 1959), pp. 254–9.
2. Adams Papers, June 20, 1801.
3. *Ibid.*, October 16, 1780.
4. Historical Society of Pennsylvania, From Adams to Van der Kemp, April 17, 1781.
5. *Ibid.*, July 13, 1801.
6. Adams Papers, June 5, 1781 (in French). An edition of this work in the Library of Congress is *Verzameling van stukken tot de dertien Verreenigde Staeten van Noord-America betrekkelijk*, Leyden, L. Herdingh, 1781.
7. *Ibid.*, December 20, 1781; also August 31, September 7, 14 and 27, 1780.
8. De Witt Clinton Papers, Columbia University, January 5, 1818.
9. Adams Papers, November 25, 1781.
10. J. Hartog, *Uit de Dagen der Patriotten* (Amsterdam, P. N. Van Kampen & Zoon, n.d.), p. 78.
11. Adams Papers, May 17, 1807.
12. *Ibid.*, April 2, 1809.
13. Van Loon, p. 332.
14. Hartog, p. 58.

NOTES TO CHAPTER V

1. R. R. Palmer, *The Age of the Democratic Revolution, A Political History of Europe and America, 1760–1800.* (Princeton: Princeton University Press, 1959), p. 329.
2. *Ibid.,* p. 330.
3. *Ibid.*
4. Fairchild, p. 57.
5. Historical Society of Pennsylvania, June 24, 1781.
6. *Ibid.,* November 27, 1781.
7. Hartog, p. 78; Fairchild, p. 59.
8. Some of the commendations of the provinces are preserved in the Van der Kemp papers in the Oneida Historical Society.
9. Historical Society of Pennsylvania, June 24, 1781.
10. Adams Papers, June 28, 1815.
11. *Ibid.,* April 25, 1782.
12. Fairchild, p. 122.
13. Blok, V, 210–12.
14. Fairchild, p. 83.
15. Palmer, pp. 334–5.
16. Adams Papers, February 18, 1812.
17. *Ibid.,* March 1, 1814.
18. *Ibid.,* January 18, 1809.
19. *Ibid.,* December 11, 1785.
20. Manuscript in Oneida Historical Society.
21. Palmer, p. 336.
22. P. Geyl, *De Patriottenbeweging, 1780–1787* (Amsterdam: P. N. Van Kampen & Zoon, N.V., 1947), pp. 139–40.
23. Adams Papers, October 31, 1786.
24. Blok, V, 240.
25. *Ibid.*
26. Adams Papers, March 14, 1788.
27. Palmer, p. 327.
28. Adams Papers, January 17, 1803.

NOTES TO CHAPTER VI

1. Adams Papers, June 20, 1801.
2. *Ibid.,* June 5, 1781.
3. Historical Society of Pennsylvania, June 24, 1781.
4. Adams Papers, November 25, 1781.
5. Historical Society of Pennsylvania, November 27, 1781.
6. Adams Papers, April 25, 1782.
7. Historical Society of Pennsylvania, February 18, 1783.
8. Adams Papers, December 11, 1785.
9. *Ibid.,* October 31, 1786.
10. *Ibid.,* December 7, 1786.
11. Historical Society of Pennsylvania, December 1, 1786.

12. Fairchild, p. 102.

13. Adams Papers, December 29, 1787.

14. Buffalo Historical Society, January 6, 1788.

15. Adams Papers, October 4, 1813.

16. *The Writings of George Washington from the Original Manuscript Sources, 1745–1799*, John C. Fitzpatrick, Ed. (Washington: U.S. Government Printing Office, 1939), Vol. 29, 504–5.

17. Massachusetts Historical Society, Van der Kemp to unknown person, July 15, 1788.

18. Adams Papers, July 25, 1788.

19. *Ibid.*, September 5, 1788.

20. *Laws of New York, 1789–1796*, Twelfth Session, Chapter 42, February 28, 1789.

NOTES TO CHAPTER VII

1. Adams Papers, September 5, 1788.

2. Fairchild, p. 116.

3. *United States Census*, 1790, Kingston Town, Ulster County, New York, p. 171.

4. Buffalo Historical Society, June 3, 1789.

5. Historical Society of Pennsylvania, Letter from Van der Kemp to LeRoy and Bayard, New York, May 9, 1793.

6. Massachusetts Historical Society, November 12, 1790.

7. *U.S. Census*, 1790, p. 171.

8. Alphonso T. Clearwater, *The History of Ulster County*, New York (Kingston: W. J. Van Deusen, 1907), pp. 142, 148.

9. Nathaniel Bartlett Sylvester, *History of Ulster County, New York*, (Philadelphia: Everts & Peck, 1880), p. 113.

10. George Dangerfield, *Chancellor Robert R. Livingston of New York, 1746–1813* (New York: Harcourt, Brace and Co., 1960), p. 102.

11. Clearwater, pp. 213–5.

12. *Travels in the Years 1791 and 1792 in Pennsylvania, New York and Vermont, Journals of John Lincklaen, Agent of the Holland Land Company with a Biographical Sketch and Notes*, Helen Lincklaen Fairchild, Ed. (New York: G. P. Putnam's Sons, 1897), p. 119.

13. Massachusetts Historical Society, October 20, 1789.

14. New-York Historical Society, August 18, 1793.

15. Dangerfield, pp. 282–3.

16. *Writings of Washington*, Vol. 30, 49–50.

17. *Ibid.*, p. 103.

18. *New-York Historical Society*, August 24, 1793.

19. Dangerfield, p. 429.

20. New-York Historical Society, January 31, 1790.

21. *Ibid.*, August 24, 1793.

22. Adams Papers, January 7, 1790.

23. Historical Society of Pennsylvania, February 27, 1790.

24. "A Bundle of Thomas Jefferson's Letters Now First Published," Edited by Frank H. Severance, *Publications of the Buffalo Historical Society*, Vol. VII (Buffalo: 1904), pp. 9–10.

25. Adams Papers, June 19, 1790.

26. *Ibid.*, October 5, 1789.

27. *Ibid.*, January 7, 1790; January 9, 1790.

28. Historical Society of Pennsylvania, February 27, 1790.

29. Thomas McKellar, *The American Printer* (Philadelphia: The McKellar, Smiths & Jordon Co., 1887), p. 23.

30. Adams Papers, November 23, 1793.

31. Historical Society of Pennsylvania, December 11, 1793.

32. Adams Papers, February 24, 1794.

33. John F. Seymour, *Centennial Address, Delivered at Trenton New York, July 4, 1876* (Utica: White & Floyd, 1877), p. 49.

34. Adams Papers, August 3, 1793.

NOTES TO CHAPTER VIII

1. The text used here is that found in Seymour, *Centennial Address,* pp. 48–128.

2. These were eel flies and they still pile up on shore several inches thick in late May or early June.

3. A plant, also called frog spit, which Robert Livingston tried to use for making paper, beginning about 1792 and resulting in a patent in 1799.

NOTES TO CHAPTER IX

1. *Works of J. Adams,* IV, p. 579.

2. Ibid., p. 585.

3. Adams Papers, April 17, 1790.

4. *Ibid.*, February 3, 1790.

5. *Ibid.*, January 7, 1790.

6. *Ibid.*, February 3, 1790.

7. Historical Society of Pennsylvania, February 27, 1790.

8. *Ibid.*

9. *Ibid.*, March 27, 1790.

10. Adams Papers, April 17, 1790.

11. *Ibid.*, June 19, 1790.

12. Historical Society of Pennsylvania, March 19, 1793; Adams Papers, February 9, 1793.

13. Adams Papers, February 9, 1793.

14. Historical Society of Pennsylvania, March 19, 1793.

15. Adams Papers, February 9, 1793.

16. *Ibid.*, August 3, 1793.

17. *Ibid.*

18. *Ibid.*, November 23, 1793.

19. *Ibid.*, February 1, 1794.

20. Historical Society of Pennsylvania, February 18, 1794.

21. Adams Papers, August 28, 1794.

22. *Ibid.*, October 4, 1794.

23. *Ibid.*, August 24, 1795.

24. *Ibid.*, June 12, 1796.
25. *Ibid.*, October 3, 1795.
26. *Ibid.*, September 1, 1796.
27. *Blok*, V, 290–303.
28. Adams Papers, September 1, 1796.
29. *Ibid.*, October 10, 1796.
30. *Ibid.*, November 10, 1796.
31. *Journal of the Senate of the State of New York*, 20th Session, 1796, p. 12.
32. Adams Papers, March 4, 1797.

NOTES TO CHAPTER X

1. Adams Papers, May 26, 1794.
2. *Fairchild*, p. 128.
3. Historical Society of Pennsylvania, June 27, 1794.
4. Adams Papers, August 28, 1794.
5. Scriba Papers, Bound Volumes, State Library, Albany, N.Y.
6. *Gazetteer of the State of New York*, Ed., J. H. French (Syracuse: R. P. Smith, 1860), p. 521.
7. Crisfield Johnson, *History of Oswego County, New York* (Philadelphia: L. H. Everts & Co., 1877), pp. 288–9.
8. *Ibid.*, p. 288.
9. Scriba Papers, October 11, 1796.
10. Historical Society of Pennsylvania, October 4, 1794.
11. *Ibid.*, January 31, 1795.
12. *Journal of the Assembly of the State of New York* 18th Session, 1795 (March 9, 1795).
13. Scriba Papers, January 24, 1795.
14. Pomroy Jones, *Annals & Recollections of Oneida County* (Rome, 1851), pp. 21–2.
15. Adams Papers, December 9, 1794.
16. Scriba Papers, Bound Volumes.
17. Adams Papers, August 28, 1794.
18. Pomroy Jones, *Annals & Recollections of Oneida County* (Rome, 1851), p. 2128.
19. Adams Papers, October 3, 1795.
20. Pomroy Jones, *Annals & Recollections of Oneida County* (Rome, 1851), pp. 22–3.
21. *Speech of Francis Adrian Van Der Kemp at a Meeting the First of June, One Thousand, Seven Hundred and Ninety-five, at Whitestown for the Institution of a Society of Agriculture* (Whitesboro: Oliver P. Easton, 1795).
22. Ulysses Prentiss Hedrick, *A History of Agriculture in New York State* (New York State Agricultural Society, 1933), p. 86.
23. Adams Papers, October 3, 1795.
24. Buffalo Historical Society, December 23, 1796.
25. *Gazeteer of the State of New York*, Ed., J. H. French (L. Johnson & Co., 1860), p. 390.

26. Nina Moore Tiffany and Francis Tiffany, *Harm Jan Huidekoper* (Cambridge, 1904), pp. 49–50.

27. D. E. Wager, *Men, Events, Lawyers, Politics and Politicians of Early Rome*, Oneida Historical Society (Utica: Ellis H. Roberts & Co., 1879), p. 15.

28. Adams Papers, December 9, 1794.

29. *Ibid.*, February 2, 1796.

30. De Witt Clinton Papers, Columbia University, March 1, 1816.

31. Scriba Papers, January 29, 1796.

32. *Ibid.*, November 20, 1796.

NOTES TO CHAPTER XI

1. *Gazeteer of the State of New York*, Ed., J. H. French (Syracuse: R. P. Smith, 1860), p. 468.

2. Seymour, p. 141.

3. Barneveld Library, unpublished MS.

4. John Andrew, "Historical Address, 1893," delivered at Trenton, unpublished manuscript owned by Mrs. Ernest S. Breed, Lyndonville, N.Y.

5. Paul Demund Evans, *The Holland Land Company* (Buffalo: Buffalo Historical Society, 1924), pp. 70–4.

6. Fairchild, p. 139.

7. *Ibid.*, p. 154.

8. Robert Anderson, "Tales of a Scholar," *New York Folklore Quarterly*, Fall, 1956.

9. *Laws of the State of New York*, 1797–1800, Vol. IV (1797), p. 64. The name appears in this record as Thomas Weeks.

10. *Records of Town Meetings*, Town of Trenton, Oneida County, New York.

11. Oneida Historical Society, Van der Kemp Papers.

12. *Records of Circuit Court and Court of Oyer and Terminer*, Oneida County, 1798–1813.

13. *Utica Patriot*, April 5, 1808.

14. Seymour, p. 27.

15. Francis Adrian Van der Kemp, "Eulogy of George Washington," pronounced at Oldenbarneveld, Oneida County, New York, February 22, 1800. *Washington Eulogies*, compiled by Margaret Bingham Stillwell (New York, Public Library, 1916), pp. 9–18. A copy of the eulogy was sent to Martha Washington and was duly acknowledged.

16. Livingston Papers, July 8, 1800.

17. *Ibid.*

18. *Ibid.*, November 20, 1800; December 26, 1800.

19. Historical Society of Pennsylvania, Van der Kemp to Livingston, June 12, 1801.

20. Adams Papers, November 11, 1802, and March 14, 1803.

21. *Ibid.*, August 20, 1810.

22. *Ibid.*, September 2, 1808.

23. Livingston Papers, January 7, 1810.

24. *Ibid.*, August 20, 1805.
25. *Ibid.*, April 15, 1806.

NOTES TO CHAPTER XII

1. *The Documentary History of New York,* Edited by E. B. O'Callaghan (Albany, 1850), III, 1134.
2. *Ibid.*, pp. 1111, 1124.
3. *Ibid,* p. 1114.
4. *Ibid.*, p. 1115.
5. This and much of the following material is from Charles Graves, *A Century of Village Unitarianism being a History of the Reformed Christian (Unitarian) Church of Trenton, Oneida County, New York, 1803–1903* (Boston: Geo. H. Ellis Co., 1904), pp. 8–49.
6. William B. Sprague, *Annals of the American Pulpit* (New York: Robert Carter & Brothers, 1865), VIII, 330.
7. *Columbian Gazette,* Utica, August 19, 1805.
8. Sprague, VIII, 327.
9. Adams Papers, July 29, 1806.
10. A. O. F. [Van der Kemp], *A Wreath for the Rev. Daniel Dow* (Utica: Merrell and Seward, 1806).
11. *Columbia Gazette,* Utica, September 30, 1806.
12. *Ibid.*, October 7, 1807.
13. Historical Society of Pennsylvania, December 29, 1807.
14. *Ibid.*, to the Reverend Abiel Abbot, November 8, 1812.

NOTES TO CHAPTER XIII

1. New-York Historical Society, Livingston Papers, November 20, 1800.
2. *Ibid.*, December 26, 1800.
3. *Ibid.*, January 18, 1801
4. Adams Papers, June 20, 1801.
5. Historical Society of Pennsylvania, July 13, 1801.
6. *Ibid.*, June 12, 1801.
7. Buffalo Historical Society.
8. Historical Society of Pennsylvania, August 20, 1801.
9. Adams Papers, October 3, 1801.
10. *Ibid.*, January 3, 1802.
11. Historical Society of Pennsylvania, January 26, 1802.
12. *Ibid.*, March 4, 1802.
13. Adams Papers, March 24, 1802.
14. Historical Society of Pennsylvania, August 20, 1801.
15. Adams Papers, October 3, 1801.
16. Historical Society of Pennsylvania, November 20, 1801.
17. Adams Papers, December 30, 1801; January 3, 1802.
18. *Ibid.*, January 3, 1802.
19. *Ibid.*, February 7, 1803.
20. Historical Society of Pennsylvania, August 1, 1803.

21. Adams Papers, September 3, 1803.
22. *Ibid.*, February 15, 1804.
23. *Works* IX, 588.
24. Historical Society of Pennsylvania, November 5, 1804.
25. Adams Papers, February 15, 1805.
26. *Ibid.*, March 14, 1803.
27. *Ibid.*, February 15, 1804.
28. *Ibid.*, August 10, 1804.
29. Buffalo Historical Society, March 6, 1802.
30. Historical Society of Pennsylvania, April 10, 1804.
31. Adams Papers, February 25, 1805.
32. Historical Society of Pennsylvania, November 5, 1804.
33. Adams Papers, February 15, 1805.
34. *Ibid.*, February 28, 1805.
35. New-York Historical Society, Livingston Papers, November 27, 1809.
36. *Ibid.*
37. *Ibid.*, December 15, 1809.
38. *Ibid.*, November 28, 1811.
39. De Witt Clinton Papers, Columbia University, XVIII, 294–6 (February 21, 1816).

NOTES TO CHAPTER XIV

1. Adams Papers, December 30, 1797.
2. *Ibid.*, January 20, 1799.
3. *Ibid.*, December 13, 1799.
4. Historical Society of Pennsylvania, December 24, 1799.
5. Adams Papers, January 19, 1800.
6. Historical Society of Pennsylvania, January 30, 1800.
7. Adams Papers, September 1, 1800.
8. *Ibid.*, September 7, 1801.
9. *Ibid.*, August 23, 1802.
10. *Ibid.*, September 1, 1800.
11. *Ibid.*, December 12, 1800.
12. Historical Society of Pennsylvania, December 28, 1800.
13. Adams Papers, February 7, 1801.
14. *Ibid.*, June 20, 1801.
15. Historical Society of Pennsylvania, July 13, 1801.
16. Adams Papers, January 3, 1802.
17. *Ibid.*, September 7, 1801.
18. *Ibid.*, March 24, 1802.
19. Historical Society of Pennsylvania, July 24, 1802.
20. *Ibid.*, September 28, 1802.
21. *Ibid.*, September 29, 1802.
22. Adams Papers, November 11 and 28, 1802.
23. *Ibid.*, December 15, 1802.
24. Historical Society of Pennsylvania, January 3, 1803.
25. Francis Adrian Van der Kemp, *A Sketch of the Achaian Republic*

in Letters to Colonel John Lincklaen, MS in Oneida Historical Society, Utica, New York. Introduction, pp. 21–2.

26. *Ibid.,* p. 23.
27. *Ibid.,* Main body, p. 135.
28. *Ibid.,* pp. 248–9.
29. *Ibid.,* pp. 251–2.
30. Adams Papers, December 15, 1802.
31. Historical Society of Pennsylvania, January 3, 1803.
32. Adams Papers, July 15, 1803.
33. *Ibid.,* January 12, 1807.
34. Historical Society of Pennsylvania, March 9, 1806.
35. *Ibid.,* April 30, 1806.
36. Adams Papers, July 7, 1806.
37. Historical Society of Pennsylvania, August 23, 1806.
38. Adams Papers, November 1, 1806.
39. *Ibid.,* May 17, 1807.
40. *Ibid.,* November 1, 1807.
41. *Ibid.,* October 3, 1801.
42. Historical Society of Pennsylvania, December 14, 1802.
43. Adams Papers, January 17, 1803.
44. *Ibid.,* July 7, 1806.
45. Historical Society of Pennsylvania, August 23, 1806.
46. Adams Papers, October 15, 1804.
47. *Ibid.,* November 28, 1802.
48. *Ibid.,* March 21, 1808.
49. *Ibid.,* January 18, 1809.
50. *Ibid.,* April 2, 1809.
51. The MS had the date 1811 on it. It is in the Adams Papers as of 1814 but Adams read it as early as July 15, 1812.

NOTES TO CHAPTER XV

1. Adams Papers, December 13, 1799.
2. *Ibid.,* September 1, 1800.
3. *Ibid.,* June 20, 1801.
4. Historical Society of Pennsylvania, July 13, 1801.
5. *Ibid.,* January 26, 1802.
6. Adams Papers, January 3, 1802.
7. *Ibid.,* September 3, 1803.
8. *Ibid.,* August 10, 1804.
9. *Utica Patriot,* July 16, 1804.
10. Adams Papers, February 15, 1805.
11. *Ibid.,* December 28, 1805.
12. *Ibid.,* February 1, 1806.
13. *Ibid.,* February 18, 1806.
14. Historical Society of Pennsylvania, January 8, 1806.
15. *Ibid.,* February 20, 1806.
16. Adams Papers, April 7, 1806.

17. *Ibid.,* July 7, 1806.
18. *Ibid.,* November 1, 1806.
19. *Ibid.,* March 15, 1807.
20. *Ibid.*
21. Historical Society of Pennsylvania, April 25, 1808.
22. Adams Papers, August 3, 1808.
23. Historical Society of Pennsylvania, August 15, 1808.
24. Adams Papers, September 2, 1808.
25. *Ibid.,* December 12, 1808.
26. *Ibid.,* April 2, 1809.
27. Fairchild, p. 188.
28. Adams Papers, November 28, 1809.
29. New-York Historical Society, Livingston Papers, August 20, 1805.
30. *Ibid.,* January 7, 1810.
31. Adams Papers, November 28, 1809.
32. *Works,* X, 625; December 15, 1809.
33. Adams Papers, August 20, 1810.
34. Historical Society of Pennsylvania, November 30, 1810.
35. Adams Papers, February 9, 1811.
36. Adams Papers, March 12, 1811.
37. Historical Society of Pennsylvania, April 4, 1811.
38. Adams Papers, June 12, 1811.
39. *Ibid.,* October 7, 1811.

NOTES TO CHAPTER XVI

1. *Utica Patriot,* October 20, 1812.
2. *Ibid.,* December 22, 1812.
3. Nina Moore Tiffany and Francis Tiffany, *Harm Jan Huidekoper* (Cambridge: 1904), p. 184.
4. *Messages from the Governors,* Ed. by Charles Z. Lincoln (Albany: 1909), II, 774.
5. *Utica Daily Press,* March 26, 1898.
6. Luther Guiteau, *Dissertation Delivered before the Medical Society of the County of Oneida, by Appointment of the President of Said Society, July 1822, On the Epidemic of 1812 & 13,* Oneida Historical Society, pp. 2–3.
7. *Ibid.,* pp. 18, 21.
8. Adams Papers, May 5, 1813.
9. Fairchild, pp. 161–2.
10. Seymour, pp. 27–8.
11. *Utica Patriot,* January 25, 1814.
12. Adams Papers, January 13, 1814.
13. *Ibid.*
14. *Ibid.,* January 14, 1814.
15. *Ibid.,* February 5, 1814.
16. Historical Society of Pennsylvania, February 19, 1814.
17. Adams Papers, March 1, 1814.
18. *Ibid.,* February 9, 1814.

19. *Ibid.*, March 1, 1814.
20. Historical Society of Pennsylvania, Letter to Benjamin Walker, March 1, 1814.
21. *Utica Patriot*, March 8, 1814.
22. *Ibid.*, March 22, 1814.
23. March 12, 1814, Nathan Williams Collection, Oneida Historical Society.
24. *Ibid.*, March 15, 1814.
25. Adams Papers, March 15, 1814.
26. *Ibid.*, March 1, 1814.
27. *Ibid.*, July 19, 1814.
28. *Ibid.*, September 12, 1814.
29. *Ibid.*
30. *Ibid.*, October 5, 1814.
31. Historical Society of Pennsylvania, October 31, 1814.
32. *Albany Gazette*, November 17, 1814.
33. Historical Society of Pennsylvania, Letter to Benjamin Walker, December 5, 1814.
34. Adams Papers, November 11, 1814.
35. *Speeches of the Hon. Morris S. Miller and Thomas P. Grosvenor of New York, on the Army Bills*, delivered in the House of Representatives of the United States, December, 1814 (Utica: Merrell & Camp, 1815).
36. New York State Library, Letter to Miller, December 14, 1814.
37. *Utica Patriot*, January 31, 1815.
38. Adams Papers, February 18, 1815.
39. *Ibid.*, March 7, 1815.

NOTES TO CHAPTER XVII

1. *Works* of J. Adams, IX, p. 625.
2. Adams Papers, January 14, 1810.
3. Historical Society of Pennsylvania, April 9, 1811.
4. Adams Papers, June 12, 1811.
5. Historical Society of Pennsylvania, January 9, 1812.
6. Adams Papers, February 18, 1812.
7. Historical Society of Pennsylvania, January 23, 1813.
8. *Ibid.*, May 20, 1813.
9. *Ibid.*, August 9, 1813.
10. This and following excerpts from Van der Kemp's two letters to his daughter are in Fairchild, pp. 162–5.
11. Historical Society of Pennsylvania, October 15, 1813.
12. Adams Papers, October 2, 1813.
13. *Ibid.*, September 21, 1813.
14. Historical Society of Pennsylvania, October 4, 1813.
15. Adams Papers, October 11, 1816.
16. Historical Society of Pennsylvania, October 4, 1813.
17. *Works* X, 70.
18. Historical Society of Pennsylvania, October 15, 1813.

19. Adams Papers, September 26, 1813.
20. *Ibid.*, September 21, 1813.
21. Historical Society of Pennsylvania, October 15, 1813.
22. Adams Papers, January 14, 1814.
23. *Ibid.*, February 3, 1814.
24. Adams Papers, May 26, 1815.

NOTES TO CHAPTER XVIII

1. Yale University Library. Van der Kemp to Jedidiah Morse, December 23, 1806.
2. *The Panoplist or the Christian's Armory*, II, No. 9 (February, 1807), p. 419.
3. *Ibid.*, II, No. 12 (April, 1807), p. 536.
4. Historical Society of Pennsylvania, Van der Kemp to Jedidiah Morse, April 16, 1807.
5. *Panoplist*, III, No. 1 (June, 1807), p. 48.
6. Historical Society of Pennsylvania, Letter to the Editors of the Panoplist, June 1, 1807.
7. Historical Society of Pennsylvania, Van der Kemp to Morse, June 1, 1807.
8. *Ibid.*, October 24, 1807.
9. *Panoplist*, II, No. 7 (December, 1807).
10. Historical Society of Pennsylvania, Van der Kemp to Morse, December 29, 1807.
11. *Panoplist*, January, 1808.
12. *Ibid.*
13. Historical Society of Pennsylvania, Van der Kemp to Morse, October 2, 1808.
14. *Ibid.*
15. Historical Society of Pennsylvania, February 20, 1811.
16. *Ibid.*, April 9, 1811.
17. *Ibid.*, January 9, 1812.
18. Adams Papers, February 18, 1812.
19. Historical Society of Pennsylvania, Jefferson to Van der Kemp, March 22, 1812.
20. Columbia University, De Witt Clinton Papers, September 14, 1812.
21. Historical Society of Pennsylvania, January 29, 1813.
22. *Ibid.*, April 20, 1812.
23. *Ibid.*, May 20, 1815.
24. Adams Papers, June 28, 1815.
25. *Ibid.*, October 6, 1815.
26. Historical Society of Pennsylvania, April 14, 1812.
27. *Ibid.*, July 15, 1812.
28. Adams Papers, August 10, 1812.
29. Historical Society of Pennsylvania, October 28, 1812.
30. *Ibid.*, Van der Kemp to Abiel Abbot, November 8, 1812.
31. Adams Papers, May 5, 1813.
32. Oneida Historical Society, Van der Kemp to Dwight, April 16, 1813.

33. *Ibid.*, September 25, 1813.

34. *The General Repository,* Vol. III (April, 1813), pp. 309–10.

35. *Ibid.*, July, 1813, pp. 31 ff. The Harvard Library is unable to locate any of the Van der Kemp Manuscripts at the present time.

36. *Ibid.*, October, 1813, pp. 388–9.

37. Historical Society of Pennsylvania, December 26, 1813.

38. Adams Papers, April 8, 1814.

39. Historical Society of Pennsylvania, May 2, 1814.

40. *Ibid.*, May 29, 1814.

41. Columbia University, De Witt Clinton Papers, January 5, 1818; Adams Papers, November 16, 1816.

42. Historical Society of Pennsylvania, March 2, 1816, and May 26, 1816.

NOTES TO CHAPTER XIX

1. *Publications of the Buffalo Historical Society,* Ed., Frank H. Severance (Buffalo: Buffalo Historical Society, 1904), VII, 11–12. The editor has a note that the punctuation and spelling is preserved as it was in Jefferson's manuscript which is the one he sent to Van der Kemp.

2. Adams Papers, October 4, 1813.

3. Historical Society of Pennsylvania, December 26, 1813.

4. Adams Papers, January 13, 1814.

5. *Buffalo Historical Society,* pp. 16–17.

6. *Ibid.*, pp. 18–19.

7. *Works of Adams,* X, 223.

8. *Ibid.*, p. 224.

9. Adams Papers, November 19 and 26, 1816.

10. *Ibid.*, March 12, 1817.

11. *Buffalo Historical Society,* pp. 20–1.

12. *Ibid.*, pp. 21–2.

13. Historical Society of Pennsylvania, November 20, 1816.

14. *Buffalo Historical Society,* pp. 19–20.

15. *Ibid.*, pp. 21–2.

16. Adams Papers, December 15, 1816.

17. *The Writings of Thomas Jefferson,* ed., Andrew A. Lipscomb (Washington: The Thomas Jefferson Memorial Association, 1905), XV, 383–4.

18. *The Monthly Repository,* October, 1816.

19. Adams Papers, October 11, 1816.

20. *Buffalo Historical Society,* p. 22.

21. *Ibid.*, pp. 22–3.

22. *Ibid.*, pp. 23–7.

23. *Ibid.*, pp. 27–8.

24. *Ibid.*, pp. 28–9.

25. *Ibid.*, pp. 29–31.

26. *Ibid.*, pp. 31–2.

NOTES TO CHAPTER XX

1. De Witt Clinton Papers. September 14, 1812.
2. *Ibid.*, May 30, 1814.
3. *Ibid.*, October 27, 1815.
4. *Ibid.*, November 20, 1815.
5. *Ibid.*, January 3 and 8, 1816.
6. *Ibid.*, February 21, 1816.
7. *Ibid.*, March 1, 1816, Van der Kemp's manuscript is among the Clinton documents.
8. *Ibid.*, October 22, 1816.
9. *Ibid.*, December 27, 1816.
10. *Ibid.*, February 12, 1817.
11. *Ibid.*, March 24, 1817.
12. Rae B. Smith, *History of the State of New York, Political and Governmental*, Vol. I (1776–1822), by Willis Fletcher Johnson (Syracuse: The Syracuse Press, Inc., 1922), pp. 374–5.
13. De Witt Clinton Papers, April 25, 1817.
14. *Ibid.*, December 6, 1817.
15. *Ibid.*, January 19, 1818.
16. *Ibid.*, January 5, 1818.
17. *Ibid.*, January, 1818.
18. *Ibid.*, February 9, 1819.
19. *Ibid.*, December 5, 1818.
20. Fairchild, pp. 182–5.
21. Buffalo Historical Society, April 20, 1822.
22. De Witt Clinton Papers, May 3, 1822.
23. *De Witt Clinton's Diary*, Columbia University.
24. De Witt Clinton Papers, July, 1822.
25. *Ibid.*, February 11, 1822; Adams Papers, January 23, 1822.
26. De Witt Clinton Papers, March 4, 1824.
27. *Ibid.*, July 13, 1824.
28. *Ibid.*, October 6, 1824.
29. *Ibid.*, April 21, 1823.
30. Buffalo Historical Society, April 8, 1823.

NOTES TO CHAPTER XXI

1. De Witt Clinton Papers, September 14, 1812.
2. *Ibid.*, January 3, 1816 with postscript, January 8.
3. Adams Papers, January 9, 1816.
4. Craig R. Hanyan, "The Erie Canal of New York State, 1784–1825," unpublished thesis, Yale University, p. 49.
5. Hanyan, p. 58.
6. De Witt Clinton Papers, October 22, 1816.
7. *Ibid.*, December 27, 1816.
8. *Ibid.*, February 12, 1817.
9. *Ibid.*, March 24, 1817.

10. *Ibid.*, April 25, 1817.

11. *Ibid.*, December 6, 1817.

12. *Ibid.*, January 5, 1818.

13. *Ibid.*, January 19, 1818.

14. *Ibid.*, February 8, 9, 1819.

15. Daniel E. Wager, pp. 185–8.

16. Historical Society of Pennsylvania, Letter from Van der Kemp to Websters and Skinners, Albany, December 18, 1819; a second letter without date was written to Websters and Skinners, a few days later.

17. De Witt Clinton Papers, December 26, 1821.

18. Adams Papers, January 23, 1822.

19. Buffalo Historical Society, April 20, 1822.

20. Historical Society of Pennsylvania, July 1, 1822.

21. De Witt Clinton Papers, November 25, 1822.

22. Historical Society of Pennsylvania, February 13, 1823.

23. De Witt Clinton Papers, April 21, 1823.

24. Oneida Historical Society, Van der Kemp to Williams, December 10, 1822.

25. *Utica Daily Press*, Van der Kemp to Seymour, March 26, 1898.

26. Buffalo Historical Society, April 22, 1823.

27. De Witt Clinton Papers, May 5, 1823.

28. *Ibid.*, September 29, 1823.

29. *Ibid.*, October 11, 1823.

30. *Ibid.*, April 19, 1824.

31. *Ibid.*, October 6, 1824.

32. *Utica Sentinel & Gazette*, November 8, 1825.

33. *Ibid.*, November 15, 1825 with a correction of text on November 22, 1825.

NOTES TO CHAPTER XXII

1. De Witt Clinton Papers, April 25, 1817.

2. Buffalo Historical Society, January 21, 1818.

3. De Witt Clinton Papers, January 26, 1818.

4. Historical Society of Pennsylvania, March 10, 1818.

5. De Witt Clinton Papers, March 20, 1818.

6. Vivian C. Hopkins, "The Dutch Records of New York: Francis Adrian Van der Kemp and De Witt Clinton," *New York History*, October, 1962, p. 387.

7. Adams Papers, August 8, 1818.

8. Historical Society of Pennsylvania, August 22, 1818.

9. Adams Papers, September 18, 1818.

10. *Ibid.*, November 1, 1818.

11. De Witt Clinton Papers, December 5, 1818.

12. Adams Papers, February 1, 1819.

13. *Ibid.*, March 4, 1819.

14. *Ibid.*, April 12, 1818.

15. *Ibid.*, June 9, 1819.

16. *Ibid.*, July 6, 1819.

17. *Ibid.*, August 24, 1819.

18. *Ibid.*, September 9, 1819.
19. *Ibid.*, September 12, 1819.
20. *Ibid.*, December 20, 1819.
21. *Ibid.*, February 7, 1820.
22. *Ibid.*
23. *Ibid.*, July, 1820.
24. Historical Society of Pennsylvania, October 10, 1820.
25. Adams Papers, September 25, 1820.
26. *Ibid.*
27. *Ibid.*, December 3, 1820.
28. Historical Society of Pennsylvania, February 12, 1821.
29. Adams Papers, June 10, 1821.
30. *Ibid.*, October 19, 1821.
31. De Witt Clinton Papers, January 3, 1822.
32. *Ibid.*, Yates to Clinton, January 16, 1822.
33. *Messages from the Governors*, II, 1116.
34. De Witt Clinton Papers, January 31, 1822.
35. Hartog, p. 68.
36. Adams Papers, May 1, 1822.
37. De Witt Clinton Papers, May 3, 1822.
38. *Albany Gazette & Daily Advertiser*, June 21 and 25, 1822.
39. Historical Society of Pennsylvania, July 1, 1822.
40. Historical Society of Pennsylvania, July 22, 1822.
41. De Witt Clinton Papers, December 16, 1822.
42. Buffalo Historical Society, January 9, 1823.
43. Historical Society of Pennsylvania, March 7, 1823.
44. *Ibid.*, March 20, 1823.
45. Hopkins, pp. 394-5.
46. De Witt Clinton Papers, February 17, 1824.
47. *Ibid.*, April 2, 1825.
48. *Ibid.*, April 7, 1825.
49. Hopkins, pp. 395-7.
50. *Messages from the Governors*, III, 162.

NOTES TO CHAPTER XXIII

1. Fairchild, p. 154.
2. Adams Papers, May 29, 1809.
3. *Ibid.*, August 20, 1810.
4. Manuscript reminiscence by John P. [?] Garrett in the Barneveld Library.
5. Historical Society of Pennsylvania, November 2, 1810.
6. *Ibid.*
7. Trenton Town Records, Town Meeting, 1824.
8. Historical Society of Pennsylvania, March 28, 1812.
9. *Ibid.*, December 30, 1812, and January 15, 1813.
10. *Ibid.*, May 22, 1814.
11. *Ibid.*, December 5, 1814.
12. Adams Papers, June 1, 1813.
13. *Ibid.*, April 8, 1814 and June 19, 1814.

14. *Ibid.*, December 17, 1814; see also John Adams to J. Q. Adams for the plagiarism, April 8, 1811.
15. *Ibid.*, February 18, 1815.
16. Historical Society of Pennsylvania, February 23, 1815.
17. *Ibid.*, September 3, 1815.
18. Adams Papers, May 7, 1815.
19. *Ibid.*
20. *Ibid.*, June 28, 1815.
21. *Ibid.*, August 16, 1815.
22. *Ibid.*, October 6, 1815.
23. *Ibid.*, November 25, 1815.
24. *Ibid.*, November 7, 1815.
25. *Ibid.*, January 9, 1816.
26. *Ibid.*, April 12, 1818.
27. *Ibid.*, April 28, 1818.
28. *Ibid.*, November 4, 1818.
29. Historical Society of Pennsylvania, May 20, 1819.
30. Adams Papers, November 4, 1816; January 24, 1817.
31. *Ibid.*, July 28, 1817.
32. *Ibid.*, September 20, 1817.
33. *Ibid.*, October 14, 1817.
34. *Ibid.*, November 29, 1817.
35. Adams Papers, January 7, 1818.
36. *Ibid.*, February 17, 1818.
37. *Ibid.*, August 3, 1816.
38. Historical Society of Pennsylvania, August 21, 1819.
39. *Ibid.*
40. Adams Papers, September 18, 1818.
41. *Ibid.*, July 6, 1819.

NOTES TO CHAPTER XXIV

1. Yale University Library, Van der Kemp to Silliman, April 6 and 28, 1818.
2. Book now in Harvard Library.
3. Adams Papers, May 21, 1821.
4. *Ibid.*, August 13, 1821.
5. Historical Society of Pennsylvania, Van der Kemp to Le Roy, Bayard, & Co., June 9, 1820.
6. *Ibid.*, March 27, 1822.
7. *Ibid.*, May 20, 1820.
8. *Ibid.*, November 29, 1821.
9. *Ibid.*, July 1, 1822.
10. Adams Papers, February 24, 1821.
11. Girelius, "Religious Controversy."
12. Historical Society of Pennsylvania, January 2, 1822.
13. Adams Papers, May 1, 1822.
14. Historical Society of Pennsylvania, November 29, 1821.
15. *Ibid.*, July 1, 1822.
16. Adams Papers, July 24, 1822.

17. *Ibid.*, August 5, 1822.

18. *Ibid.*, November 20, 1822.

19. Historical Society of Pennsylvania, Caroline de Wint to Van der Kemp, February 14, 1823.

20. Buffalo Historical Society, April 20, 1822.

21. De Witt Clinton Papers, May 3, 1822.

22. Winslow C. Watson, *Men and Times of the Revolution or Memoirs of Elkanah Watson* (New York: Dana & Co., 1856), pp. 434–5.

23. Historical Society of Pennsylvania, January 3, 1823.

24. Adams Papers, January 20, 1823.

25. Historical Society of Pennsylvania, February 4 and 13, 1823; Adams Papers, February 13, 1823.

26. Historical Society of Pennsylvania, Van der Kemp to Websters, December 30, 1822.

27. De Witt Clinton Papers, November 3, 1823.

28. *Ibid.*, April 12, 1824.

29. Historical Society of Pennsylvania, December 1, 1823.

30. Adams Papers, December 13, 1823 (incorrectly marked November 13).

31. Adams Papers, November 18, 1824.

32. *Ibid.*, February 15, 1825.

33. *Ibid.*, February, 1825.

34. Historical Society of Pennsylvania, February 24, 1825.

35. Adams Papers, December 27, 1825.

36. Historical Society of Pennsylvania, July 29, 1826.

37. Oneida Historical Society.

38. Adams Papers, September 18, 1825.

39. *Ibid.*, November 13, 1825.

40. De Witt Clinton Papers, July 28, 1824.

41. *Ibid.*, April 2, 1825.

42. *Ibid.*, April 7, 1825.

43. Historical Society of Pennsylvania, Van der Kemp to a friend, probably Abraham Varick, April, 1829.

44. *Ibid.*, April 25, 1827.

45. Buffalo Historical Society, February 11, 1828.

46. Van der Kemp's notation of the event in the old Family Record Book, Oneida Historical Society.

47. Historical Society of Pennsylvania, April 27, 1827.

48. *Ibid.*, July 17, 1829.

49. *Ibid.*, April, 1829.

50. Family Record Book.

51. MS copy of the oration in Betsy's handwriting in Oneida Historical Society records.

52. *A Gazeteer of the State of New York*, Ed., Horatio Gates Stafford (New York: Packard & Van Benthuysen, 1824).

Index